Design Concepts for a Virtualizable Embedded MPSoC Architecture

Alexander Biedermann

Design Concepts for a Virtualizable Embedded MPSoC Architecture

Enabling Virtualization in Embedded Multi-Processor Systems

Springer Vieweg

Alexander Biedermann
Darmstadt, Germany

Technische Universität Darmstadt, 2014

Darmstädter Dissertation, D17

ISBN 978-3-658-08046-4   ISBN 978-3-658-08047-1 (eBook)
DOI 10.1007/978-3-658-08047-1

Library of Congress Control Number: 2014954234

Springer Vieweg

Printed on acid-free paper

Springer Vieweg is a brand of Springer Fachmedien Wiesbaden
Springer Fachmedien Wiesbaden is part of Springer Science+Business Media
(www.springer.com)

für meine Eltern

Abstract

In the present work, a generic hardware-based virtualization architecture is introduced. The proposed virtualization concept transforms an array of off-the-shelf embedded processors into a system with high execution dynamism. At any point in time, tasks may be shifted among the processor array transparently. Neither the software of tasks nor the processor cores have to be modified in order to enable this feature. The work details task-processor interconnection, virtualized task communication as well as means for energy awareness and fault tolerance in a virtualizable MPSoC.

Based on this architecture, concepts for the design of embedded multi-processor systems with the ability for a dynamic reshaping of their initial configuration are highlighted. This includes energy aware systems, fault tolerant systems as well as parallelized systems. For the latter, the so-called Agile Processing scheme is introduced, which enables a seamless transition between sequential and parallel execution schemes of tasks. The design of virtualizable systems is furthermore aided by a dedicated design framework, which integrates into existing, commercial design flows.

Application examples taken from different domains in embedded system design feature specific optimization goals and demonstrate the feasibility of the proposed design concepts and of the virtualization architecture. For this purpose, prototyped virtualizable multi-processor designs have been successfully synthesized for FPGAs.

Abstract

Zusammenfassung

Die vorliegende Arbeit stellt ein generisches hardware-basiertes Virtualisierungskonzept vor, das aus einem Array aus eingebetteten Standardprozessoren ein System mit hoher Ausführungsdynamik schafft. Tasks können zur Laufzeit zu jedem Zeitpunkt transparent zwischen den Prozessoren im Array verschoben werden. Weder existierende Software der Tasks, noch die Prozessoren bedürfen hierbei einer speziellen Anpassung. Die Arbeit detailliert die skalierbare Task-Prozessoranbindung, virtualisierte Task-Kommunikation, sowie Maßnahmen zur Energieverwaltung und Fehlererkennung bzw. -maskierung in virtualisierbaren Systemen.

Auf Basis des vorgestellten Virtualisierungskonzepts können eingebettete Multi-Prozessorsysteme unterschiedlicher Ausprägung designt werden. Dies beinhaltet energie-bewusste Systeme, fehlertolerante Systeme oder parallel verarbeitende Systeme. Bei letzterem wird das sog. Agile Processing-Schema als nahtlose Transition zwischen sequentieller und paralleler Ausführung von Tasks eingeführt. Das Design virtualisierbarer Systeme wird durch ein eigens bereitgestelltes Design-Framework unterstützt, das eine nahtlose Anbindung an existierende, kommerzielle Design Flows bietet.

Das Entwurfskonzept wird durch Anwendungsbeispiele aus eingebetteten Systemen mit jeweils unterschiedlichen Optimierungszielen demonstriert. Hierfür wurden entsprechende Designs prototypisch für FPGAs synthetisiert.

Acknowledgments

This thesis would not exist without the help, advice, and guidance by a lot of people. First of all, I would like to thank Prof. Sorin A. Huss for supervising my thesis. For more than half a decade, Prof. Huss guided me on the journey towards this thesis by giving advice when I was stuck, by pointing out links I had not seen and by sharing experience I was lacking. I am grateful for having had the opportunity to research and work at the Integrated and Circuits Lab where I could pursue and evolve my ideas.

Second, I would like to thank Prof. Jörg Henkel for taking the time to be second assessor of this thesis.

At the Integrated Circuits and Systems Lab, I especially thank Maria Tiedemann, who always provided kind and experienced support in all matters I still consider being mysterious and inscrutable, such as travel expense accounting.

Ideas evolve both in phases of secluded thinking as well as in lively debates. For the latter, I thank my colleagues Tom Aßmuth, Attila Jaeger, Felix Madlener, Gregor Molter, and Qizhi Tian for delightful hours of fervid discussions about Life, the Universe and Everything. I also thank my other colleagues at the Integrated Circuits and Systems Lab and at the Center for Advanced Security Research Darmstadt (CASED), in particular Tolga Arul, Carsten Büttner, Thomas Feller, Annelie Heuser, Adeel Israr, Zheng Lu, Sunil Malipatlolla, André Seffrin, Abdulhadi Shoufan, Marc Stöttinger, Hagen Stübing, and Michael Zohner.

Tens of thousands lines of implementation work by a lot of students have enabled that this work is not solely a construct of ideas, but is based on working prototypes, which allowed to test and to demonstrate the opportunities arising from the proposed virtualization concept. In this connection, I especially thank Boris Dreyer for discussing ideas and providing exceptional work over the last three years. I furthermore thank Clemens Bergmann, Antonio Gavino Casu, Hieu Ha Chi, Quoc Hien Dang, Johannes Decher, Binh Vu Duc, Nicolas Eicke, Steffen Fleckenstein, Sebastian Funke, Peter Glöckner, Maik Görtz, Christopher Huth, Inac Kadir, Michael Koch, Thorsten Jacobi, Dan Le, Randolph Lieding, Wei Lin, Kevin Luck, Mischa Lundberg, Amir Naseri, Joel Njeukam, Jan Post, Andreas Rjasanow, Lucas Rothamel, Tobias Rückelt, Gregor Rynkowski, Daniel Schneider, Kai Schwierczek, Omid Pahlevan Sharif, Johannes Simon, Niels Ströher, Markus Tasch, Do Thanh Tung, Manuel Weiel, and Matthias Zöllner.

Finally, I thank my beloved family for never demanding too much detail about my research about "something with computers" at the coffee table.

Alexander Biedermann

Acknowledgments

Contents

List of Figures

List of Tables

List of Algorithms

List of Abbreviations

AP	Auto Pilot
API	Application Programming Interface
APT	Air Pressure Tracking
AR	Audio Response
ASAP	As Soon As Possible
AST	Abstract Syntax Tree
AXI	Advanced eXtensible Interface Bus
BRAM	Block Random Access Memory
BS	Blind Spot Detection
BV	Binding Vector
C2T	CO_2 Level Tracking
CAN	Controller Area Network
CD	Collision Detection
CIL	Code Injection Logic
CISC	Complex Instruction Set Computer
CORDIS	Community Research and Development Information Service
DMR	Dual Modular Redundancy
ECC	Error-Correcting Code
ESL	Electronic System Level Design
FF	Flip-Flop
FLA	Fog Light Assistant
FPGA	Field-Programmable Gate Array
FSL	Fast Simplex Link
GC	Ground Communication
GHD	Ground Heat Detection & Analysis
GPS	Global Positioning System
HBA	High Beam Assistance
HDL	Hardware Description Language
ILP	Integer Linear Programming
IP	Intellectual Property
ISM	Instruction Stream Monitor
LCS	Lane Change Support
LKS	Lane Keeping Support
LUT	Look-up Table
MIC	Microphone

MPSoC	Multi-Processor System-on-Chip
MSR	Machine Status Register
NMR	n Modular Redundancy
NoC	Network-on-Chip
NUMA	Non-Uniform Memory Access
ODP	Organic Design Pattern
PA	Parking Assistant
PC	Program Counter (Chapter 2)/Position Control (Chapter 4)
RAM	Random Access Memory
RISC	Reduced Instruction Set Computer
RT	Radiation Level Tracking
SCCC	Single-Chip Cloud Computer
SI	System Initialization
SIMD	Single Instruction, Multiple Data
SoC	System on Chip
SOL	Sources of Light
SPE	Synergistic Processor Element
Tcl	Tool Command Language
TCM	Task Context Memory
TDM	Task Data Matrix
TG	Task Group
TMR	Triple Modular Redundancy
TSD	Traffic Sign Detection
TT	Temperature Tracking
VBR	Visual Body Recognition
VHDL	Very High Speed Integrated Circuit Hardware Description Language
VLIW	Very Long Instruction Word
VMR	Virtualized Modular Redundancy

1 The "Nulticore" Dilemma

For almost half a century, one of the first principles beginners in computer technology are taught is the infamously accurate "Law" of engineer Gordon Moore. He predicted a doubling of the transistor count in chips every two years [Moore 1965]. While the time interval has been adjusted several times, the prediction about a steady, exponential growth holds still true. However, besides being an estimate in semiconductor development and serving as introduction of hardware-related texts such as the present one ad nauseam, the ongoing growth in terms of available logic resources predicted by Moore is a matter of concern in recent system design.

The growing number of transistors – or of logic resources when speaking of Field-Programmable Gate Array (FPGA) technology – is theoretically accompanied by gain in performance. However, several aspects prove that in reality, the increase in terms of transistors or logic resources outbalances the growth in performance one would expect. One reason for this is the so-called Design Gap, cf. Figure 1.1. The productivity of designers cannot cope with the fast increase in theoretical computational power available [Belanovic 2003]. Productivity covers programming paradigms as well as design tools and hardware layout. Speaking of programming paradigms, another "Law" emerged in 1995. Wirth's Law postulates that more complex hardware leads to more complex software, which in turn is less efficient than software with less complexity. In [Wirth 1995] this is subsumed in the quote: "Software is getting slower more rapidly than hardware becomes faster."

Besides the struggle with inefficient software design, also the hardware view raises problems, which prohibit fully profiting from the growth in logic resources. A huge transistor count indeed allows building processors with tremendous complexity. However, a growth in complexity of the chip design implies an additional complexity in verifying such designs, not speaking of the difficulties of efficiently programming for such architectures. With Wirth's Law in mind, the yield in performance by more complex processor cores could be nullified by inefficient software design. A solution to this vicious circle is seen in developing methodologies for System Level Design, which exploit multi-processor or multi-core architectures [Henkel 2003].

A multi-core architecture is usually regarded as a processor, which features several instances of a processing core on its die. These cores have independent register sets and caches, but share cache memory at some point. There are multi-core chips featuring different types of processor core on the die, such as the Cell chip by IBM, which features a Power processor core as well as eight so-called synergistic processor elements (SPE) [Chen 2007].

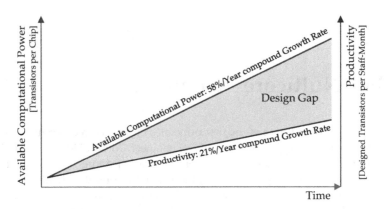

Figure 1.1: The Design Gap: Growth of available Computing Power outperforms the Productivity of System Designers [Belanovic 2003].

In contrast, a multi-processor architecture is a system consisting of a set of processors. The processors themselves may be multi-core architectures. Usually, it is assumed that the processor instances in a multi-processor architecture are able to collaborate. If a multi-processor architecture features several auxiliary components, such as co-processors or other hardware modules on chip, these systems are called Multi-Processor System-on-Chip (MPSoC). According to [Wolf 2008], the first system to be seen as an MPSoC is the Daytona architecture, which was presented in 2000 [Ackland 2000].

Thus, a trivial solution to cope with the growth in available transistors or logic resources appears to be the instantiation a set of processors in order to form a multi-processor system. However, despite the comparatively simplicity in creating a multi-processor architecture – several instances of a well-performing processor architecture from the last years, which now fit on a common chip, are instantiated and equipped with some communication solution – the original problems persist. For decades, software was written in the intention to be executed on a machine, which executes instructions in a sequential fashion. Therefore, few paradigms are tailored yet to target multi-processor architectures. Moreover, even when assuming suited paradigms for parallelizing software, not all software contains parallelizable code. Consequently, the missing improvement in performance expected from multi-processing is already called the "Nulticore" effect [Ganssle 2008].

In order to overcome this effect, this work will highlight a methodology for the design of embedded MPSoC, which is based upon the introduction of a dedicated *Virtualization Layer* placed between an array of off-the-shelf embedded processors and their corresponding memories. Chapter 2 will demonstrate how this Virtualization Layer will enable virtualization properties, such as the transparent shift of task execution among the processor array. The behavior of the Virtualization Layer as well as its inner structure consisting, e. g., of a dedicated task-processor interconnection network and infrastructure for virtualized task communication, are detailed.

Chapter 3 will then focus on design concepts, which may exploit the virtualization features introduced by the insertion of the Virtualization Layer. For this purpose, the design framework FripGa will be highlighted, which acts as a seamless expansion to existing vendor design suites in order to design virtualizable systems. Beneath design flows for reliable and parallelized systems, a flow for the hereby introduced *Agile Processing* scheme is presented as well. Here, the virtualization features enable a seamless transition from sequential and parallel execution of tasks. The degree of parallelism may be tailored dynamically at runtime.

Finally, Chapter 4 demonstrates some selected application examples, which prove the feasibility of the virtualization concept. These application examples feature different design goals, such as reliability or energy awareness. For the application examples, prototype designs were synthesized for FPGAs featuring between eight and twelve virtualizable processors. The application examples will highlight the yield in terms of execution dynamism provided by the exploitation of the virtualization properties.

Chapter 5 will summarize the comprehensive approach consisting of a generic, scalable virtualization solution, a set of design concepts covering different design optimization goals and a concise workflow provided by the design framework FripGa on top of vendor workflows. The work finishes with an outlook regarding further work remaining in the scope of virtualizable embedded multi-processor systems.

2 Virtualizable Architecture for embedded MPSoC

2.1 The Term Virtualization

Virtualization is a concept, which enables transparent resource sharing by strictly encapsulating modules. These virtualized modules behave as being the sole user of a resource. As each virtualized module has no knowledge about actually not being the sole user of a resource, malicious interference between virtualized modules is avoided by design. A survey lists the IBM VM Facility/370 to be the first machine realizing this concept [Goldberg 1974]. When the virtualized modules are software tasks, virtualization may be regarded as being a very strict interpretation of multi-tasking.

The use of virtualization is widespread among personal computers, servers, and mainframes. The isolated environment of virtualized operating systems, e. g., enable the simple cloning of systems or the backup and recovery of entire system states. For parallel architectures, approaches as the Parallel Virtual Machine exist, where virtualized tasks may share a pool of processors [Sunderam 1990]. This led to approaches as the SDVM [Haase 2004], which allows virtualized tasks to spread among a cluster of processors. However, in the field of embedded computing, especially regarding multi-processor architectures, the trend of exploiting virtualization is adopted with a certain delay. At least, in 2011, hardware-supported virtualization has been proposed for the ARM architecture, which is one of the most common processor architecture in today's embedded systems [Varanasi 2011]. In [Cohen 2010], processor virtualization accompanied by runtime compiling enables migrating software to heterogeneous processor platforms. This tool chain aims at the redistribution of software, but does not account for actual multi-processing.

Virtualization of software is usually accompanied by a virtualization host, i. e., a kernel or operating system, which manages the virtualized software. However, as embedded systems often face the constraints of harsh timing requirements as well as a limited amount of available memory, the overhead introduced by a virtualization solution may render its application as not feasible for most designs. In [Heiser 2008], this overhead is reduced by the introduction of microkernels, i. e., kernels with a very small memory footprint. As discussed before, in [Heiser 2008] two requirements are stated for embedded virtualization: A strong encapsulation of virtualized modules as well as a high communication bandwidth. The work of [Kopetz 2008] furthermore states principles for component composability in System-on-Chip (SoC) which are crucial in order to maintain the system's stability: interface specification, stability of prior services, non-interfering interactions, error containment, fault masking. In order to provide a virtualization scheme, these requirements and principles have to be considered. Thus, the strict encapsulation of virtualized modules and the transparency property of the virtualization procedure have to be maintained at all times.

Since virtualization is not exclusively limited to software being virtualized, several works regarding hardware module virtualization exist. As a first step, multi-tasking schemes known from the software world were adopted for hardware modules in [Brebner 1996]. In the succeeding work, the abilities of this task management are expanded by the partial reconfiguration feature of FPGAs [Brebner 2001]. The work of [Huang 2009] virtualizes hardware components in HW-SW designs. In doing so, several tasks can access virtualized instances of the same hardware component and, thus, reduce the waiting time arising from resource sharing. Task switching procedures for hardware tasks were proposed, e. g., in [Simmler 2000, Jozwik 2012, Stoettinger 2010], with the last one explicitly targeting virtualization features. Another approach targets the virtualization of whole FPGAs [Figuli 2011, Sidiropoulos 2013]. Here, so-called virtual FPGAs may be mapped to different underlying hardware. In doing so, a re-use of hardware blocks written for the virtual FPGA on different target devices is enabled.

Besides virtualization in live systems, virtual platforms may also be exploited for rapid system prototyping, test, and verification [Leupers 2012]. For virtual platforms, an accurate virtual image of an envisaged SoC is created, on which debugging and verification takes places. Accuracy may cover, e. g., execution time behavior and a power model of the underlying SoC.

Nevertheless, only few comprehensive approaches for virtualization in an embedded multi-processor environment exist. E. g., the concept of the SDVM was transferred to FPGAs by providing a dedicated firmware running on embedded processors in order to execute virtualized tasks [Hofmann 2008]. Another virtualization solution exploiting an MPSoC based on heterogeneous processor arrays was addressed in [Hansson 2011]. There, an underlying operating system acts as a host for virtualized software. However, this virtualization concept adds a fair amount of complexity to the system, hardening debug and verification. This architecture is exploited in [Ferger 2012] to host virtualizable, self-adaptable tiles. Splitting the computational power provided by the underlying MPSoC into tiles is one way to cope with the complexity of such architectures.

As the presented approaches often either rely on dedicated architectures or add a decent amount of complexity, which hardens design and testing, the following sections will, thus, introduce a very fast, simple, and memory-efficient virtualization concept for an array of embedded off-the-shelf processors, which will form a virtualizable MPSoC. As the virtualization properties are inserted by means of a hardware layer, the tasks may run natively on the processors without need for an underlying kernel.

2.2 Virtualization for Embedded Multi-Processor Architectures

Before motivating, why a virtualization procedure for an embedded multi-processor system is desirable, the characteristics of embedded processors are outlined in short. These characteristics as well as the desired properties lead to a set of requirements, which are defined in Section 2.2.3 and which have to be fulfilled by a virtualization procedure. Consequently, the steps necessary to meet these requirements are then outlined.

2.2.1 Characteristics of Embedded Processors

Despite the fact that we see ourselves surrounded by computer devices in our everyday's life, such as personal computers, notebooks, or tablet computers, the overwhelming number of computers is embedded.[1] In almost all powered devices, we may find digital circuits. The more functionality a device offers, the higher is the probability, that at least one embedded processor is exploited for this purpose. As embedded devices often have a very narrow scope of predefined uses, and, moreover, face several constraints, which will be addressed below, the characteristics of processors exploited in embedded devices differs from those employed in personal computers.

A personal computer serves a wide range of applications, e. g., writing documents, managing photos of the last vacation, listening to music, or playing video games. Therefore, a personal computer is designed to fulfill all these needs in an acceptable manner. Thus, the processor employed in a personal computer is equipped with a huge instruction set in order to speed up a broad range of applications.[2] This design concept is known as Complex Instruction Set Computer (CISC). In order to further boost execution speed by executing several applications in parallel, modern processors feature more than one processor core on the chip. A CISC design in combination with multi-core layout comes at price. Recent processors for personal computers are implemented on more than 2 billion transistors [Intel Corporation 2011]. Moreover, such processors are outlined for a Thermal Design Power of 77 W and above [Intel Corporation 2013a, p. 43]. For embedded designs, however, such characteristics are often unwanted.

Embedded computers are designed to handle a specific, reduced set of applications based on the intended use of the device. In contrast to variability and maximum performance, other aspects are of higher importance. As the range of applications is narrow and known during design of the device, a smaller instruction set for a so-called Reduced Instruction Set Computer (RISC) architecture may be exploited.[3] A

---

[1] According to the Community Research and Development Information Service (CORDIS) of the European Commission, embedded processors account for 98 % of all produced processors in 2006 [Research 2006].

[2] For reference, the "Intel 64 and IA-32 Architectures Software Developer's Manual" lists 434 different processor instructions [Intel Corporation 2013b].

[3] The manual for the Xilinx MicroBlaze RISC processor, which will be exploited for the prototype implementation in the scope of this work, lists 87 instructions [Xilinx, Inc. 2012] – a fraction of the 434 instructions provided by the Intel 64 and IA-32 CISC architectures.

simplified chip design furthermore reduces the transistor count. Consequently, the most significant constraint for embedded designs may be met: device cost. An embedded processor has to be as cheap as possible in order to lower the overall device cost. At the expense of this constraint, the performance of embedded processors is usually lower than that of those employed in personal computers. As a consequence of a lower transistor count and a simpler chip design, the power consumption is also lower. Since many of today's embedded computers, such as smartphones or mp3 players, are mobile, reducing energy consumption is an essential requirement to lengthen battery life. The simpler chip design is further accompanied by a fairly reduced interfacing. This will be an important property regarding the envisaged shift of task execution.

As low device cost is desired, embedded soft-core processors may be targeted. In contrast to usual, hard-wired integrated circuits, the so-called hard-cores, a soft-core processor is solely represented either by a behavior description given in a hardware description language (HDL), such as Verilog or VHDL or by a netlist. The description of a soft-core processor may be transformed into a hardware design by a synthesis process. Here, the description is mapped to primitives of the targeted chip, e. g., to look-up tables and registers of an FPGA.

Soft-core processors feature advantages, which are not present for hard-core processors. Due to their representation in an HDL, their behavior may be modified by altering their corresponding hardware description. However, the vendors of commercial soft-core processors may restrict the modification, e. g., by encrypting the files containing the hardware description. Nevertheless, open-source processors, such as the PicoBlaze [Xilinx, Inc. 2013b] or the Secretblaze [Barthe 2011], offer the modification of their hardware description.

Besides this manual adaption, soft-core processors may feature several pre-defined customizations. Based on the intended use, e. g., floating-point units, multipliers, or barrel shifters may be activated. During synthesis, the corresponding hardware descriptions of the desired functionality are included. Therefore, in contrast to a hard-wired processor, a soft-core processor may be tailored to the application purpose by disabling unnecessary functions and, thus, cost is reduced by a resulting lower resource consumption.

As a soft-core processor is available by its hardware description, multi-processor systems may easily be designed by instantiating the processor description multiple times in a top-level hardware description. Thus – given sufficient resources of the targeted FPGA – a multi-processor system may be designed without an increase in cost for the additional soft-core processors, whereas for a hard-core processor design, each additional core also causes additional cost. However, there are currently no common multi-core soft-core processors available yet. Therefore, multi-processing on soft-core processors relies on instantiating a set of soft-core processors.

Main drawback of soft-core processors is performance, which is usually lower than that of hard-wired embedded processors. A hard-wired processor, whose placement has underwent several optimization steps will always outperform a processor with

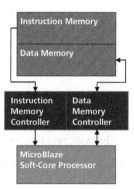

Figure 2.1: A MicroBlaze Processor System.

similar behavior, whose description has to be mapped onto existing chip primitives. For the first one, structures and routes on the chip may be tailored to the processor, whereas for the latter one, the processor is tailored to the target chip.

This work will demonstrate the virtualization concept by exploiting the commercial MicroBlaze soft-core processor, which is provided by the device vendor Xilinx, Inc. [Xilinx, Inc. 2013a]. The files containing the hardware description are encrypted and cannot be modified by a designer. However, since this work will demonstrate an approach to enable virtualization features without modifying existing processor designs, a modification of the hardware description is neither necessary nor desired.

The MicroBlaze is a common 32-bit RISC processor, which features a five stage pipeline in its default set-up. It is designed as Harvard architecture; therefore, instruction and data memory are separated from each other. After synthesis, instructions and data reside in BlockRAM (BRAM), memory primitives on FPGAs. Instructions and data are transferred between memory and the processor by two dedicated memory controllers. A processor system containing the MicroBlaze IP core, as well as instruction and data memories with their corresponding memory controllers is depicted in Figure 2.1. Further details of the processor architecture are provided later in this work as they get of particular importance.

Before highlighting the enhancements of the processor architecture depicted in Figure 2.1 towards a virtualizable multi-processor design, the intended purpose of the virtualization procedure is motivated.

2.2.2 Purpose of Virtualization in Embedded Multi-Processor Arrays

As highlighted above, virtualization enables transparent task handling on a host processor. While this functionality is well-established in the field of personal computing and server systems, embedded systems, especially soft-core processor-based designs, often lack of a virtualization property. To motivate why a virtualization concept

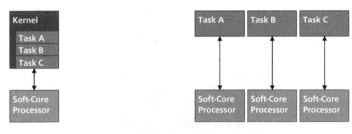

(a) Kernel.   (b) Dedicated Processor Resources.

Figure 2.2: Task Management by a Kernel (a) compared to dedicated Processor Resources for each Task (b).

enhances embedded system design, two common design alternatives for embedded processor systems are discussed.

In the first alternative, a kernel manages the access of tasks to a processor, cf. Figure 2.2, left hand side. Both kernel and tasks reside in the same memory area. In this system, all the tasks and the kernel are statically bound to the processor. The employment of a kernel eases the scheduling of tasks on the processor. Furthermore, individual tasks may dynamically be excluded from processor access or may temporarily get a higher priority assigned. Unlike for personal computers, memory in embedded devices is often of limited size. Therefore, despite the convenient task handling, a kernel may add an unwanted overhead in terms of memory. Additionally, the switching process between tasks is time consuming. The Xilkernel, a kernel for the MicroBlaze processor provided by the device vendor Xilinx, Inc. takes approximately 1.360 clock cycles to switch between tasks. As embedded systems may face harsh timing constraints, the additional time required for a task switch is possibly not acceptable. In addition, if an embedded system is employed in a safety-critical environment, the usage of a kernel may pose a significant safety risk in case of address space violations of tasks if no memory management is exploited. All the tasks in the system reside in the same memory. A faulty task might thus alter memory sections of a task relevant to security. Therefore, in many systems that feature safety-critical tasks, switching tasks by a kernel is avoided and the second alternative as follows is chosen.

In the second alternative, each task features a dedicated processor, cf. Figure 2.2, right hand side. Since there are no other tasks running on a processor, there is no need for scheduling or for an underlying kernel. This eliminates the overhead both in terms of memory and time caused by a kernel. Moreover, aside from task communication, e.g., via buses, tasks are logically and physically separated from each other. This prevents harmful mutual task interference. Furthermore, since each task may occupy all of the processor time of its processor, performance may be higher compared to a single processor system that features a kernel. Drawback of this solution is the tremendous resource overhead.

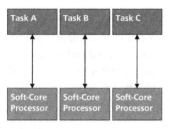

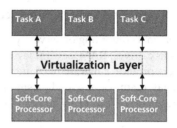

(a) Static Bindings.   **(b)** Virtualization Layer.

Figure 2.3: Resolving static Task-to-Processor Bindings (a) by Introduction of a Virtualization Layer between Tasks and Processors (b).

As an alleged solution, a hybrid solution could be exploited. Here, each safety-critical task might be bound to a dedicated processor, while other tasks in the system might share processor access via a kernel. However, the two design alternatives as well as this hybrid solution face the same major drawbacks. Due to the static bindings, it is not possible to either compensate for a defective processor at runtime or to adapt the task-processor bindings depending on current computing requirements. None of these solutions exploits the benefits arising from multi-processing, such as dynamically binding tasks to processors or executing a task in parallel on several processor instances.

As a consequence, a desired system has to feature the benefits of both designs. Tasks may share a processor resource despite avoiding the overhead caused by a kernel. In addition, strict task encapsulation has to be ensured to prevent task interference. Moreover, the solution has to exploit multi-processing, i. e., tasks may be dynamically allocated to and scheduled on a set of processors. In order to compensate for faulty devices, mechanisms for fault detection and the ability to switch from a faulty to a functioning processor have to be provided without the need to allocate a set of resource-wasting spare processors.

Virtualization as a mean of transparent task handling may enable all these features. This is achieved by the introduction of a so-called *Virtualization Layer* between tasks and processors. Otherwise isolated single-processor systems are thereby transformed into a flexible multi-processor system, cf. Figure 2.3. The static binding between tasks and processors is replaced by the ability to dynamically define new task-to-processor bindings.

As detailed in the previous section, embedded processor designs often face other constraints than processor systems for personal computers. Thus, in the following section, out of the characteristics of embedded processors and the intended purpose of a virtualization processor for an embedded processor array, a set of requirements is derived.

2.2.3 Requirements for Embedded Virtualization

For personal computing or server systems, cheap memory is available in huge numbers. Hard-disk drives, RAM, several levels of on-chip cache, and, last but not least, a set of registers provide a hierarchy of memory. In embedded systems, where cost reduction is crucial, memory is scaled as small as possible. Therefore, enabling virtualization features may not lead to a significant increase in memory needed for the multi-processor system.

Additionally, embedded systems may face timing constraints. Thus, a virtualization concept may not add a significant timing overhead and may not delay task execution. Consequently, if several tasks share a processor resource, the interruption of a running task in order to activate a task that has to fulfill its timing requirement has to be supported at any point in time.

Furthermore, embedded systems may be employed in safety-critical environments, such as in autopilots for plane navigation or, as outlined in Chapter 4.1, as driver assisting systems in an automotive environment. Correct system behavior is required since faulty computations may lead to severe incidents. This leads to two considerations. First, in an embedded system in a safety-critical environment, a task may not be harmfully affected by any other task in the system. Typical solutions completely, i.e., physically and logically, separate safety-critical tasks from other tasks in the system. Thus, mutual task interference has also to be strictly avoided for a system with virtualization features. Second, intrinsic mechanisms to detect or even mask faults are desired.

If multiple tasks are involved in an embedded system, the question about scheduling these tasks on the processor resources arises. A typical solution for scheduling issues is the exploitation of an embedded operating system or, with less overhead in terms of resources and time, a kernel. For the targeted MicroBlaze, several kernel types are available, such as the Xilkernel or Linux kernels. These kernels reside in the same memory as tasks and manage task scheduling. However, as discussed above, the overhead both in time and memory resources by a kernel is often unwanted. Thus, the usage of an existing kernel or operating system has to be avoided.

Enabling virtualization features for a set of processors will require enhancements to existing single-core processor designs. However, a solution that relies on the modification of a given processor architecture is limited to this specific processor type. Moreover, not all soft-core processors, despite being deployed as a textual hardware description, are modifiable, such as the MicroBlaze. Therefore, the virtualization features have to be as processor-independent as possible without dependence to processor-specific properties. At least, a possible migration to other processor types has to be supported with reasonable effort.

As for the processors, also the software of the tasks should not be undergo the need of a modification. Since most of embedded code is legacy code that is reused, a solution that required the re-writing of entire software projects is not feasible.

Given all these considerations, the following requirements towards an embedded virtualizable multi-processor system may be postulated:

1. Fast and transparent switch of task execution

2. No significant memory overhead caused by virtualization features

3. Guaranteed activation and interruption of task execution at any point in time

4. Strict encapsulation and isolation of tasks

5. Mechanisms for fault detection and masking

6. Avoidance of a common operating system or kernel residing in task memory

7. No modification of the processor core, usage of off-the-shelf processors

8. Minor or no modification of existing software code of tasks

In order to fulfill these requirements, the following sections will present the prerequisites necessary to enable virtualization features.

2.2.4 Prerequisites to enable Virtualization Features

In order to enable virtualization features under consideration of the requirements postulated above, some prerequisites have to be taken. As the virtualization concept is built around the transparent switch of tasks, it has to be defined at first, which information of a task has to be considered and preserved during a task switch. Second, the enhancements to existing default soft-core processors systems as depicted in Figure 2.1, which will enable virtualization properties, are detailed.

Consideration of Task Context

As the virtualization procedure is intended to interrupt and resume task execution at any point in time, the current state of a task has to be saved during its deactivation. The current state of a task is defined by its *context*.

A context typically includes the instruction memory, the current content of the data memory, the current program counter address of the processor pointing to the next instruction to be fetched, and, last but not least, the internal state of the processor, i. e., the content of its registers, during task execution. Figure 2.4 illustrates the context of a task running on a MicroBlaze processor for the two points in time t_1 and t_2. Changes in the context that arise during execution of the task are highlighted in red for t_2. The arrow indicates the current program counter address.

Given the context information at a certain point in time, the current state of a task is exactly defined. In a common multi-tasking operating system, the switch between tasks is handled in software. Here, e. g., the contents of the processor's registers, which hold data of the task to be deactivated, are written in a stack memory.

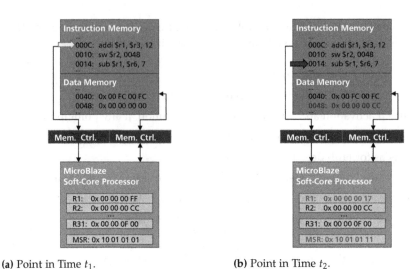

(a) Point in Time t_1.   (b) Point in Time t_2.

Figure 2.4: Dynamic Context of a Task over Time.

Upon this task's reactivation, the content is read back into the processor's register set. Accordingly, the proposed virtualization solution aims at extracting a task's context during the deactivation phase and at restoring this context during its reactivation. A comparable approach for an embedded multi-processor system was highlighted in [Beaumont 2012]. However, only a subset of the processors' registers was considered. In contrast, the virtualization procedure will take the full context inside a processor core into consideration. For hardware modules with internal states, the works of [Kalte 2005] and [Levinson 2000] highlight context extraction, which is based on a readback of the FPGA's configuration. While a readback of the FPGA configuration could also be exploited to determine the current state of a software task, this would limit the presented approach to FPGA architectures and, furthermore, would require an off-chip resource managing this context extraction. Thus, the present approach will handle task context extraction in a more convenient way independent of the actual chip architecture. The context elements to be saved during a virtualization procedure are now discussed in short.

Instruction and Data Memory The instruction memory is a read-only memory and, therefore, its state does not change during task execution. Thus, no special treatment is needed for the instruction memory. During task execution, the data memory is read and written, cf. Figure 2.4. With each write operation, the state of the data memory is altered. During deactivation of a task, the current state of the data memory has to be preserved and prevented from being altered. This may easily be achieved, e. g., by detaching the data memory from the processor during the deactivation phase.

Program Counter   The program counter is managed by the processor. By default, after executing an instruction, the program counter is set by the processor to point to the next instruction in the instruction memory. This is depicted by the arrow pointing at the instruction memory in Figure 2.4. A task may alter the program counter address, e. g., by jump or branch instructions. Here, the specific instruction or the result of its computation defines the new value of the program counter. As processors may feature a pipeline and, additionally, the computation of a new program counter address may take several clock cycles, predicting the program counter address is complex. During computation of a new program counter address, the instructions immediately following the jump or branch instruction are usually not executed by the processor. Some branch instructions may explicitly activate the execution of the first instruction following immediately after by setting a "delay slot" parameter. Thus, when interrupting a task's execution, it has to be ensured that all program counter address calculations have been completed before saving the program counter address. The saved program counter address has to point at the instruction that will be executed right after the reactivation of the task. Failing this, gaps in the instruction execution or duplicated execution of instructions will occur. Both scenarios cause an erratic behavior of the task and have to be strictly avoided. Section 2.2.5 will detail the procedure of saving the program counter address.

Internal Processor State   The part of the task context, which is represented by the internal state of the processor executing this task is defined by the content of the processor's registers. The register set of a processor consists of several general purpose registers, which may be addressed by a task, and state registers. State registers save information about past instructions, such as carry information after arithmetic operations. Changes in the register content of the processor are highlighted in Figure 2.4, lower portion of right hand side. To preserve the context of a task, the content of the registers has to be extracted out of the processor when deactivating a task. A solution is to output the register content on the data memory interface of the processor and to save it in a dedicated memory. For this purpose, a so-called *code injection* approach will be exploited. This includes the injection of a dedicated portion of machine code into the processor in order to output its register contents on the data memory interface.

Introduction of a Virtualization Layer

After having defined, which information has to be preserved during a task switching procedure, the Virtualization Layer is now introduced that implements the task switch. For demonstration purposes, the Virtualization Layer is highlighted for a single-processor system at first. For this system, a transparent deactivation and reactivation of a single task is detailed. Afterwards, this concept will be expanded to feature an array of processors and tasks.

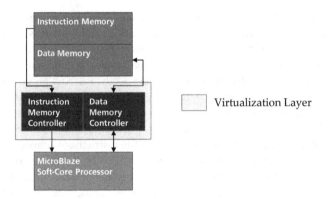

Figure 2.5: A MicroBlaze Processor System with the Virtualization Layer encapsulating the Memory Controllers.

The Virtualization Layer is implemented by means of a wrapper around the memory controllers, which connect the processor to its data and instruction memory, cf. Figure 2.5.[4] The Virtualization Layer is now expanded to feature the task context extraction and preservation. A hardware IP-Core called *Code Injection Logic* (CIL) is added. This core contains the machine code representation of the software, which will cause the processor to output its register contents. A detailed overview about the CIL's functionality is given in Section 2.2.5. The CIL is depicted in Figure 2.6.

To store the internal processor state, a dedicated memory region is instantiated inside the Virtualization Layer. The size of this so-called *Task Context Memory* (TCM) is shaped to fit the size of the register set of the processors.[5] The TCM is depicted in Figure 2.6.

In order to inject the machine code from the CIL into the processor and to store the register content into the TCM, the CIL and the TCM, respectively, need to be multiplexed onto the corresponding interfaces of the processor. Thus, two multiplexer structures may route the TCM and CIL to the data memory interface and to the instruction memory interface, respectively, of the processor. The control signals of the multiplexers are connected to the CIL, cf. Figure 2.6. This enables the CIL to initiate the task deactivation procedure.

The interface between the processor and the memory controllers consists of several signals of various bit widths. Besides data signals, control signals manage communication between processor and memory controller. For the prototype implementation

---

[4]As a side effect, commercial design tools of the device vendor Xilinx, Inc. recognize the entire structure as a valid processor system. Adding the Virtualization Layer instead as an IP core between the memory controllers and the processor or the memories, respectively, causes synthesis errors due to failing the so-called Design Rule Checks, i. e., automatic procedures, which check for valid system designs.

[5]For the MicroBlaze, there are 32 general purpose registers as well as the Machine Status Register (MSR). However, general purpose register R0 is a register containing the static value '0' and, thus, has not to be saved explicitly.

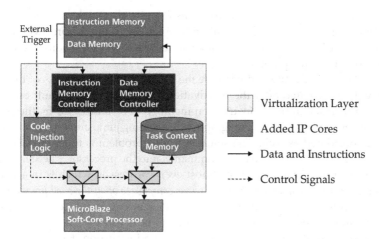

Figure 2.6: The Virtualization Layer with Code Injection Logic and Task Context Memory.

based on the MicroBlaze processor, all these signals sum up to a bit vector of the width of 296 bit. Therefore, the display of a multiplexer in Figure 2.6 is a simplified representation. Details of the processor-task memory interconnect are given in Section 2.3. An external signal connected to the CIL may now trigger the virtualization procedure, which will halt the task's execution and extract its context. Upon triggering the external signal again, the context is restored and the task resumes its execution from the point of its interruption. The following section will highlight this procedure in detail.

2.2.5 Virtualization Procedure

A first prototype implementation of the virtualization procedure has been presented in [Biedermann 2011b]. The procedure may be structured into three distinct phases. Phase 1 handles the deactivation of a running task. This includes extracting and saving its context. In phase 2, the actual task switch occurs. Section 2.3 will present a sophisticated solution to enable task switches on a processor array by means of a dynamically reconfigurable task-to-processor interconnection network. Phase 3 handles the reactivation of a task including restoring the task context up to resuming the task's execution at the position of its last deactivation.

Phase 1: Transparent Halt

As soon as the Virtualization Layer receives a signal from the external trigger depicted in Figure 2.6, the halting sequence is invoked. The instruction memory is immediately detached from the processor interface. Instead the CIL is routed to the processor. The CIL thereby mimics the behavior of the instruction memory controller. Therefore, the

processor assumes to further fetch instructions from its instruction memory. As at this
point in time, still some instructions wait in the pipeline inside the processor for being
executed.[6] The task's execution will be interrupted after the instructions queued in the
pipeline have passed the pipeline.

The first step is to identify and preserve the program counter address of the instruction that will be executed after the reactivation of a task. In the default case, this is
just the next instruction in the instruction memory to be addressed by the program
counter. However, as outlined in Paragraph 2.2.4, ongoing jump and branch instructions
have to be considered as well. The solution to this problem is to let the CIL inject a
sequence of `save word immediate` commands into the processor. These instructions
are part of default instruction set of almost every processor, which is in accordance
with Postulate 7 (*No modification of the processor core, usage of off-the-shelf processors*). The
instruction `save word immediate` outputs the content of a processor register on
the data memory interface. This value is then to be written to the data memory to
the address defined in the `save word immediate` instruction. However, as soon as
the instructions originally queued in the pipeline have passed the pipeline, the data
memory is detached from the processor. Thus, data eventually being output on the
data memory is not actually written into the data memory, but discarded. Instead, the
sequence of `save word immediate` instructions is exploited to determine, which instruction from the instruction memory would actually be executed next. This procedure
is denoted in Algorithm 1.

A special treatment is needed, if a branch instruction featuring a delay slot, a return
statement or an `immediate` instruction is detected in the instruction stream as last
instruction to regularly enter the processor pipeline before a virtualization procedure is
triggered. In this case, the procedure is being withheld for one clock cycle. Otherwise,
the instruction in the delay slot would be marked to be the instruction to be executed
right after the task's reactivation. While this would be the correct address, the program
would then continue with the instruction following the delay slot. The original branch
target addressed by the branch instruction would be lost. In delaying the procedure
by one clock cycle, i. e., by interrupting the execution after the delay slot entered the
pipeline, the instruction at which the task's execution will resume is the one addressed
by the branch instruction.

Another issue when interrupting task execution may arise by atomic instruction
sequences. Such sequences may not be interrupted in order to ensure correct system
behavior. If a processor detects an atomic instruction sequence, e. g., the invocation of
interrupt service routines is blocked despite occurrence of an interrupt. The purpose
of such sequences is, e. g., to realize transferring bursts of data to a communication
partner that expects to receive or send a data word every instruction cycle. The
behavior of the Virtualization Layer may be adapted to wait for the end of such an
atomic instruction sequence by monitoring the instruction stream before invoking the

---

[6]The MicroBlaze features a five stage pipeline.

Algorithm 1 Phase 1a of Virtualization Procedure: Determining the Program Counter Address at which to continue Task Execution after Reactivation.

Require: A processor system as depicted in Figure 2.6 consisting of a task t being executed on a processor p; a Virtualization Layer with Code Injection Logic CIL and dedicated memory TCM for the context of t; an external trigger En activating the virtualization procedure.
Ensure: Program counter address at which the task's execution will be resumed.

  1: **if** En triggers virtualization procedure **then**
  2:     **while** Branch/Return/Immediate instruction with delay slot detected in instruction stream **do**
  3:         Withhold procedure for one clock cycle
  4:     **end while**
  5:     Detach t's instruction memory from p and route t's CIL to p's instruction memory interface
  6:     Detach data memory after last instruction regularly fetched from instruction memory passed pipeline
  7:     Inject sequence of store word immediate instructions addressing data memory addresses 0, 4, 8, ...   ▷ Length of sequence determined by length of p's pipeline.
  8:     Store program counter addresses corresponding to save word immediate instructions in temporary variables $pc[0]$, $pc[4]$, $pc[8]$, ... inside Virtualization Layer
  9:     **while** No write on p's data memory interface **do**   ▷ E. g., due to ongoing branch target
 10:   computations.
 11:     **end while**
 12:     Write access via data memory interface of p at address x detected
 13:     Define address in variable $pc[x]$ to be the instruction memory address at which to resume task execution after reactivation
 14:     Save value of $pc[x]$ in TCM
 15: **end if**

---

virtualization procedure. However, as the length of the instruction sequence is not known to the Virtualization Layer, the virtualization procedure might be delayed for a substantial amount of time. As this would violate Postulate 3 (*Guaranteed activation and interruption of task execution at any point in time*) from Section 2.2.3, the usage of atomic instruction sequences is restricted.

As a next step, the task context stored inside the processor is extracted and saved in the TCM. Thus, the TCM is now routed to the data memory interface of the processor. Accordingly, the CIL may inject the machine code sequence to output the processor's register content. The instruction sequence being now inserted consists again of save word immediate instructions and outputs the register content sequentially on the data memory interface. Consequently, the register contents are saved inside the TCM.

In its default configuration, the only relevant status register of the MicroBlaze processor is the Machine Status Register (MSR). In the instruction set of the MicroBlaze, the content of the MSR may be copied into a general purpose register, which is then read-out by the context extraction routine. However, when the MicroBlaze is configured to feature, e. g., a floating point unit, other status registers are activated. For these registers, no instructions to output their content exist. Furthermore, other processor types might not feature the output of any status register on their data memory interface. In this case, the content of the status registers can be determined indirectly by executing

---

Algorithm 2 Phase 1b of Virtualization Procedure: Transparent Halt of Task Execution.

Require: A processor system as depicted in Figure 2.6 consisting of a task t being executed on a processor p; a Virtualization Layer with Code Injection Logic CIL and dedicated Memory TCM for the context of t; completion of Algorithm 1.

Ensure: Interruption of t's execution, register context of t stored in TCM.

1:   Attach t's TCM to p's data memory interface
2:   **for all** General purpose registers of p **do**
3:       Inject store word immediate command via CIL that outputs register content on p's data memory interface
4:       Write output of p's data memory interface sequentially into TCM
5:   **end for**
6:   **for all** Status registers of p **do**
7:       Inject instruction sequence via CIL that outputs p's status register on p's data memory interface
8:       Write content of status register into TCM
9:   **end for**

---

a predefined sequence of instructions stored in the CIL, whose result depend on the current value of the status bits in the status registers. Based on the result, the value of the status registers may be derived.

By now, all relevant context elements, which were identified in the previous Section, are stored. The steps performed in order to extract and preserve a task's context are denoted in Algorithm 2.

Processor Condition

When having extracted the task's context, the processor remains attached to the CIL and TCM. After executing the last command injected by the CIL, the processor is requesting the next instruction via its instruction memory interface. As long as the CIL does not input another instruction, the processor remains in this state. Instead of triggering a task switch as highlighted in the following section, a processor may also be deactivated at the end of phase 1. This may be achieved by disabling its clock input. In doing so, the energy consumption in a (multi-)processor system may be reduced. Section 2.7 will give details about the energy management features and measurements regarding the amount of energy saving by temporarily disabling a processor.

Phase 2: Transparent Switch of Execution of Tasks

In favor of a clear illustration, from now on, the CIL and TCM as well as the memory controllers, which correspond to a task are now referred as a *Virtbridge*, cf. Figure 2.7, right hand side. A Virtbridge is statically assigned to a dedicated task, i.e., its instruction and data memory. By now, only a single-processor system is considered. This system is expanded in the sequel to feature a second or third processor and corresponding tasks, cf. Figure 2.8. Note that each task resides in a dedicated memory region and the memories are completely disjoint. An additional controller now manages

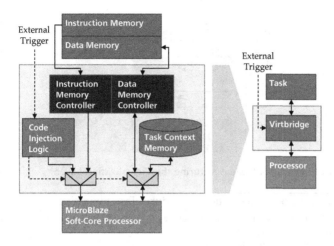

Figure 2.7: The IP Cores to facilitate Context Extraction and Restoration are subsumed to a Virtbridge.

the evocation of the virtualization procedures. After a task has been halted by the virtualization procedure denoted in Algorithms 1 and 2, it is not reliant to resume its execution on its original processor. Instead, the task's context may be restored on another processor in the system that is connected to the Virtualization Layer, i.e., the task-processor binding may be updated. A task-processor binding is defined in Definition 1; a convenient notation for bindings is given by the so-called Binding Vectors (BV), cf. Definition 2. Consequently, if now two or more tasks are halted by means of the virtualization procedure, the halted tasks may switch their corresponding processor. As depicted in Figure 2.8, this may be achieved, e.g., by means of a switching element that changes the routing of task memories to processors. Section 2.3 will introduce a sophisticated interconnect solution.

Definition 1 (Task-Processor Binding). *A task-processor binding B_i is a bijective function, which maps a task t_i of a set of tasks $t_1, t_2, \ldots, t_n \in T$ to a processor p_i of a set of processors $p_1, p_2, \ldots, p_m \in P$: $B : T \to P, t \mapsto p$.*

Definition 2 (Binding Vector). *A binding vector $BV_i = (t_w \mapsto p_x), (t_y \mapsto p_z), \ldots$ is composed of bindings B_i.*

Note that in a multi-processor system featuring the Virtualization Layer, a task does not have to be bound to a processor all the time. Instead, a task may be halted by the virtualization procedure and may then remain disconnected from a processor for an arbitrary amount of time. Furthermore, processors do not necessarily have to be bound to a task. These two features enable transparent sharing of a processor resource, cf. Section 2.2.6. In consequence, a binding vector BV_i does not necessarily cover all tasks

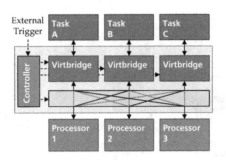

Figure 2.8: A Multi-Processor System featuring the Virtualization Layer.

Algorithm 3 Phase 2 of Virtualization Procedure: Task Switching.

Require: A set of tasks T, a set of processors P, a task-processor binding vector BV_1, an external trigger denoting a new binding vector BV_2.

Ensure: A new task-processor binding vector BV_2 realized by Virtualization Layer.

1: **for all** Tasks $t \in BV_1$ currently being executed on a processor **do**
2:     Halt t's execution by virtualization procedure denoted in Algorithms 1 and 2
3:     Detach t from its original processor p_i
4:     Mark p_i as idle
5: **end for**
6: **for all** Tasks $t \in BV_2$ **do**
7:     **while** Processor p_j that will be assigned to t in B_2 is not yet marked as idle **do**
8:         Wait for virtualization procedure of the task currently occupying P_j to finish phase 1
9:     **end while**
10:     Route memory of t to p_j ▷ cf. Algorithms 6, 11, 13
11:     Unmark p_j as idle
12: **end for**
13: Disable all processors still marked as idle   ▷ cf. Section 2.7

---

and processors present in the multi-processor system. Tasks and processors not covered by a binding vector BV_i remain unconnected. Without the prevenient virtualization procedure, just routing a task to another processor during normal task execution would lead to erroneous task behavior as parts of the task's context, which are stored inside the registers of the original processors, would not be transferred to the newly bound processor.

Algorithm 3 outlines the steps performed by the controller depicted in Figure 2.8 in order to facilitate a task switch. As the controller is implemented as an hardware IP-core, all the steps in the for-loops are executed in parallel. The question about when and how to define a new binding will be discussed in Chapter 3. For now, the new binding is given as additional information via the external trigger signal. After the binding is updated by means of adapting the routing of task memories to processors, the tasks are still halted. In order to resume task execution, phase 3, the context restoration is triggered.

Algorithm 4 Phase 3 of Virtualization Procedure: Context Restauration.

Require: A halted task t, its context inside the TCM of its virtbridge, a processor p routed to t via t's virtbridge.
Ensure: Seamless continuation of t's execution.
  1: **if** TCM of t is not empty **then**   ▷ i. e., t had already been active at least once
  2:     **for all** Status registers of p **do**
  3:         Inject instruction sequence that will set p's status register based on value saved inside TCM
  4:     **end for**
  5:     **for all** General purpose registers of p **do**
  6:         Inject `load word immediate` via CIL into p that reads from t's TCM into p's register
  7:     **end for**
  8:     Detach TCM from p's data memory interface and attach t's data memory
  9:     Inject branch instruction to program counter address saved in TCM
10:     Detach CIL from p's instruction memory interface and attach t's instruction memory
11: **else**   ▷ i. e., the task is being activated for the first time
12:     Attach t's instruction and data memory to p's memory interfaces
13:     Reset p ▷ optional step to clear p's register contents of the previous task
14: **end if**

Phase 3: Context Restoration and Resuming Task Execution

As detailed before, a task may either be just halted or a new processor binding may be realized by the virtualization procedure. In order to resume task execution, the context of the task has to be restored on the processor, which is now connected to the task. Therefore, `load word immediate` instructions injected by the CIL access the TCM and load its content sequentially into the register set of the processor. Again, the MicroBlaze features a dedicated instruction to set the MSR. In case that such an instruction is not available for other status registers or other processor types, a sequence of instructions may be inserted whose execution sets the bits in the status register(s) accordingly. Since the current content of the status registers is unknown until task deactivation, this instruction sequence would have to be set dynamically in order to trigger the specific bit pattern in the status registers after its execution. For the prototype based on the MicroBlaze processor, this special treatment is not necessary in the processor's standard configuration. After having restored the context information, the data memory of the task is reattached to the processor. An unconditioned jump to the beforehand saved program counter address and routing the instruction memory to the processor's instruction memory interface conclude the virtualization procedure. The execution of the task then seamlessly continues from the point of its previous interruption. Algorithm 4 denotes the steps performed during context restoration.

2.2.6 Analysis and Characteristics of the Virtualization Procedure

The virtualization procedure detailed in the previous Section is now discussed in short regarding its characteristics and possible limitations. At first, the possibility to enable transparent processor resource sharing is highlighted.

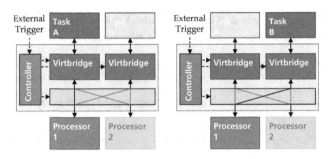

Figure 2.9: Sharing of a Processor Resource via Virtualization Procedure over Time.

Transparent Multi-Tasking by Virtualization Procedure

As detailed in the previous Section, the task-processor bindings may be updated by the virtualization procedure. In consequence, a processor may be occupied by several tasks over time. Altering the tasks that are bound to a processor is equivalent to common multi-tasking schemes. However, due to the properties of virtualization, neither the tasks nor the processor have or need knowledge about the fact, that more than one task makes use of the processor resource. As an advantage, the tasks' memories remain strictly separated all the time. Even during a virtualization procedure, their contexts are kept separate by design. This prevents harmful memory access violations by faulty tasks and is compliant to Postulate 4 (*Strict encapsulation and isolation of tasks*). Figure 2.9 depicts the processor resource sharing between two tasks over time via the Virtualization Layer. In Section 2.4, the benefits of an interconnection network will be exploited in order to enable convenient and fast processor resource sharing among tasks. Feasibility of the transparent resource sharing cannot be evaluated without regarding timing characteristics of the virtualization procedure. Furthermore, interrupting tasks at any time is a prerequisite to enable reliable processor resource sharing.

Guaranteed Interruption of Task Execution

The design of the Virtualization Layer guarantees that tasks can be interrupted at any point in time. This is achieved by detaching the instruction memory as soon as a virtualization procedure is triggered. However, to guarantee this property, several constraints apply. Interrupt and exception handling may come into conflict with the virtualization procedure as interrupts and exceptions do also intermit normal task execution. In consequence, an interrupt or exception may distort the virtualization procedure. Moreover, since the instruction memory is detached during the virtualization procedure, the interrupt service routine or the exception handling routine, which are usually stored inside the instruction memory, cannot be evoked in case of occurrence of an interrupt or exception. As a solution, interrupts and exceptions can be suppressed during the virtualization phase. However, for some interrupt-based systems, this may

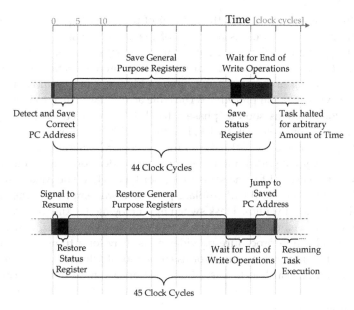

Figure 2.10: The Timing of the Virtualization Procedure for Halting and Resuming Task Execution for a Xilinx MicroBlaze Soft-Core Processor.

be accompanied by erroneous behavior of the module triggering the interrupt that expects the processor to handle the interrupt accordingly. Another solution is an external interrupt handler that forwards interrupts as soon as the corresponding task is active. For the reference implementations, interrupts and exceptions are disabled.

Another issue might be atomic instruction sequences. As discussed earlier, a virtualization procedure can not start until this atomic sequence has been executed. As the Virtualization Layer has no knowledge about the length of the atomic sequence, the time until the interruption of the task's execution via the virtualization procedure cannot be predicted. For time critical systems, atomic sequences have either to be limited in size to guarantee an interruption in a fair amount of time or their use has to be restricted completely. The following section will give details about the timing properties of the virtualization procedure.

Timing Properties

The timing of the virtualization procedure is mainly affected by the size of the register set of the processor type employed. As visible from Figure 2.10, which denotes the timing of phases 1 and 3 of the virtualization procedure for a MicroBlaze soft-core processor, the transfer of the processor registers' contents into the TCM takes the largest amount of time spent during the virtualization procedure. The duration of the procedure scales linearly with the number of processor registers. Time spent for flushing the pipeline, as well as handling of the status register is negligible. Not depicted in Figure 2.10 is the time needed for the actual switch of the task-processor bindings. Section 2.3 will introduce a task-processor interconnection network, which computes the routing of the next task-processor binding to be applied in parallel to phase 1 of the virtualization procedure. Thus, the actual task switch can be performed within one clock cycle as soon as phase 1 has been completed. For the prototype implementation, a complete task switch, i. e., the context extraction of one task as well as the reactivation of another task on the same processor is, therefore, handled within 89 clock cycles. For comparison reasons, the time needed for a conventional kernel-based task was measured for the same processor type. Here, the Xilkernel, a kernel provided by Xilinx, Inc. for the MicroBlaze processor, was employed. Measurements have revealed that a conventional task switch by employing the Xilkernel takes around 1.400 clock cycles, i. e., up to fifteen times longer than the virtualization procedure. Thus, the virtualization procedure provides a fast way for a transparent update of task-processor bindings, which outperforms conventional solutions and, thereby, offers significant advantages such as task isolation and transparent resource sharing.

Task Memories

In the presented approach, tasks are stored into completely disjoint memory areas. Even during binding updates, these memories remain strictly separated all the time. A task cannot access the memory region of any other task. Furthermore, each TCM is statically assigned to a dedicated task. In doing so, no mix-up of task contexts can occur. This prevents harmful memory access violations. In safety-critical systems, it is strictly avoided to schedule safety-critical tasks with other tasks of the system. A task might either corrupt the processor's state or even block the entire processor system due to an unforeseen stall. In this case, the safety-critical task would also be affected. However, the strict separation of task memories and contexts as well as the guaranteed task interruption of the virtualization approach may enable processor resource sharing even for safety-critical tasks. In an application example in Chapter 4.1, tasks relevant to safety with harsh timing constraints will be taken into consideration.

A byproduct of the disjoint memory design is a simplified placement on the target chip. FPGAs are not optimized to feature large multi-port memories that would be necessary if the chosen memory design would be abandoned. In this case, the inefficient synthesis as well as the hardened placement of such a memory might significantly deteriorate the performance of the system.

Modification of Processor Core or Memory/Memory-Controller

As detailed above, the context extraction is an essential step to enable virtualization features. The extraction of register contents is realized by a sequential readout via the data memory interface. The readout is initialized by an instruction sequence injected into the processor via the instruction memory interface. The original instruction memory and data memory are detached during this procedure. Instead of the proposed procedure, two implementation alternatives are discussed in short.

First, instead of detaching instruction and data memory, the corresponding instruction sequence might reside in a dedicated area of the instruction memory and the content of the registers might be saved into a reserved area within the data memory. To trigger a task deactivation, the program counter could be forced to point to the section containing the code for the register readout. However, this would require the designer to add the dedicated portion of machine code to each software task in the system. Additionally, for each task, a reserved area in its data memory had to be defined. These alterations conflict with Postulate 8 (*Minor or no modification of existing software code of tasks*) in Section 2.2.2. Therefore, this alternative is discarded.

Second, instead of relying on the memory interfaces of the processor, a soft-core processor might be expanded in order to feature a dedicated register interface that is triggered by a newly created virtualization instruction. Instead of reading the contents of registers out sequentially via the data memory interface, a dedicated register interface could then output all register values in parallel. This would significantly speed up the content read out.[7] However, this solution violates Postulate 7 (*No modification of the processor core, usage of off-the-shelf processors*) of Section 2.2.2, since this solution would be very processor-specific. Furthermore, not every soft-core processor's hardware description is modifiable. Moreover, a radical modification of the processor's behavior and interface would be required. This modification of a core that is otherwise optimized to be efficiently mapped onto the primitives of the target chip may lead to a significant performance drop due to an inefficient synthesis. For this reasons, this implementation alternative is also discarded.

Given these issues, the proposed work relies on a solution that detaches instruction and data memories and reroutes the signals to the instruction and data memory interface of the processor dynamically. This solution fulfills Postulates 6 (*Avoidance of a common operating system or kernel residing in task memory*), 7 (*No modification of the processor core, usage of off-the-shelf processors*), and 8 (*Minor or no modification of existing software code of tasks*) of Section 2.2.2 as neither the processor IP core nor the software tasks have to be modified.

Synthesis Results and Limitations

A prototyped system consisting of three processors and tasks has been implemented for a Virtex-5 FPGA from vendor Xilinx Inc. Table 2.1 compares the synthesis results of a static three-processor solution, i. e., processors that do not feature any task migration or resource sharing, to a three-processor system that is connected by a Virtualization Layer.

---

[7]In its default configuration, the MicroBlaze features 32 general purpose registers as well as the MSR. Instead of 33 consecutive reads, 1 read would be sufficient to extract the complete context.

Table 2.1: Comparing Static and Virtualizable 3-Processor Solutions for a Virtex-5 LX110T
FPGA.

	Conventional System	Virtualizable System
System Frequency	125 MHz	96 MHz
Resource Overhead	–	4,649 LUT 3,222 FF

The TCMs are implemented in flip-flop memory. The overhead introduced by the
Virtualization Layer occupies just about 5 % of the available resources on the employed
Virtex-5 LX110T FPGA. The maximum frequency of the virtualizable solution is lower
than for a static processor system. This is due to two reasons. The virtualization logic
adds a combinatorial delay to the task-processor path. Moreover, the multiplexer logic
that is exploited to adapt the routings between tasks and processors further elongates
combinatorial paths. As Section 2.3.4 will discuss, adding buffers into the path between
tasks and processors is not feasible.

Figure 2.11 depicts a placement map for a design on a Virtex-5 FPGA, which features
three soft-core processors highlighted by numbers as well as the Virtualization Layer,
which is highlighted in light grey. Although one can clearly derive from the Figure
that the design is far from exceeding the logic resources available on the FPGA, ex-
panding the design to feature more than three processors leads to unresolvable routing
constraints. This is caused by the interconnection of tasks and processors. An overlay
in dark grey depicts the connectivity of the design. As every task has to be connected
to each processor, a high wiring complexity is caused by the employed multiplexer
structures. As this limits scalability of the solution, the following section will introduce
a sophisticated task-to-processor interconnection scheme. This interconnect will not
only ease the routing but also feature intrinsic mechanisms for task scheduling and
updating bindings during runtime.

2.2.7 Intermediate Conclusions

By now, a procedure was detailed that features a transparent shift of task execution
without exploiting an underlying operating system or kernel. The speed of a task
switch by the virtualization procedure significantly outperforms common kernels.

An arbitrary number of tasks may transparently share a processor resource. Due
to disjoint task memories and task context memories, a strict separation of tasks is
guaranteed. Furthermore, evoking a context switch is possible at any point in time.
Therefore, even safety-critical tasks might share a processor resource with other tasks.
This is achieved without the need for modifying neither the processor nor the software
tasks. Based on the Postulates from Section 2.2.3, the following requirements are met:

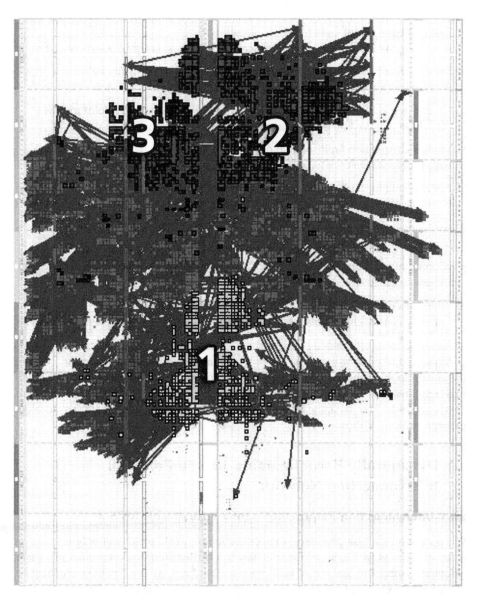

Figure 2.11: Floorplan of a virtualizable System featuring three Processors and the Virtualization Layer (light grey) on a Virtex-5 LX110T FPGA. The Area in dark grey depicts the Connectivity.

1. Fast and transparent switch of task execution ✔
   Faster than SW-based kernels; processors and tasks have no knowledge about switch

2. No significant memory overhead caused by virtualization features ✔
   For each task a small TCM stores program counter and processor registers

3. Guaranteed activation and interruption of task execution at any point in time ✔
   Virtualization procedure is able to interrupt task execution at any point in time

4. Strict encapsulation and isolation of tasks ✔
   Fully disjoint design of task memories and TCMs

5. Mechanisms for fault detection and masking ✖
   Will be handled in Section 2.6

6. Avoidance of a common operating system or kernel residing in task memory ✔
   Context switch is HW-based

7. No modification of the processor core, usage of off-the-shelf processors ✔
   Default processor with default instructions

8. Minor or no modification of existing software code of tasks (✔)
   Currently none; slight changes necessary for virtualized task communication, cf. Section 2.5

At present, the usability of the approach is limited, as routing constraints prevent the system to scale above the number of three processors. Moreover, as Section 2.5 will highlight, inter-task communication needs special treatment in a virtualizable system. To overcome the first issue, the following section introduces an advanced task-processor interconnection solution.

2.3 Dynamically Reconfigurable Task-to-Processor Interconnection Network

2.3.1 Interconnection Requirements for a virtualizable MPSoC

When designing a task-processor interconnection network, which not only features an array of tasks as well as of processors, but has furthermore to accomplish processor resource sharing and updates of task-processor bindings, as, e. g., by the virtualization procedure, several requirements come into play. An interconnection solution is needed, where at any point in time, all of the processors are able to work in parallel, i. e., a solution where in each clock cycle instructions may be fetched by each processor. Without this requirement, the advantages of a parallel processor array can not be fully exploited, since the throughput is significantly reduced, if processors have to wait for several clock cycles until they receive an instruction from the instruction memory of their adjacent task. This renders interconnection solutions unfeasible that would sequentially deliver the processors with instructions. Therefore, the envisaged solution has to feature a simultaneous interconnection of all processors to task memories. The virtualization procedure, which was introduced in the previous Section, may update the task-processor bindings during runtime. In consequence, this requires dynamically routing a task to another processor. As not only the binding of one task-processor relation may be updated, but, in contrast, all of the processors may feature a new task assignment, the routes from tasks to processors may differ completely among two different binding vectors. As routing may be a problem with high complexity, e. g., running an on-demand synthesis, which computes the routes necessary for a binding to be applied, and applying this result by a dynamic partial reconfiguration on an FPGA is not feasible. This is due to both the time needed for synthesis, which lies in the range of minutes, if not hours, and the computation effort that requires a strong processor as well as a decent amount of RAM – both are not in the usual equipment of an embedded system. Another solution would be to precalculate all binding possibilities on a workstation and to store these routing results in an off-chip memory. From there, the required routing may be selected and applied, again by dynamic partial reconfiguration. However, even when automating the step of synthesizing different bindings, the number of routings, which would be generated increases drastically with the size of the processor array. For a design featuring eight processors and eight tasks, there would be about 40,000 possible routings, which have to be precalculated, as well as stored somewhere in the embedded design.[8] Again, this is not a feasible solution due to the overhead in terms of time and memory. This leads to the requirement that an interconnection solution has to feature a fast online-rerouting of task-processor connections, which does not rely on pre-synthesized results.

A fast and simple update of task-processor bindings is further required in order to provide an efficient mean for scheduling several tasks on the same processor resource by exploiting the virtualization procedures. The time needed for establishing a task-processor route may not significantly exceed the time needed for the virtualization procedure to accomplish a context switch. Otherwise, scheduling of tasks would be drastically slowed down by setting up the corresponding task-processor routes.

Moreover, the interconnection solution has to handle not only the transport of single signals, but of complete processor-task interfaces. As highlighted in the previous Section, the virtualization solution encapsulates the memory controllers of a task. Therefore, all the signals on the memory interface between the memory controllers and a processor have to be routed by the interconnection solution.[9] As the fundamental design of FPGAs, which are exploited for the reference implementation, is not optimized to dynamically route interfaces of huge bit widths, the synthesis of such an interconnection

---

[8]For the number of processors n, the number of tasks m and the assumption that $m \geq n$, the number of possible bindings is $\frac{m!}{(m-n)!}$.

[9]For the prototype design based on MicroBlaze soft-core processors, the interface plus a set of trace signals features a width of 296 bit.

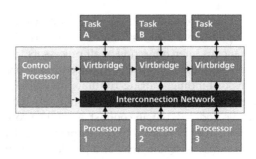

Figure 2.12: A virtualizable System featuring a dedicated Soft-Core Processor for Binding
      Management.

solution – almost regardless of its type – may lead to inefficient synthesis results.
Section 2.3.5 will discuss the outcomes of this issue.

Last but not least, aside from the interconnection between tasks and processors, an
instance is required, which will manage the update of task-processor routes. For this
purpose, a dedicated soft-core processor, which is not part of the parallel processor array,
is introduced, cf. Figure 2.12. On this processor, the management of bindings as well as
commands that will trigger an update of the task-processor routes is accomplished.

2.3.2 Architectural Alternatives

In the following, several interconnection alternatives for multi-processor designs are
discussed in short. A plethora of architectural solutions exist to solve the problem of
efficiently connecting processors to task memories. Here, however, only some of the
most prominent solutions are highlighted in short and discussed with special regard to
the requirements, which were identified above.

Static Interconnect

In the beginning of the era of processors, a chip usually featured a single processor,
which was sometimes accompanied by a set of co-processors. As there was just one
processor there, the interconnection to the corresponding task memory was static.
Today's embedded design most often still rely on the static interconnect of a task
memory to a processor. Despite being still predominant for many embedded designs,
such a static interconnect is obviously completely unsuited for the targeted virtualizable
multi-processor system.

However, other static interconnects, such as busses, may be exploited for multi-
processor interconnection. Processor architectures such as the IBM Cell [Chen 2007]
feature, e. g., a ring-based bus system to enable intra-processor communication. For
the interconnection between a set of task memories and an array of processors, busses
have the disadvantage of complex access management. A bus may realize only one

connection at one point in time. However, each processor is expected to receive an instruction from the task memory almost each clock cycle. Thus, in order to connect a set of task memories to a set of processors in parallel, a bus is not well suited. To overcome this issue, a set of busses in parallel may be exploited. However, this foils the initial idea of a bus providing a common communication interface for a set of connected modules. Other approaches rely on globally addressable memory. Here several problems arise. At least on FPGA architectures, large multi-port memories are hard to synthesize efficiently. The usage of off-chip memory may increase the latency, which is not acceptable for instruction fetch. When exploiting caches, keeping cache memories coherent becomes an issue.

Network-on-Chip

The increasing communication overhead arising from many-core architectures some-times referred to as "sea of processors" [Yamauchi 1996] has led to new communication paradigms in complex SoC. In a Network-on-Chip (NoC), techniques known from the area of computer networks are applied in embedded system design [Hemani 2000, Benini 2002]. This may involve, e. g., packet-based transfers, dynamic routes instead of static interconnects and a runtime scalability. While NoC provide a solution for intra-task communication or for links to external components, their applicability for the task memory-processor interface is restrained by several factors. A processor usually fetches new instructions every clock cycle, thus, the instruction interface has to be fed continuously. Depending on the NoC type, this requirement cannot be met all the time depending on the current route between the task memory and the processor. Furthermore, most NoC rely upon a protocol, i. e., a control overhead is introduced, e. g., by adding a header to every instruction, which has to be truncated before the instruction is fed into an off-the-shelf processor.

There are dedicated chip architectures providing NoC. The TILE64 architecture [Bell 2008], e. g., exploits a mesh design, which consists of five NoC connecting the grid of 64 processor tiles on the chip. Here, local caches for each processor compensate for the latency when accessing the external DDR memory. The Single-chip Cloud Computer (SCCC) [Howard 2010] by Intel takes a similar, mesh-based approach. Another approach provides non-uniform memory access (NUMA) across a set of memory types and an architecture explicitly aimed at Invasive Programming, cf. Section3.4 [Henkel 2012]. However, all these architectures require a decent overhead in terms of software and hardware in order to provide coherent cache levels among the processor cores in the grids. Furthermore, as these solutions exploit dedicated chip designs, it is difficult to transfer these concepts to other target architectures, such as FPGAs. Moreover, a common memory access model may pose a significant safety risk arising from malicious address space violations. The virtualization procedure of Section 2.2, thus, relies on strictly disjoint task memories.

Figure 2.13: A Crossbar Switch in its two Configuration Modes.

Crossbars and Multistage Interconnection Networks

One of the oldest interconnection solutions based on telephone interconnects are non-blocking switching networks [Clos 1953]. Here, arrays of crossbars are interconnected in a way so that every input-output permutation can be realized. By its non-blocking structure, each input is guaranteed to be routed to its designated output. In contrast to full crossbars, switching networks reduce the overhead in switching elements and are, thus, less resource-expensive. Since the structure of a switching network may be purely combinatorial, these networks are well-suited for communication, which is based upon 1-1 relations and require a continuous data transfer without delay caused by register stages within the network. The concept of switching networks of Clos was later expanded to permutation networks [Waksman 1968]. Permutation networks introduce several distinct advantages, such as fast routing algorithms and a generic, scalable layout. Thus, permutation networks will be the interconnection type of choice for virtualizable MPSoC.

2.3.3 Permutation Networks

As for other multi-stage networks, the concept of permutation networks is known for many years as they were already proposed in 1968 [Waksman 1968]. In the past, they have been exploited for processor-memory interconnection, e. g., in [Goke 1973], [Patel 1981]. They may be regarded as a compromise between full n-to-n crossbars and point-to-point interconnects. For the first ones, they consume fewer resources but also do not always offer full flexibility, and for the last ones, they at least offer some flexibility.[10] Usually, permutation networks feature the same number of inputs and outputs and their number is a power of two. As their structure is generic, networks with a higher number of inputs may be constructed recursively out of networks with lower numbers of inputs. The fundamental structure of permutation networks consists of reconfigurable crossbar switches connected by a static interconnect.

A crossbar switch is a small switching element featuring two inputs and two outputs. It may either route both inputs to their corresponding outputs or route the inputs to the

---

[10]Indeed, according to its original definition in [Waksman 1968], they are supposed to be able to realize all possible $n!$ input-output relations for n inputs and outputs. Some of the now discussed networks, such as Butterfly networks, do not fulfill this property and are, hence, strictly speaking no permutation networks. In the following the term permutation network is applied to networks, whose crossbar switches are connected by static interconnects.

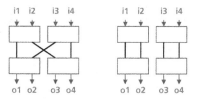

Figure 2.14: Two Networks with different static Interconnects between Crossbar Switches.

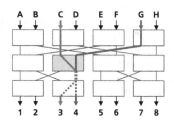

Figure 2.15: A Butterfly Network of Size 8×8 with Occurrence of a Blockade: C and G cannot establish their desired Routes at the same Time.

outputs in a cross manner. Figure 2.13 depicts a crossbar switch in its two configuration modes. The configuration of a crossbar switch may be toggled during runtime.

The actual type of a permutation network is defined by the pattern of static interconnects, which connect the crossbar switches. The interconnect is chosen at the design phase and is not altered at runtime. For four crossbar switches, in Figure 2.14, two different types of permutation networks are established by choosing two static interconnects. Depending on the permutation network type, the number of crossbar switches as well as the static interconnect between crossbar switches may vary.

In the following, different permutation network types are evaluated in short in order to identify the most suited type for being employed in a virtualizable MPSoC regarding the prerequisites defined in Section 2.3.1. The selection for the specific network types to be discussed was made in order to highlight differences among them in terms of flexibility, routing complexity, scalability and resource consumption. A further in-depth discussion of other well-known permutation network types, such as Omega networks, adds no insight regarding the employment in the virtualizable MPSoC. So, an exhaustive discussion of different permutation network types is not the goal of this work and is, therefore, omitted.

Selected Types of Permutation Networks

Butterfly Networks *Butterfly networks*, cf. Figure 2.15 feature fair resource consumption and a modest length of their combinatorial paths. The resource consumption is $n_{i \times i} = n_{(i/2) \times (i/2)} \cdot 2 + \frac{i}{2}$ crossbar switches, with i being the number of inputs of the

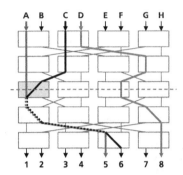 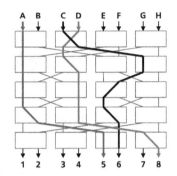

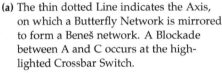

(a) The thin dotted Line indicates the Axis, on which a Butterfly Network is mirrored to form a Beneš network. A Blockade between A and C occurs at the highlighted Crossbar Switch.

(b) Blockade resolved by alternate Route.

Figure 2.16: A Beneš Network of Size 8×8.

network.[11] For the smallest network size with $i = 2$ the number of crossbar switches is $n_{2 \times 2} = 1$. Because of the relatively few stages[12] of the Butterfly network, it offers only a low interconnectivity, i. e., not every input-output relation may be established. This is depicted in Figure 2.15 as well. In this example, inputs C and G cannot be routed to outputs 3 and 4 at the same point in time. There, a so-called *blockade* occurs. Thus, if the inputs are seen as tasks and the outputs of the network as processors, not all task-processor bindings would be realizable. As the flexibility of task migration would, therefore, be limited by employing Butterfly Networks, they are not considered further. However, they might be well-suited for scenarios with harsh resource constraints and few dynamic binding configurations, where their low connectivity does not raise problems. Routing is fairly easy by applying a bisection method.

Beneš Networks A *Beneš network* may be constructed out of a Butterfly network, which is doubled and mirrored along a horizontal axis at the lowermost stage of crossbar switches, cf. Figure 2.16. The resource consumption may, therefore, be derived from the formula given for Butterfly networks. The number of crossbar switches necessary to form a Beneš network of the size $i \times i$ is given as $n_{i \times i} = (m_{i \times i} - i/2) \cdot 2 + i/2$ with $m_{i \times i}$ being the number of crossbar switches employed in a Butterfly network of the size $i \times i$. This number may be calculated by the formula given in the previous paragraph. As for the Butterfly network, for $i = 2$, $n_{2 \times 2} = 1$. Due to the increased number of stages, the flexibility increases, therefore lowering the risk of impossible input-output relations.

---

[11]The formula containing $n_{(i/2) \times (i/2)}$ to compute $n_{i \times i}$ hints to the recursive structure of permutation networks.

[12]The maximum number of crossbar switches between an input and an output of the network.

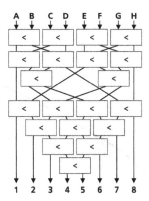

Figure 2.17: A Max-Min Sorting Network of Size 8×8.

Algorithm 5 Sorting Property of a Crossbar Switch.

Require: A value x on left input i_l, a value y on right input i_r of crossbar switch CS.
Ensure: Left output o_l and right output o_r of CS output x and y in ascending order.
 1: **if** $x \leq y$ **then**
 2:     Configure CS to route i_l to o_l and i_r to o_r
 3: **else**
 4:     Configure CS to route i_l to o_r and i_r to o_l
 5: **end if**

However, finding blockade-free routes is difficult in a Beneš network. Moreover, with increasing numbers of inputs and outputs, calculating the configuration of the crossbar switches in order to set up routes becomes even more complex. A self-routing algorithm for Beneš networks is presented in, e. g. [Nassimi 1981], a Matrix-based algorithm in [Chakrabarty 2009]. There are expansions of Beneš networks, which are proven to not produce blockades, [Arora 1990]. These multi-Beneš networks, however, require far more complex interconnects and crossbar elements. As the network configuration in the virtualizable MPSoC will vary at runtime based on the current task-processor binding, a fast and easy routing algorithm is needed. Since this is not the case for Beneš networks, this network type is also discarded.

Sorting Networks   Next, *Sorting Networks* are considered. In a sorting network each crossbar switch acts as a comparator element as detailed in Algorithm 5. By applying a sorting behavior at each crossbar switch, in consequence, at the output stage all values from the input ports will be sorted in order. Therefore, establishing routes is very easy, if the outputs are labeled in ascending order and the inputs use these labels to identify their desired output. Since sorting networks are able to sort any input sequence, they consequently are also able to realize every possible input/output relation. They are, therefore, true permutation networks in its original sense.

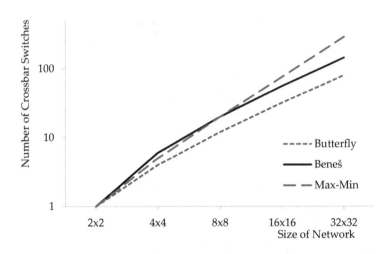

Figure 2.18: Growth of Resource Consumption in Terms of Crossbar Switches for different Permutation Network Types and Sizes.

Batcher proposed several concurrent sorting networks in 1968 such as an Odd-Even Mergesort and Bitonic Sort [Batcher 1968]. An implementation and evaluation of a generic bitonic sort on a massively parallel multi-core chip was done, e. g., in [Biedermann 2008]. Another sorting network was proposed by Parberry [Parberry 1992]. A plethora of other sorting network types, which map existing sorting algorithms to a network representation, exist, as proposed, e. g., in [Ajtai 1983, Rudolph 1985]. When sorting a sequence of the length of n, with n being a power of two, sorting networks mainly differ in terms of the number of crossbar switches employed and the delay from input to output. For the reference implementation, a sorting network called *Max-Min network*, whose structure was developed in the scope of the diploma thesis of Wei Lin [Lin 2012], is exploited, cf. Figure 2.17. While an optimal solution for a network of the size 8×8 features 19 crossbar switches [Knuth 1997], the employed Max-Min network is built upon 20 crossbar switches. Despite not being the optimal network for the given size, a reshaping procedure will be highlighted for the Max-Min network in Section 2.3.5, which creates an asymmetric shape, i. e., a network, which is able to feature more inputs than outputs.

As visible from Figure 2.17, a sorting network is not necessarily balanced, i. e., the number of crossbar switches, which are traversed varies for different input-output paths. This results in different combinatorial lengths of the routes. For the reference implementation of FPGAs, unbalance is not an issue, since the maximum clock frequency is derived from the slowest, i. e., longest combinatorial path. Therefore, all routes are guaranteed to match timing requirements albeit some routes could tolerate higher clock frequencies due to their shorter paths.

Table 2.2: Evaluation of different Permutation Network Types.

	Butterfly	Beneš	Max-Min
Interconnectivity	low	medium	**high**
Resource Consumption	low	medium	high
Combinatorial Delay	low	high	high
Routing Complexity	medium	high	**low**

The number of crossbar switches necessary for a Max-Min network of the size $i \times i$ is $n_{i \times i} = n_{i/2 \times i/2} \cdot 2 + \sum_{x=1}^{i/2} x$. Figure 2.22 of Section 2.3.4 illustrates the derivation of this formula.

Figure 2.18 depicts the resource consumption in terms of crossbar switches for the discussed permutation networks. The Butterfly network features the lowest resource consumption at the expense of a high risk of blockades. Up to size 8×8, the Max-Min network maintains a lower resource consumption than a Beneš network. Beginning with sizes 16×16, the growth of the Max-Min network's resource consumption distinctly surpasses those of Beneš and Butterfly networks. Section 2.3.4 will document, however, the limited necessity of network sizes of 16×16 and beyond. Furthermore, Section 2.3.5 proposes design alternatives by clustering networks of lower size. Thus, the objection of a step growth in resource consumption for the Max-Min network with larger network sizes has not to be considered.

Table 2.2 summarizes the characteristics of the evaluated permutation networks. This is further depicted by Figure 2.19, which visualizes the advantages of the different network types. Despite their higher resource consumption, whose impact is subsequently lowered by Moore's Law, Max-Min networks are the type of choice for the virtualizable MPSoC, because of the fast routing algorithm and the full flexibility. This routing algorithm enables the quick setup of new task-processor relations. In the following, the adoption of the Max-Min network as a task-processor interconnection is detailed. In the scope of a virtualizable MPSoC, this enhancement was proposed in [Biedermann 2012c].

2.3.4 A Sorting Permutation Network as Task-Processor Interconnect

In the following, tasks are seen as the inputs, processors as the outputs of the network. Despite referring to tasks as *input* and to processors as *output* of the network, task-processor connections remain bidirectional, as some data, such as the program counter address, are routed from the processor towards the task memory and other data, such as an instruction from the instruction memory is routed from the task's memory to the processor. Tasks are labeled in alphabetical order beginning with A, while processors are labeled in numerical order beginning with 1.

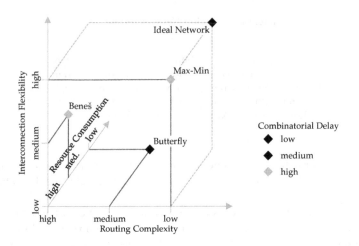

Figure 2.19: Individual Properties of different Permutation Network Types.

Structure

For the virtualization architecture, the sorting network is implemented in a two-layered structure, cf. Figure 2.20. The first layer realizes the physical connection between the task memories and the processor cores. The second layer acts as a shadow copy of the network. It is exploited to precalculate new routes at runtime, which are then applied to the first layer. In doing so, the physical connection between tasks and processors will not be interrupted by a routing update. This feature will be important for the later-discussed transparent processor resource sharing.

Binding Updates for 1-to-1 Relations

This Section will outline the behavior of the interconnection network to establish a task-processor Binding Vector. As defined in Section 2.2.5, a Binding Vector denotes, which task is to be executed on which processor. For example, the Binding Vector

$$BV_1 = (A \mapsto 1), (B \mapsto 2), (C \mapsto 3)$$

defines that task A is bound to processor instance 1, B to processor instance 2 and C to processor instance 3.

Binding Vectors are managed by a dedicated soft-core processor inside the Virtualization Layer, cf. Figure 2.20. The processor may enter a new Binding Vector into the system at any time. The decision about which binding to activate is application specific and may either be statically defined by the designer or by applying binding

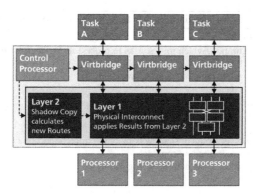

Figure 2.20: The two-layered Structure of the Task-Processor Interconnection Network.

optimization strategies, which is detailed in Section 3.2. An example use of exploiting binding optimizations to define suited bindings for the virtualizable architecture is given in the application example in Section 4.1.

In order to establish a Binding Vector in the virtualizable MPSoC, it is mapped to a configuration of the interconnection network. As soon as the control processor outputs a new Binding Vector, the execution of all tasks currently running on the set of processors is interrupted by the virtualization procedure detailed in Algorithm 2 in Section 2.2.5. Meanwhile, the configuration of the permutation network is calculated by the shadow copy of the interconnection network as defined by Algorithm 6. Here, the sorting property of the Max-Min network is exploited to quickly calculate a new configuration. Figure 2.21 depicts the routing process.

Consequently, the configuration information is passed to the physical layer of the interconnection network as soon as the execution of all tasks has been interrupted by the virtualization procedure. The new configuration of the network is then applied. This configuration establishes routes from tasks to processors in accordance with the Binding Vector entered by the control processor. As a result of the routing algorithm also tasks, which are not listed in the current binding vector are routed to processors. Those processors are marked to be temporarily deactivated as denoted in Algorithm 3, cf. Figure 2.21d. As a result, the clock input of these processors is temporarily disabled by the Virtualization Layer. In doing so, the tasks not featured by the binding vector are prevented from being executed.

Timing of the routing process is as follows: A Binding Vector is transferred sequentially from the control processor to the interconnection network. For a system featuring n tasks, of which are m listed in the Binding Vector, this takes $m \cdot 2$ clock cycles. For tasks not listed in the Binding Vector, unused processor labels are sequentially assigned. This takes $n - m$ clock cycles. Afterwards, the shadow copy sorts the input data. Each stage of the interconnection network is buffered. As the depth of the Max-Min network of the size $n \times n$ is $n - 1$, after $n - 1$ clock cycles the inputs are routed to the outputs

---

Algorithm 6 Mapping of a Binding Vector to a Network Configuration.

Require: A binding vector BV_j.
Ensure: A network configuration, which routes tasks to processors in accordance with BV_j.
1: **for all** Tasks listed in BV_j **do**
2:     Set RoutingID of task to label of assigned processor
3: **end for**
4: **for all** Tasks not listed in BV_j **do**
5:     Set RoutingID to a processor label unused so far
6: **end for**
7: Set RoutingIDs of tasks as inputs of shadow copy of the interconnection network
8: **for all** Crossbar Switches in shadow copy **do**
9:     Behave as sorting elements as defined in Algorithm 5
10:    Output current configuration of CS
11: **end for**
12: Accumulate all configurations of crossbar switches
13: Apply configuration information at physical network layer

---

of the network. The complete configuration information is passed in parallel to the physical layer. The information for the Virtualization Layer about disabling clock inputs of processors is passed in parallel as well. In summary, the complete network reconfiguration process takes $m \cdot 2 + (n - m) + (n - 1) + 1$ clock cycles with n being the number of tasks in the system and m the number of tasks listed in a Binding Vector. For a 8×8 network, in its worst case, i. e., if each task is assigned to a processor, the configuration process takes $8 \cdot 2 + 8 + 7 + 1 = 32$ clock cycles. The configuration process is started in parallel with the virtualization procedure, which is triggered for each task as soon as a new Binding Vector is entered. As the suspension of tasks by the virtualization procedure takes 44 clock cycles, cf. Section 2.2.6, the introduction of the interconnection network of sizes up to 8×8 does not elongate the time needed for binding updates.

At the moment, only 1-1 relations between tasks and processors are considered. Besides system featuring redundant modules, most real-world scenarios will presumably barely benefit from the ability to swap processors among tasks. Therefore, Section 2.4 will introduce advanced binding and routing concepts, which will enable, e. g., convenient task scheduling mechanisms. At first, however, the characteristics of the employed Max-Min network as well as optimization strategies are discussed in the following sections.

Scalability of the Network

The network is symmetric in terms of number of inputs and outputs, i. e., in the number of attached tasks and memories. It is designed to scale to an arbitrary power of two of inputs and outputs. This is achieved by the generic structure of the network. Larger networks contain smaller networks as building elements, cf. Figure 2.22. Despite this theoretical scalability, the feasibility of large-scaled permutation networks is limited. This is due to the fact, that the permutation network features only combinatorial, un-

$$BV_1 = (A \mapsto 4), (B \mapsto 2), (C \mapsto 7), (D \mapsto 3), (E \mapsto 1), (H \mapsto 5)$$

(a) An example Binding Vector.

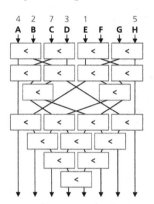

(b) Naming of Inputs according to Processor Assignments.

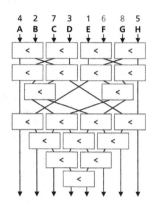

(c) Remaining Inputs filled with unused Processor Labels.

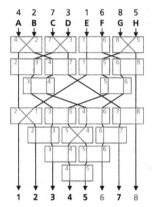

(d) Applying the Sorting Behavior of Algorithm 5. Processors 6 and 8 are marked for being temporarily deactivated.

Figure 2.21: Illustration of the Routing Algorithm performed in the Shadow Copy of the Interconnection Network.

buffered signals between tasks and processors. The lengths of the longest combinatorial path, i.e., the longest route between two register elements determine the maximum clock frequency achievable for the system. If a higher clock frequency is chosen than defined by the longest combinatorial path, a signal being output at a clock event onto this path can be altered by the succeeding clock event before being saved to the register

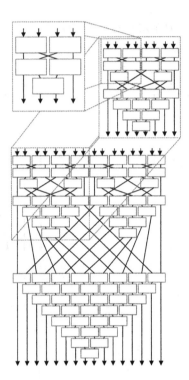

Figure 2.22: A 4 × 4 Network is Building Block of a 8 × 8 Network, which in turn is Building Block of a 16 × 16 Network.

at the end of the path. Thus, the results are incorrect register values and system misbehavior. The larger the permutation network is scaled, the more stages of crossbar switches exist in the network and, consequently, the longer the combinatorial path gets. With increasing network size, the system's clock frequency therefore decreases.

The depth of a Max-Min network can be derived from its generic structure. A Max-Min network of the size $n \times n$ consists of two Max-Min networks of the size $\frac{n}{2} \times \frac{n}{2}$ placed beside each other and a funnel shaped sequence of crossbar switches placed below these nets, cf. Figure 2.22. This "funnel" has the width of $\frac{n}{2}$ crossbar switches on top. Therefore, for a $n \times n$ network, the funnel adds $\frac{n}{2}$ additional stages of crossbar switches. The overall depth of the network may now be derived recursively as denoted in Algorithm 7.

Figure 2.23 gives an impression about the correlation of network size and maximum clock frequency. The numbers are given for a Xilinx Virtex-6 FPGA. As a network size of 16 × 16 causes placement errors on the target chip due to resource constraints, the frequency given for size 16 × 16 is an estimation. One may derive from the numbers of Figure 2.23 that the employment of a permutation network causes a significant

---

Algorithm 7 Computation of the Depth of a Max-Min Network.

Require: A Max-Min network of the size $n \times n$ with n being a power of two and $n \geq 2$.
Ensure: The depth d of the Max-Min network.
1:   $d = \text{ComputeDepth}(n \times n)$
2: **function** ComputeDepth($n \times n$)
3:     **if** $n \times n = 2 \times 2$ **then**
4:       **return** 1
5:     **else**
6:       **return** $\frac{n}{2} + \text{ComputeDepth}(\frac{n}{2} \times \frac{n}{2})$ ▷ the size of the "funnel" plus the size of the smaller
7:       network used as building block
8:     **end if**
9: **end function**

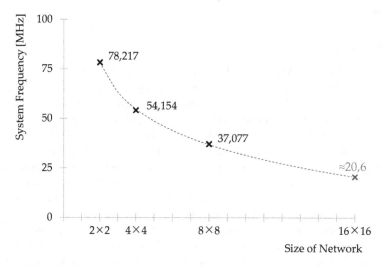

Figure 2.23: The Correlation between Network Size and System Frequency for Network Sizes 2×2 to 16×16.

performance drop in the system. The first prototype of a Virtualization Layer between three processors without dedicated interconnection scheme achieved 91 MHz on a Virtex-5. When employing the permutation network, already the 2×2 version is slower as the first prototype without the interconnection network. Obviously, the permutation network is, therefore, a performance bottleneck.

Adding buffers into the combinatorial paths of the network seem to solve the problem at first sight. Here, one or several register stages are added into the network. Indeed, this significantly shortens the critical paths and, therefore, raises the clock frequency. However, adding registers between task memories and processors causes a system behavior that is hard to handle and error-prone. Usually, the instruction fetch, i. e., reading an instruction out of a memory location of the instruction memory, which is defined by the program counter is accomplished within one clock cycle. Adding registers to the instruction memory-processor route causes the instruction fetch to take several clock cycles. As a consequence, the correlation between program counter address and the instruction to be executed is lost. This may cause erroneous behavior in case that branch executions perform branches with relative branch targets, whose resulting branch target address depend on the current program counter address. Therefore, buffering the network route is not an applicable solution.

A significant drop in system frequency is only tolerable, if the system gains other, distinct advantages in return. The most prominent gain by exploiting a permutation network is the full flexibility with regard to the task-processor bindings. The following section discusses, under which circumstances flexibility is a valuable tradeoff against system frequency.

Flexibility of the Network

By exploiting the Max-Min network, a task inside this network may be shifted to any processor that is connected to the network. Chapter 3 will highlight the benefits of exploiting this flexibility. In short, dynamically adapting task-processor bindings may not only enable a convenient method of sharing of processor resources, but also allow for module redundancy or even advanced concepts, such as the Agile Processing paradigm, which is introduced in Section 3.4. However, the flexibility comes at the price of significantly reduced system frequency as discussed above. Therefore, it is not feasible to design a virtualizable design with a processor number larger than eight. For more than eight processors, a frequency of about one fifth or less of the maximum clock frequency is expected. In return, the execution of a task could be shifted, e. g., among sixteen processors. The design concepts in the following chapter will point out that tasks in a complex embedded design indeed benefit from at least *some* flexibility but do not need *full* flexibility, i. e., there is no need to assure that any task in an embedded design may be executed on any processor of the system. For redundancy issues, for example, it is important that at least one or two processor resources can take over the execution of a task relevant to safety in case its processor failed. The Agile Processing scheme will also profit from dynamic binding updates, but will not rely on a very large permutation network in which each task might be shifted to any processor. In conclusion, for smaller network sizes, e. g., a 4x4 network, the performance drop is still distinct, yet significantly lower than for lager network sizes. In return, all of the discussed design concepts that will be discussed in Chapter 3 are enabled already for this network size. In case that a system with more processors is desired, instead of scaling the permutation network to larger sizes, and, therefore, further lowering the system performance, building clusters of processor arrays which feature each a Virtualization Layer is a viable solution.

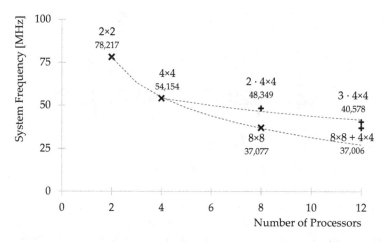

Figure 2.24: Clustering improves System Performance. All clustered Designs depicted are close Clusters.

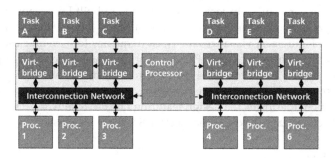

Figure 2.25: A close Cluster of two virtualizable Systems.

2.3.5 Optimization

Clusters of Virtualizable Networks

As discussed above, a certain degree of freedom regarding the processor instance on which a task is executed is desired, but a full flexibility, which requires shifting the execution of a task to any processor in the system, is not needed. Instead of one huge processor array, which would cause a very large and, therefore, unusable network due to the large combinatorial paths, structuring the design into clusters is a solution to avoid large network sizes, i. e., maintaining a reasonable system frequency and yet keeping the advantages arising from the virtualization features. In this case, smaller processor arrays are instantiated of which each features a dedicated Virtualization Layer. Here, two design alternatives exist.

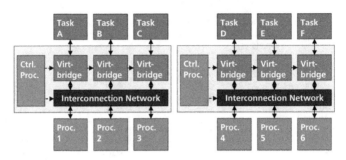

Figure 2.26: A loose Cluster of two virtualizable Systems.

In the first alternative, the *close clusters*, several processor arrays with independent Virtualization Layers feature the same control modules, which, e. g. manage and update the binding definitions for the processor array. Close clusters are depicted in Figure 2.25.

In *loose clusters*, each processor array is a self-contained virtualizable system with dedicated control modules. In fact, loose clusters are built by instantiating a virtualizable design as depicted in Figure 2.8 several times. Loose clusters are depicted in Figure 2.26. Figure 2.24 visualizes the clock frequency for several close clusters of various sizes for a Virtex-6 LX240T FPGA.[13] For designs featuring eight processors, the frequency drop is lower for a $2 \cdot 4 \times 4$ system compared to an 8×8 solution. Furthermore, a solution featuring twelve processors structured in three close clusters of four processors outperforms the design featuring one 8×8 network. The application example in Section 4.2 will exploit such a close $8 \times 8 + 4 \times 4$ cluster.

Asymmetric Shaping

As discussed above, the Max-Min network that is employed for the virtualizable multi-processor architecture features the same number of inputs and outputs, i. e., of processors and of tasks. Indeed, in many embedded designs, assigning a dedicated processor for each task is not uncommon to prevent malicious interference with other tasks and to maintain system safety. However, for multi-processor designs that feature sharing of processor resources, the need to feature as many processors as tasks is not desired. In most scenarios, which employ resource sharing, there will be more tasks than processors. Even if some processor instances are held ready as spare resources in case of errors, the overall number of processors is usually lower than the number of tasks. In order to overcome the shortcomings of a conventional symmetric network design, an asymmetric shaping of the interconnection network is now proposed. This

---

[13]It is assumed that loose clusters will achieve slightly better results. This will be due to the increased degree of freedom for module placement as loose clusters do not share access to a common control processor.

Algorithm 8 Asymmetric Shaping of a Max-Min Network.

Require: A Max-Min network of the size $n \times n$, desired output width m with $m < n$.
Ensure: A Max-Min network of the size $n \times m$.

1: $u = n - m$;   ▷ number of outputs (i. e., processors) to be discarded
2: $x = \frac{n}{2} + 1$;   ▷ start at the xth output of the network's output stage
3: **for** $i = 1 \to i \leq u$ **do**
4:      CheckCB(crossbar switch leading to output at position x);
5:      Delete all marked Crossbar Switches;
6:      Delete output on position x at output stage;
7:      $x = (i\%2 = 0)?(x + i) : (x - i)$;   ▷ In turns go left or right
8:      $i + +$;
9: **end for**
10: **function** CHECKCB(crossbar switch)
11:      **if** One of the crossbar switch's outputs is unconnected **then**
12:          Mark current crossbar switch for deletion; ˊ
13:          CheckCB(crossbar switch preceding current switch on its left input)
14:          CheckCB(crossbar switch preceding current switch on its right input)
15:      **end if**
16:      **return**
17: **end function**

---

optimization will allow featuring more tasks than processors in a Max-Min network. Foundation of the optimization is a Max-Min network of the size $n \times m$, where n is the number of inputs, i. e., of tasks and m the number of outputs, i. e., of processors. As detailed above, in the beginning $n = m$ holds. Result of the optimization will be a network of the size $n \times m$ with $m < n$. Algorithm 8 lists the step performed to modify the interconnection network. This algorithm has to be executed during system design.

The algorithm starts at the middle of the output stage, where the combinatorial path is the longest.[14] This is depicted in Figure 2.27. In doing so, by discarding parts of the network, the most time critical path is eliminated at first. The algorithm now continuously removes outputs and crossbar switches that are not needed any more for the desired number of outputs. The algorithm works from the inner to both outer sections of the output stages, alternating between going left and right. This ensures evenly reducing the longest paths in the network. Figures 2.27 and 2.28 depict the process of reshaping a 8×8 down to a 8×1 network.

The result of this procedure is accompanied by several characteristics. First, less processor instances as well as less crossbar switches have to be synthesized. Crossbar switches are removed, which cannot be a section of a route to a remaining processor. This leads to a significant decrease of occupied logic slices on the target FPGA, cf. Figure 2.29. The LUT consumptions of an asymmetrical shaped network is, however, higher than for an unmodified network of a smaller size. This can easily be explained by a visual comparison of, e. g., a 4×4 network as depicted on the top of Figure 2.22 with an asymmetrical shaped 8×4 network as depicted in Figure 2.27, lower portion of

---

[14]As discussed in Section 2.3.3, some routes pass more crossbar switches than others.

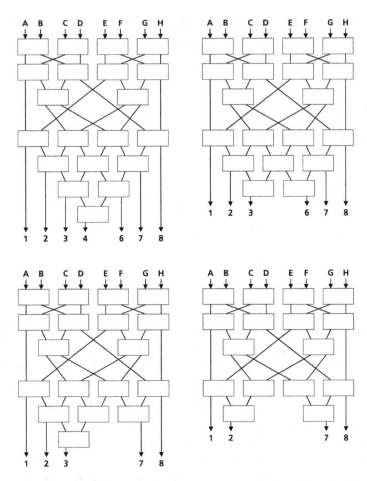

Figure 2.27: Reshaping a Max-Min Network of the size 8×8 by Algorithm 8.

the right hand side. One immediately sees that given the same number of processors, the number of crossbar switches is higher for an asymmetrical shaped network than for an unmodified network.

Second, depending on the number of remaining processors, the longest path of the system is shortened accordingly, leading to an increase in system frequency and, thus, performance, compared to the original network size. The combinatorial delay t_{cd} of routes from task memories to processors via the interconnection network may be written as

$$t_{cd} = t_{mem\_to\_icn} + t_{icn} + t_{icn\_to\_proc}$$

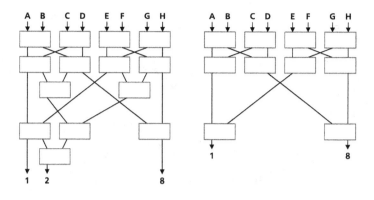

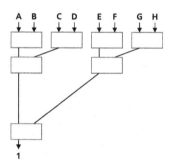

Figure 2.28: Reshaping a Max-Min Network of the size 8 × 8 by Algorithm 8.

where $t_{mem\_to\_icn}$ is the delay caused by the route from task memories to the inputs of the interconnection network, t_{icn} is the delay caused by the interconnection network and $t_{icn\_to\_proc}$ is the delay caused by the route from the output of the interconnection network to the input of the processors. The asymmetric reshaping reduces t_{icn}, while $t_{mem\_to\_icn}$ and $t_{icn\_to\_proc}$ remain unchanged.[15] This effect is depicted in Figure 2.30.

Third, those crossbar switches, which now only feature one output behave like a normal multiplexer. If the left output remains connected, the input with the lower ID is

---

[15] Indeed, due to reshaping and the resulting decrease in occupied logic, a slightly better placement of task memories and processors might be achieved, resulting in a decrease of $t_{mem\_to\_icn}$ and $t_{icn\_to\_proc}$. These deviations are not considered further.

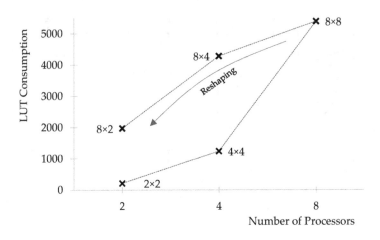

Figure 2.29: Reshaping a Max-Min Network leads to a Decrease in LUT Consumption.

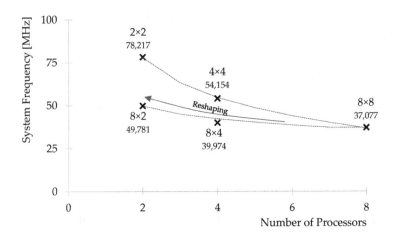

Figure 2.30: Increasing Frequency by Shortening Combinatorial Paths due to Asymmetrical Shaping.

routed to this output. If the right output remains connected, the input with the higher ID is routed to this output.

Care has to be taken that with a reduced size of the network, only the remaining processors may be addressed as a target of a binding definition. As the processors are removed starting from the middle of the network, the remaining processors are not numbered in a continuous sequence any more, cf. Figures 2.27 and 2.28, where the remaining processors are, e. g., 1, 2, and 8. This cluttered sequence has to be maintained

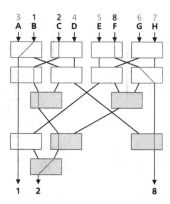

Figure 2.31: An asymmetrically shaped 8×3 Network realizing the Binding $BV_1 = (B \mapsto 1), (C \mapsto 2), (F \mapsto 8)$.

in order for the routing algorithm to work correctly. Aside from this fact, no adaptions regarding the binding or scheduling of tasks have to be considered.

To realize a given binding, e.g., in a network of the size 8×3 the same routing algorithm as denoted in Algorithm 6 applies as for an unmodified symmetrical network. In consequence, the processors, which have been removed by the reshaping process, are treated just like processors, which are not considered in a binding. Figure 2.31 depicts a network configuration for the 8×3 network with the active binding:

$$BV_1 = (B \mapsto 1), (C \mapsto 2), (F \mapsto 8)$$

Crossbar switches, which only feature one output as result of the reshaping process, behave as a 2:1 multiplexer and are highlighted in Figure 2.31.

Dynamic Task Replacement

Reshaping an otherwise symmetrical network is one way to feature more tasks than processors in a system. As mentioned in the previous Section, multi-tasking systems usually do have far more tasks than processors. Reshaping the network may not be a feasible solution to handle a huge number of tasks. The scalability of the interconnection network decreases system performance with increasing inputs and outputs, even when reducing the overall network size by the asymmetric reshaping process. Thus, in order to support an arbitrary number of tasks in the system, another solution has to be found.

Tasks consist of instructions, data, and the current context. Instructions are stored inside an instruction memory, data inside a data memory. For an FPGA-based implementation, both memories are mapped to a so-called BlockRAM (BRAM) module, existing memory banks on the FPGA device with two ports. Usually instruction and data memory are mapped into the same chain of BRAM modules, and, therefore,

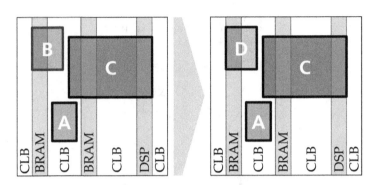

Figure 2.32: A partial Reconfiguration on an FPGA allows switching Modules B and D at Runtime without interrupting the Execution of Modules A and C.

occupy one of the memory ports each. As discussed, the design and the size of the interconnection network and, consequently, the number of tasks attached to the system, are defined during the design phase and cannot be altered during runtime.

One solution might be to fill other BRAM banks, which are not occupied by the design, with tasks and route them as inputs to the network by means of a multiplexer structure. This solution, however, would be nothing more than an inefficient expansion of the interconnection network. Moreover, an FPGA's BRAM resources are usually limited, which would then be the upper boundary for the number of possible tasks.

Now the runtime partial reconfiguration features for FPGAs is exploited to overcome this issue. Partial reconfiguration is a technique, which alters only parts of the FPGA's configuration. This is achieved by applying a partial bitstream onto the device. This partial bitstream only contains the configuration update of the chip region to be reconfigured. As a significant side effect, those areas, which are not affected by the partial reconfiguration, may continue their execution even during the partial reconfiguration phase. Figure 2.32 depicts a partial reconfiguration of a design, where module B is replaced by module D, whereas modules A and C continue their execution all the time. This allows building systems with high execution dynamism. The partial reconfiguration technique has, therefore, contributed to a wide range of applications such as [Hübner 2006, Paulsson 2006b, Ullmann 2004, Lanuzza 2009]. Inter-FPGA reconfiguration was proposed in [Wichman 2006], which in consequence led to complex, reconfiguration-based FPGA networks [Biedermann 2013a].

The left hand side of Figure 2.33 depicts a virtualizable system with two *task memories*. These memories are not explicitly bound to a specific task, but may be filled over time with different tasks. On the right hand side of Figure 2.33, task B residing in task memory 2 is replaced by task C by means of a partial reconfiguration. In order to replace a task by dynamic reconfiguration, the task that is currently being executed is halted by the virtualization procedure detailed in Section 2.2.5. In doing so, the processor is detached from the task's memory. After the virtualization procedure has

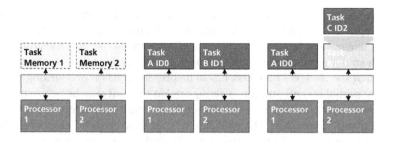

Figure 2.33: Over Time, the Task Memories in the System can be filled with different Tasks by performing a partial Reconfiguration.

stopped the task's execution, the control processor outside the processor array triggers the partial reconfiguration by calling a dedicated function, which denotes the partial bitstream to be applied and the target region on the FPGA. The new partial bitstream contains the machine code of a new task. Target area are the BRAM cells on the FPGA, which host the original task. The reconfiguration is then applied by a dedicated IP-core, the so-called ICAP, which is provided by the device vendor Xilinx Inc. While a full reconfiguration of an FPGA of the size of a Virtex-6 takes about 12 to 20 seconds via a serial PC connection, the duration of a partial reconfiguration depends on the size of the partial bitstream and on the speed of the storage medium, which contains the partial bitstream file. For altering the BRAM cells, which form a task memory, the partial reconfiguration takes about 2 seconds. Indeed, this includes the time needed for the data transfer of the bitstream from a personal computer. When exploiting a fast, off-chip memory, which stores the bitstreams, a reconfiguration process is significantly accelerated. Recent works demonstrated a huge speedup in the transfer of partial bitstreams [Bonamy 2012]. However, dynamic task replacement is still slower than a conventional virtualization procedure, where the tasks are already stored in the chips memory. Therefore, this approach is not suited for frequent task scheduling events while facing harsh real-time constraints.

As soon as the reconfiguration process is finished, the memory is reattached to the processor by the virtualization procedure. Additionally, the content of the TCM, which still features the context of the now overwritten task, is erased. Consequently, the new task may start its execution without any interference with the old task. Strict isolation of task contents as required by Postulate 4 (*Strict encapsulation and isolation of tasks*) is preserved.

The dynamic task replacement procedure enables the employment of an unlimited number of tasks. However, as soon as a task is being replaced, its current content, which was stored in its TCM is erased. Therefore, when this task is configured onto the FPGA again, it has to restart its execution from start. Section 2.4.4 will highlight a feature, where a task may indicate that it has finished one execution cycle.[16] Consequently, tasks are replaced not until they have completed their current processing. The Agile Processing scheme highlighted in Section 3.4 will modify this approach slightly in order to enable a smooth transition between sequential and parallel task execution.

In case that the context of the task has to be preserved when overwriting the task's memory by partial reconfiguration, a configuration readout may be performed. Here, the ICAP may read out the current configuration of the TCM, before applying a new partial bitstream to the BAM. The extracted context may be saved elsewhere off-chip. Alternatively, every task, which may be mapped into the system may feature a dedicated TCM. However, this would cause a significant resource overhead, as the number of tasks being applicable by a dynamic task replacement is almost unlimited. For the prototype implementation, TCM readout or dedicated TCMs for each and every task are not implemented.

Please note that despite the partial reconfiguration technique is necessary in order to efficiently feature an unlimited number of tasks on a FPGA-based virtualizable design, the approach is not limited to FPGAs. For other target architectures, which do not offer any runtime reconfiguration features, but whose structures may be outlined by the designer – in contrast to an FPGA – the same approach may be implemented by means of a suited memory design. Here, a dedicated port in each task memory may be added in order to externally replace the memory contents.

Dynamic Network Replacement

The partial reconfiguration feature might not only be exploited to replace tasks, but also to exchange the entire processor-task interconnection network during runtime. Depending on the current flexibility requirements, a network with fewer stages and, consequently, less flexibility, such as a butterfly network, could replace the max-min network at runtime. In theory, fewer combinatorial stages would lead to an increase in system frequency. By dynamically replacing the max-min network, the system's frequency could be increased. However, this is not considered by the design tools. Moreover, a methodology about when to apply which interconnection network is missing. If many exchanges of the interconnection network would be required during runtime, the advantage of the theoretical increase in system frequency would disappear. Although the work of [Pionteck 2006] has already demonstrated the implementation of NoC reconfiguration on FPGAs – however for networks, which feature off-line routing in contrast to the proposed runtime routing – a dynamic exchange if the interconnection network seems not feasible when considering the constraints discussed above.

---

[16]In embedded designs, many tasks run "infinitely", i.e., are encapsulated in a loop to continuously process input data. In this context, one cycle in this loop is called an execution cycle. Often, no data dependencies are carried between two execution cycles.

Influence of FPGA Place&Route on System Frequency Drop

Figure 2.34 depicts a floorplan of a loose cluster, cf. Section 2.3.5, which consists of an array of eight processors plus an array of four processors. Target chip is a Virtex-6 LX240T FPGA. Processors are marked by numbers, task memories are indicated by letters. The corresponding control processors are highlighted in light gray. The dark grey backgrounds, respectively, depict the FPGA's resources occupied by the interconnection networks. In grey, the network connectivity is depicted. The clusters are spatially separated indicated by the dashed line. One may clearly see, however, that the networks are scattered over almost the entire area of the FPGA. This is due to the combinatorial structure of the interconnection network, which is mapped into LUTs. The combinatorial networks occupy 20 % and 45 %, respectively, of the FPGA's LUT resources. In only about 30 % of occupied slices both LUT and registers are exploited. This hints to an inefficient placement caused by the structure of the interconnection network. The scattered placement, furthermore, elongates routes between registers and, thus, cause long critical paths, which in return lower the system's overall frequency.

The exploitation of multi-stage interconnection networks, however, not automatically implies a reduction of a system's performance. Multi-processor systems, such as the Plurality architecture [Plurality 2013] feature a multi-stage interconnection network as dispatcher between processors and memories, which is depicted in [Green 2013]. Plurality's interconnect is advertised featuring "low latency". However, they do not state whether the routes from processors to memories are buffered, a solution that is unsuited for the virtualizable architecture as discussed above. Nevertheless, transferring the design from the prototype FPGA platform to a custom chip whose layout is optimized to realize the multistage structure may significantly shorten combinatorial paths and, thus, result in an articulate increase of system performance. Therefore, the performance drop is not seen as a weakness of the advocated virtualization structure, but as a limitation arising from the FPGA platform being exploited for the prototype implementations.

2.3.6 Intermediate Conclusions

This section has introduced a dedicated task-processor interconnection network, which features a fast online routing and offers fully flexibility. Thus, by exploiting the virtualization procedure, a task's execution can be shifted to any other processor in the array. This is achieved by a runtime reconfiguration of the task-processor interconnection network, which updates the routes from task memories to processors.

However, there is little use for a system, which only permutes 1-to-1 relations between tasks and processor resources. Thus, the virtualization concept will further be expanded in order to allow for sharing a processor resource among a set of tasks. This will not only require an enhancement of the routing algorithm but also the introduction of a scheduling scheme for tasks, which share a processor resource. These features will be introduced in the following section.

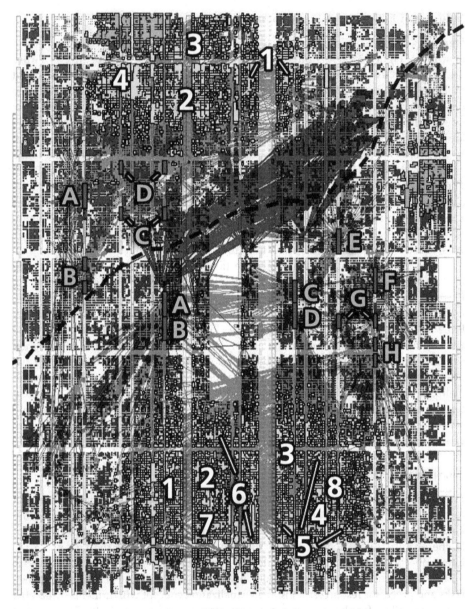

Figure 2.34: The Floorplan clearly depicts the two Clusters of the System. Processors are marked by Numbers, Task Memories by Letters. The control processors are depicted in light grey. The corresponding networks (dark grey) are depicted with an Overlay of the Connectivity (grey.)

Figure 2.35: Binding BV_1 over Time.

2.4 Task Scheduling via Interconnection Network

By now, an interconnection network between processors and tasks has been detailed, which is able to update task-processor routes during runtime. However, the anticipatory benefit from being able to just alter 1-1 bindings between processors and tasks is limited. The powerfulness of the architecture comes into play when the interconnection network and the virtualization procedure are combined to feature a transparent and dynamic processor resource sharing between several tasks. In doing so, a multi-processor array, which intrinsically supports multi-tasking is formed.

At first, the definition of n-1 bindings is explained, where n is the number of tasks mapped to one processor instance. Additionally, the basic multi-tasking scheduling scheme, the so-called *Task Group Scheduling* is highlighted. Afterwards, the routing algorithm to realize n-1 bindings is detailed. At last, a self-scheduling scheme for tasks is introduced. Here, tasks will be able to trigger scheduling events by themselves without the need of an external scheduling instance.

2.4.1 Binding Definitions of Task Groups and Task Budgets

Section 2.2.5 has introduced Binding Vectors to denote the assignments of task to processors. In the example Binding Vector

$$BV_1 = (A \mapsto 1), (B \mapsto 2), (C \mapsto 3)$$

the task A is bound to processor instance 1, B to processor instance 2 and C to processor instance 3. This binding is depicted over time in Figure 2.35. As tasks do not share access to a processor resource, no scheduling is required.

This representation is now expanded. To denote that several tasks share a processor instance, a so-called *Task Group* may be formed:

Definition 3 (Task Group-Processor Binding). *A task group-processor binding B_i is a surjective function, which maps a set of tasks $t_1, t_2, \ldots, t_n \in T_g \subseteq T$ to a processor p_i from a set of processors $p_1, p_2, \ldots, p_m \in P$: $B : T \to P, T_g \mapsto p$.*

Definition 4 (Binding Vector with Task Groups). *A binding vector $BV_i = \{((t_v, t_w, \ldots) \mapsto p_x), (t_y \mapsto p_z), \ldots\}$ is composed of bindings B_i.*

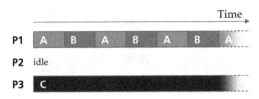

Figure 2.36: Binding BV_2 over Time.

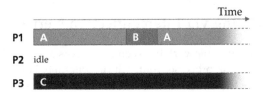

Figure 2.37: Binding BV_3 over Time.

In the Binding Vector

$$BV_2 = ((A, B) \mapsto 1), (C \mapsto 3)$$

the tasks A and B form the Task Group (A,B). This denotes that both tasks will share processor instance 1. Processor resource sharing in its basic form is realized as a time division Round-Robin scheme, cf. Figure 2.36. In this scheme, the execution of a task is halted after a certain time and another task of the same task group is activated on the targeted processor instance. The virtualization procedure thereby allows for a transparent interruption of task execution at any point in time as outlined in Section 2.2.5.

The designer defines the time interval, after which a task's execution is interrupted in favor of another task. Additionally, for each task of a Task Group, in the Binding Vector a so-called task budget parameter may be optionally given. The Binding Vector

$$BV_3 = ((A : 3, B) \mapsto 1), (C \mapsto 3)$$

denotes a task budget of 3 for task A. This defines that task A is assigned three times more processing time in each turn than task B before being interrupted, cf. Figure 2.37. The procedure for the time division scheduling is denoted in Algorithm 9.

Besides the sequential eradication of tasks as denoted in a task group, the binding for each processor may feature an execution sequence. This sequence is set along with the binding in the control processor. It defines the order, in which tasks are activated. The Binding Vector

$$BV_4 = ((A : 1.5, B, C) \mapsto 1 | (A,B,A,C))$$

Algorithm 9 Time Division Scheduling.

Require: A task group TG with tasks featuring budget parameters.
Ensure: A time division scheme for TG.
 1: Point to first task listed in TG
 2: **loop**
 3:     Set budget counter to value initially defined by designer
 4:     **if** Current task of TG features a task budget parameter **then**
 5:         Override budget counter with value denoted by budget paramter
 6:     **end if**
 7:     **while** Budget counter > 0 **do**
 8:         Execute task on processor
 9:         Decrease budget counter by one each clock cycle
10:     **end while**
11:     **if** Current task of TG is the last task denoted in TG **then**
12:         Trigger virtualization procedure in order to activate first task listed in TG
13:     **else**
14:         Trigger virtualization procedure in order to activate next task listed in TG
15:     **end if**
16: **end loop**

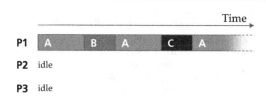

Figure 2.38: Binding BV_4 with the Task Execution Sequence A, B, A, C.

maps tasks A, B, and C to processor 1. Additionally, the execution sequence A, B, A, C is given. This sequence will be repeated during execution as depicted in Figure 2.38. In the control processor, the execution sequence for each task group is denoted with its particular length. Algorithm 10 outlines the behavior of the execution sequence handling. Advantage of this enhanced task group scheduling is that some tasks may be evoked more frequently than other tasks. Depending on the application scenario this may be crucial in order to meet, e. g., timing constraints of a system. The application example in Section 4.1 will demonstrate the need for this advanced feature.

2.4.2 Scheduling an n-to-1 Relation

This Section now details how the virtualization procedure in combination with the dynamically reconfigurable interconnection network enables the time division scheme of Algorithms 9 and 10.

A Binding Vector, which features a Task Group and, optionally, a task execution sequence, is sent from the control processor, cf. Figure 2.12, into the Virtualization Layer. As soon as a new Binding Vector is received, a virtualization procedure for

---

Algorithm 10 Enhanced Time Division Scheduling with dedicated Execution Sequence.

Require: A task group TG with tasks featuring an execution sequence TG_{ES}.
Ensure: A time division scheme for TG according to execution sequence TG_{ES}.
  1: Point to first task denoted in TG_{ES}
  2: **loop**
  3:     Set budget counter to value initially defined by designer
  4:     **if** Current task of TG features a task budget parameter **then**
  5:         Override budget counter with value denoted by budget parameter
  6:     **end if**
  7:     **while** Budget Counter > 0 **do**
  8:         Execute task on processor
  9:         Decrease budget counter by one each clock cycle
 10:     **end while**
 11:     **if** Current task is the last task denoted in TG_{ES} **then**
 12:         Trigger virtualization procedure in order to activate first task listed in TG_{ES}
 13:     **else**
 14:         Trigger virtualization procedure in order to activate next task listed in TG_{ES}
 15:     **end if**
 16: **end loop**

Algorithm 11 Network Configuration for a Binding Vector with a Task Group.

Require: A binding vector BV_i, featuring a task group TG.
Ensure: An network configuration, which routes one task of TG to its designated processor and all other tasks denoted in BV to their corresponding processors.
  1: **for all** Tasks listed in BV_i, which are not part of TG **do**
  2:     Set RoutingID of task to label of assigned processor
  3: **end for**
  4: Set RoutingID of first task in TG to label of assigned processor
  5: **for all** Other tasks in TG and Tasks not listed in BV_i **do**
  6:     Set RoutingID to a processor label unused so far
  7: **end for**
  8: Set RoutingIDs of tasks as inputs of shadow copy of the interconnection network
  9: **for all** Crossbar Switches in shadow copy **do**
 10:     Behave as sorting elements as defined in Algorithm 5
 11:     Output current configuration of all crossbar switches
 12: **end for**
 13: Accumulate all configurations of crossbar switches
 14: Apply configuration information to physical network layer

---

all active tasks is triggered. In doing so, the execution of all tasks in the system is halted. For a Binding Vector not featuring a Task Group, the routing Algorithm 6 of Section 2.3.4 will apply in order to setup according task-processor routings in the interconnection network. This Algorithm is now modified in order to support Task Groups. Algorithm 11 notes the initial setup of the network for a Binding Vector, which features a Task Group.

In doing so, the first task of a Task Group and all tasks of 1-1 relations will be activated, cf. Figure 2.39, left hand side. As soon as the budget of the first task of the

---

Algorithm 12 Task Group Scheduling.

Require: A scheduling event within a Task Group TG.
Ensure: Activation of the next task in TG.
1: Select next task of TG either by Algorithm 9 or, in case an explicit task execution sequence is given, by Algorithm 10
2: Trigger virtualization procedure of Algorithm 2 for currently active task of TG
3: Compute new network configuration by executing Algorithm 11 or Algorithm 13 ▷ line 2 is executed
4:   in parallel with line 3.
5: Trigger virtualization procedure of Algorithm 4 to activate the next task of TG

Task Group runs out, a scheduling event is triggered. Consequently, this task is being interrupted by the virtualization procedure. Meanwhile, a new network configuration is computed in parallel. This new configuration will feature a route from the next task of the task group to the targeted processor instance. With the new network configuration, this next task of the Task Group may start or resume its execution. Algorithm 12 denotes the steps for a Task Group scheduling event. For Task Groups, scheduling events are internally managed by timers inside the Virtualization Layer as well as registers keeping track of task execution sequences. Therefore, the control processor is relieved from managing scheduling events.

As mentioned before, new network configurations are calculated in a shadow copy of the interconnection network at runtime. During Task Group Scheduling events, the bindings of tasks not part of the Task Group are not altered. Hence, as soon as the new network configuration is found, it may immediately be applied to the network without the need for interrupting the tasks outside the Task Group. Thus, all tasks bound to other processors in the array are not affected by this procedure, even if the route between their task memory and their corresponding processor is adapted by the network reconfiguration, cf. Task D in Figure 2.39, right hand side.

2.4.3 Scheduling several n-to-1 Relations

A Binding Vector may feature several Task Groups. The algorithm to setup an initial configuration is analogous to the case with only one Task Group, cf. Algorithm 13. Here, for the first task in each Task Group, the label of the corresponding processor is set, while all other tasks in the Task Groups are fed with labels of unused processors.

Task Group scheduling events are also treated in the same way. For each scheduling event, a new network configuration is computed, while the current task of the Task Group is deactivated by the virtualization procedure. Besides the free choice of a target processor, featuring Task Groups in a Binding Vector contributes to a plethora of different network configurations, which may occur at runtime. This would render solutions unfeasible, which rely on preliminarily calculated network configurations.

An ongoing computation of a new network configuration in case of a scheduling event of a Task Group might delay a scheduling event of another Task Group. It is not started until the previous scheduling event, i. e., calculation of a network reconfiguration

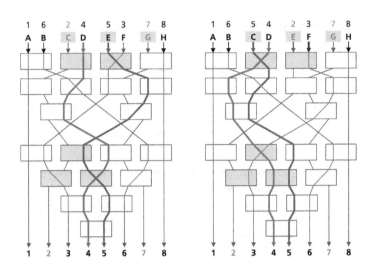

Figure 2.39: Task Group Scheduling Event for the Binding Vector $BV_1 = (A \mapsto 1), (B \mapsto 6),$ $((C, E, G) \mapsto 5), (D \mapsto 4), (F \mapsto 3), (H \mapsto 8)$. The Task Group's tasks are highlighted as well as the Crossbar Switches reconfigured during a Task Group Scheduling Event. The Route of the Binding $(D \mapsto 4)$, which is unrelated to the Task Group, is adapted without affecting D's Execution.

is completed. The designer may choose task budgets in a way, that scheduling events occur at common factors of these budgets. If two or more scheduling events are triggered within the same clock cycle, all scheduling events are handled simultaneously. Consequently, only one new network configuration is computed for these scheduling events. Nevertheless, due to the speed of the virtualization procedure and the fast routing algorithm, such delays are in the range of 90 clock cycles.

2.4.4 Self-Scheduling of Tasks

Drawbacks of Budget-based Scheduling

By now, a time division scheme for processor resource sharing has been detailed. However, by performing such a scheme, the execution of a task is disrupted into several parts. This is an issue, if tasks have dependencies among each other. Here, a task may only start its execution if it has received data from the tasks it is depending on. As commonly adopted, a task is assumed to at first receive data from preceding tasks. Then it may resume its computations. At the end of its execution cycle, the task sends its result to subsequent tasks. Besides this, no communication occurs during its computation. This is depicted for a simple task graph in Figure 2.40. A time division scheme may lead to a significant delay in the overall system execution time. This is

---

Algorithm 13 Network Configuration for a Binding Vector, featuring several Task Groups.

Require: A binding vector BV_i, which features a set of task groups $TG_1, TG_2, TG_3, \ldots$.
Ensure: A network configuration, which routes one task of each task group TG_j to its designated processor and all other tasks denoted in BV to their corresponding processors.
1: **for all** Tasks listed in BV_i, which are not part of any task group TG_j **do**
2:     Set RoutingID of task to label of assigned processor
3: **end for**
4: **for all** Task groups TG_j **do**
5:     Set RoutingID of first task in TG_j to label of assigned processor
6:     **for all** Other tasks in TG_j **do**
7:         Set RoutingID to a processor label unused so far
8:     **end for**
9: **end for**
10: **for all** Tasks not listed in BV_i **do**
11:     Set RoutingID to a processor label unused so far
12: **end for**
13: Set RoutingIDs of tasks as inputs of shadow copy of the interconnection network
14: **for all** Crossbar Switches in shadow copy **do**
15:     Behave as sorting elements as defined in Algorithm 5
16:     Output current configuration of all crossbar switches
17: **end for**
18: Accumulate all configurations of crossbar switches
19: Apply configuration information on physical network layer

---

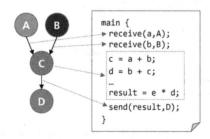

Figure 2.40: A Task, here C, at first receives Data from the Tasks it is dependent on, here A and B. Afterwards, it may start its Computation. Finally, it sends its result to the Tasks, which depend on it, here D.

highlighted in Figure 2.41. Here, a task graph consisting of the four tasks A, B, C, and D is mapped to processor P_1. The individual task execution times are given in Figure 2.41 as well. P_{1_1} to P_{1_4} illustrate different scheduling alternatives. The default time division interval is t.

P_{1_1} realizes the simple binding

$$BV_1 = ((A, B, C, D) \mapsto 1)$$

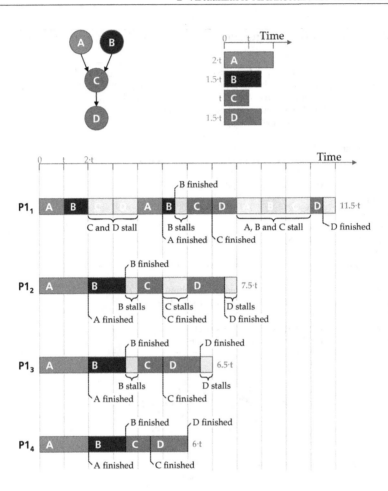

Figure 2.41: A Task Graph with given Task Execution Times is executed in four different Ways.

where each task is interrupted after t by the virtualization procedure to activate the next task. A and B are interrupted without having completed their computation, i. e., without production of a result. As C and D, however, rely on the results of A and B, C and D stall during their first invocation. During the next invocation of B, B finishes its computation after $\frac{t}{2}$. B stalls for the rest of this time slot. Not until the next invocation, C may start its execution for the first time. Afterwards, D may start its execution. If C would have featured an execution time longer than t, the start of D's execution would have been further delayed. Besides task stalling, because they are waiting for other tasks to produce results, tasks being invoked despite already having completed their computation further elongate the overall system execution time. Altogether, the execution time for the task graph is $11.5 \cdot t$ for P_{11}.

The system execution time may be reduced, if the time division interval is skillfully adapted to the task execution times. For P_{12}, the time division interval in the architecture is set to $2 \cdot t$, which is exactly the execution time of the slowest task, A, in the task system. Now, each task is guaranteed to finish its execution within its first invocation. For tasks B, C, and D, which feature shorter execution times than A, stalls occur after they have finished their execution. Nevertheless, the overall system execution time may be lowered to $7.5 \cdot t$ for the given task graph.

For P_{13}, the budget parameter of the Virtualization Layer is exploited to further optimize the system execution time. The basic time division interval is reset to t, however, the Binding Vector now features a budget parameter for A, B, and D:

$$BV_2 = ((A : 2, B : 2, C, D : 2) \mapsto 1)$$

In doing so, for each invocation, A, B, and D feature double as much execution time as task C. As a result, the behavior is somewhat similar to P_{12}, as C features only a time slot of t, the stall after C's execution disappears. By defining $2 \cdot t$ as time interval for A, B, and D, all three tasks are still guaranteed to finish their computation during their first invocation. The system execution time is now lowered to $6.5 \cdot t$.

At first sight, a simple solution would be to assign each task a budget, which exactly correlates with its execution time. However, task execution times may vary during runtime. If a task unexpectedly stalls, e. g., because a communication participant does not provide or consume data in time, the execution time is elongated. Though, the Virtualization Layer interrupts the task after its budget runs out without accounting for the stall. Thus, relying on static registered task execution time seems not to be feasible.

P_{14}, finally, provides an optimal scheduling. Here, each task is interrupted exactly after it has finished its execution. The system execution time is the optimal as $6 \cdot t$ is the sum of the execution times of A, B, C, and D.[17] This scheduling behavior is established by the so-called *self-scheduling* features of the Virtualization Layer.

Self-scheduling is a term originally aimed at the decentralized, manual organization of work shifts of nurses [Burke 2004]. In the field of computing, the term is used several times for the automatic or partially guided mapping of parallelized loop-sections to parallel processor architectures [Polychronopoulos 1987, Liu 1993, Tang 1986]. In the scope of virtualizable MPSoC, self-scheduling was proposed in [Biedermann 2012b].

Dedicated Scheduling Instructions

By exploiting the self-scheduling scheme, a task may indicate the end of its computation. This indication is provided by means of dedicated scheduling instructions, which may

---

[17]For the entire example, the timing overhead generated by the virtualization procedure, which performs task switching, is neglected. The basic time interval as well as task execution times are assumed to be a magnitude above the duration of the virtualization procedure.

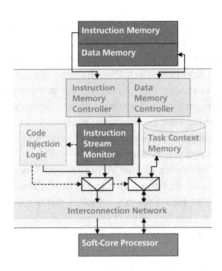

Figure 2.42: The Instruction Stream Monitor scans the Instruction Interface and catches dedicated Scheduling Instructions.

be included into the program code of the task. A combinatorial *Instruction Stream Monitor* (ISM) is placed in the instruction interface between the task's instruction memory and the processor. It is able to observe the instructions being sent to the processor. It is exploited to detect these dedicated scheduling instructions and passes this information to the Code Injection Logic (CIL), cf. Figure 2.42. Consequently, the CIL triggers a virtualization procedure, which is similar to the invocation after the task's budget would have run out. As the scheduling instructions are based upon instructions available for the given processor and employ as parameters values, which are defined by the designer, these instructions can be compiled by existing compilers without modification. Furthermore, as these instructions are catched by the ISM and are not forwarded to the processor, no modification of the processor itself is necessary. These properties are in accordance with Postulates 3, 7, and 8 (*Guaranteed activation and interruption of task execution at any point in time; No modification of the processor core, usage of off-the-shelf processors; Minor or no modification of existing software code of tasks*).

For the self-scheduling instruction, the two alternatives *nap* and *sleep* exist. By indicating the end of the execution via *nap*, a task is disabled and the next task given in the Task Group or its execution sequence register, respectively, is activated on the target processor. After all tasks in the Task Group have been worked off, the first task of the Task Group is activated for the second time and the eradication of the Task Group is repeated. For the *sleep* alternative, a task is not only deactivated, but deleted from the Task Group. Therefore, for the next eradication of the Task Group, a task terminated by a sleep instruction is not considered further. The behavior of the nap

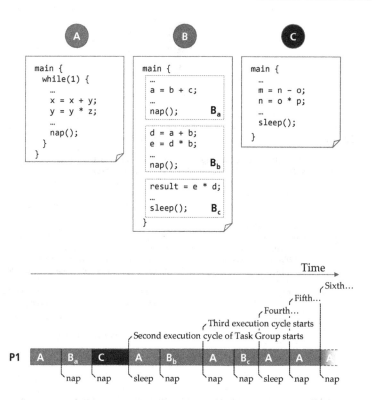

Figure 2.43: The three Tasks A, B, and C are mapped via the Binding Vector BV_1 = $((A,B,C) \mapsto 1)$ as a Task Group to Processor 1. The Insertion of Nap and Sleep Instructions leads to the Timing Behavior illustrated in the lower Portion.

and the sleep instruction is detailed in Figure 2.43. By combining such instructions, tasks may indicate a pause halfway through their execution by a nap instruction and after their execution is resumed at this point during the next invocation, the end of the tasks execution may be indicated by a sleep instruction. In doing so, the designer can define reasonable points for interrupting a task's execution. These two instructions are now being exploited in order to self-schedule task graphs. A prototype implementation for self-scheduling instructions for Xilinx MicroBlaze processors was accomplished in [Eicke 2012].

A Self-Scheduling Scheme for the virtualized MPSoC

Figure 2.44 depicts a simple task graph consisting of two tasks, whereas task B is dependent on the data sent by A. After A has completed its computation, it sends its result to B in a blocking manner. In doing so, task A assures that the subsequent

```
           main {
 A            ...                    \\normal task execution
 ID 0
              x = y + z;
              sendP2P(x, 1, blocking);   \\send data to B in blocking manner
              sleep();                    \\terminate task

           }
```

```
           main {
 B            int flag = 1;
 ID 1         while(flag) {
                recvP2P(x, 0, nonblocking); \\non-blocking semantics
                if(readSuccessful()) {      \\indicated by Status Bit
                  flag = 0;                  \\leave loop, start task execution
                } else {
                  nap();                     \\disable task, if no data received
                }                            \\entry point at reactivation
 Entry point  }
 at task
 reactivation                                     Self-Scheduling Routine

              ...                         \\normal task execution

           }
```

Figure 2.44: By adding a dedicated Portion of Software Code, a Task is only executed further, if preceding Tasks in the Task Graph provide Data. If not, the Task is suspended. After a task has successfully served succeeding tasks, it terminates itself by the *sleep* Instruction.

task B has received the data before task A disables itself by the sleep instruction. The receiving task, however, reads the data sent by A in a non-blocking manner. In non-blocking semantics, a carry bit indicates, whether a successful data transfer occurred or not.[18] The dedicated self-scheduling routine wrapped around the receiving command determines by checking this carry bit, whether B has received the data of A necessary to start its own computations. If this is not the case, B suspends itself by the nap instruction. Thus, the next task in the Binding Vector would be activated. If blocking semantics would have been applied for the receiving command, the task would stall until the data are delivered by the preceding task. Non-blocking semantics, however, allows for a self-induced suspension of the task. If the current task depends on the data of more than one preceding task, the self-scheduling code routine is slightly expanded

---

[18]For MicroBlaze architecture employed for the prototype implementation, this carry bit is set in the Machine Status Register of the processor.

Algorithm 14 Self-Scheduling Code Routine.

Require: A task in a task graph.
Ensure: A code routine inserted into the task enabling a self-scheduling scheme.
1: Initialize flag $f = 0$
2: Initialize flag $f_i = 0$ for each preceding task in the task graph
3: **while** Flag $f = 0$ indicates that not all preceding tasks have delivered data **do**
4:      **for all** Preceding tasks in the task graph **do**
5:          **if** $f_i = 0$ **then**
6:              Read from preceding task in non-blocking manner
7:              Check (e. g., by a carry bit) whether Receive was successful
8:              **if** Read was successful **then**
9:                  Set flag $f_i = 1$
10:             **end if**
11:         **end if**
12:     **end for**
13:     $f ==$ and-concatenation of all f_i
14:     **if** $f = 0$ **then**
15:         nap()
16:     **end if**
17: **end while**

---

to a sequential evaluation of the receive commands of all the predecessors in the task graph, cf. Algorithm 14.

Figure 2.45 depicts a task graph and the corresponding task execution times. At first, a conventional, pre-calculated as-soon-as-possible (ASAP) scheduling is applied (a). This scheduling scheme minimizes the overall execution time of the task graph. For a minimal execution time, three processor instances are necessary. In order to realize this scheme on an actual system out of the task graph, a corresponding task-processor binding as well as the sequence, in which the tasks will be activated on their corresponding processor, is derived. These two properties, i. e., the binding and the task sequence, may either be calculated in some instance inside the system right before the task graph is being executed or may be a pre-calculated result. In both variants, the scheduling instance of the system has to ensure to activate the tasks in the defined sequence and on the processors. After a task has completed its computation, it might either be disabled by the scheduling instance, e. g., because the scheduling instance keeps track of the execution times of the tasks or the task itself might indicate the end of its computation, e. g., by the sleep instruction introduced above. While this procedure is common for embedded designs, which feature multi-tasking, the self-scheduling scheme allows discarding any information about the task graph at the slight expense of a small timing overhead.

In (b), the same binding is applied for demonstration purposes. Consequently, the Binding Vector

$$BV_b = ((A, C, F, H, G) \mapsto 1), (D \mapsto 2), ((B, E) \mapsto 2)$$

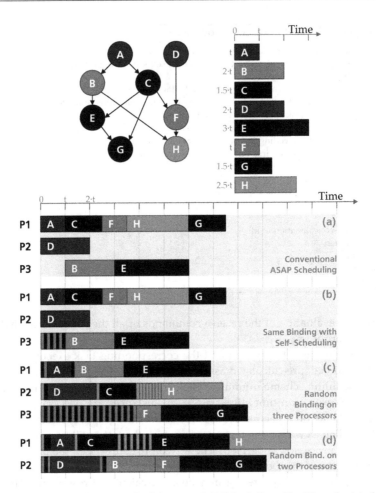

Figure 2.45: Conventional ASAP Scheduling vs. Self-Scheduling. The Time depicted for an unsuccessful Task Activation is exaggerated.

is fed into the virtualizable MPSoC. Now, every task features the self-scheduling code section detailed in Algorithm 14. Thus, if a task is activated and the preceding tasks have not yet provided the necessary data, it suspends itself with the nap instruction and the next task in the Task Group is being activated.[19] In consequence, the same behavior as for a conventional ASAP-scheduled system is observed. As the only deviation, tasks B and E, which are mapped to processor instance P3, are activated in turn until task

---

[19]Without denoting a task execution sequence, the Virtualization Layer activates tasks in the order they are entered into the system. Thus, for the Binding Vector $BV_1 = ((A, B) \mapsto 1)$, A is activated first. Entering $BV_2 = ((B, A) \mapsto 1)$ instead, leads to B being the first task being activated.

B receives data produced by A. In this case, the self-scheduling procedure exploits the binding and task sequence generated by the ASAP algorithm. For the proposed self-scheduling scheme, this information may be omitted.

Therefore, in (c), a completely random binding and task sequence is chosen. Thus, all information generated by the ASAP algorithm are discarded and not considered further. The corresponding Binding Vector for (c) is:

$$BV_c = ((E, B, A) \mapsto 1), ((H, C, D) \mapsto 2), ((F, G) \mapsto 3)$$

Now, task H, which is one of the last tasks to be executed in the task graph due to its dependencies, is being activated first in the system. As no data are available yet, it immediately suspends itself. This applies to the subsequent tasks of the Task Group as well, until tasks A and D are being activated. As they feature no dependencies to other tasks, they may start their execution. The same behavior occurs after A and D having completed their execution. Consequently, a slight timing overhead is added to the overall execution time, as e. g., task H is being activated at varying points in time despite B and F have not yet finished their computation, which will provide data for H.

As no information about the actual task graph has to be considered for the self-scheduling scheme, the designer cannot easily determine the optimal amount of processors in the system. Figure 2.45 depicts a self-scheduling for two processors in (d). Again, the binding was chosen arbitrarily to be:

$$BV_d = ((H, E, C, A) \mapsto 1), ((F, G, B, D) \mapsto 2)$$

As for the previous cases, the correct task execution sequence is self-adjusted due to the self-scheduling procedures in each task. However, the task execution time is expected to be higher than for a conventional ASAP scheduling, as for a minimal execution time three processor instances are required. Moreover, the self-scheduling routines cause a slight timing overhead. Nevertheless, a self-organizing task execution sequence is established without any control overhead.

An unsuccessful activation of a task, i. e., the activation and immediate suspension due to missing data, also causes a small timing overhead. This is due to the time needed to invoke and suspend a task by the virtualization procedure, as well as due to executing Algorithm 14. Figure 2.46 depicts a simple task graph consisting of n tasks mapped to processor P1. The task execution order in the following binding vector is the worst-case scenario, when self-scheduling is employed.

$$BV_{WC} = ((T_n, T_{n-1}, T_{n-2}, \ldots, T_5, T_4, T_3, T_2, T_1) \mapsto 1)$$

Here, every other task is evoked and immediately suspended until T1 may start the actual eradication of the task graph. T1 is removed from the task graph by a sleep instruction when it has finished its computation. However, now T2 has to wait until every remaining task has been evoked and suspended.

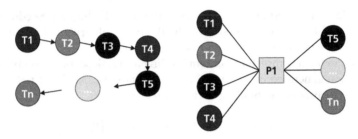

Figure 2.46: An example Task Graph and Architecture Graph for determining the Worst-Case Timing Overhead caused by the Self-Scheduling Scheme.

In an optimally scheduled binding, the execution time t_{TG} of the entire task graph would be

$$t_{TG} = \sum_{i=1}^{n} t_i$$

with t_i being the execution time of task Ti. When employing binding BV_{WC}, however, the execution time is

$$
\begin{aligned}
t_{TG_{WC}} =& (n-1) \cdot t_{ss} + t_n + (n-2) \cdot t_{ss} + t_{n-1} + \ldots + \\
& (n-(n-1)) \cdot t_{ss} + t_2 + \underbrace{(n-(n-0)) \cdot t_{ss}}_{=0} + t_1 \\
=& (n-1) \cdot t_{ss} + (n-2) \cdot t_{ss} + \ldots + \underbrace{(n-(n-1))}_{=1} \cdot t_{ss} + \underbrace{\sum_{i=1}^{n} t_i}_{=t_{TG}} \\
=& \sum_{i=1}^{n-1} i \cdot t_{ss} + t_{TG} = \frac{n \cdot (n-1)}{2} \cdot t_{ss} + t_{TG} = \underbrace{\frac{n^2-n}{2} \cdot t_{ss}}_{\text{overhead } t_{TO}} + t_{TG}
\end{aligned}
$$

with t_{ss} being the time for an unsuccessful evocation and immediate suspension of a task as denoted in Algorithm 14. Actually, this time may differ for each task depending on the number of inputs and amount of input data the corresponding task has to accumulate before being able to start its execution. When assuming that each task awaits one word from its preceding task, t_{ss} was measured to be 99 clock cycles. 44 clock cycles are needed to invoke the task and 45 to suspend it, cf. Figure 2.10. An implementation of the self-scheduling routine denoted in Algorithm 14 when awaiting one word from one input takes 10 clock cycles to evaluate. Thus, for eight tasks, i. e., $n = 8$ and $t_{ss} = 99$ clock cycles, the worst case timing overhead t_{TO} for the eradication of the entire task graph via the self-scheduling scheme is

$$t_{TO} = \frac{8^2 - 8}{2} \cdot 99 = 2,772 \text{ clock cycles.}$$

For many scenarios, the time for unsuccessful task activations of $t_{ss} = 99$ clock cycles will usually be negligible in comparison to the execution times of individual tasks, which will lay in the range of thousands of clock cycles. Even the worst overall timing overhead t_{TO} for the eradication of the entire task graph may be acceptable, as in embedded kernels, a simple task switch between two tasks may already consume more than $1,000$ clock cycles. Thus, the timing overhead generated by the self-scheduling scheme depicted in Figure 2.45 is displayed highly exaggerated in comparison to real-word applications.

As a result of the self-scheduling scheme, no explicit knowledge about the actual task graph and the individual task execution times is needed. Thus, besides entering an initial Binding Vector, which, moreover, may be chosen completely arbitrarily, the central processor is relieved from scheduling management and might, therefore, be completely skipped. Self-scheduling is, therefore, a solution, which may be applied for systems, whose timing constraints allow for a slight overhead caused by the self-scheduling procedures. In return, the self-scheduling leads to a drastic decrease in control overhead, as there are not dedicated scheduling algorithms to apply and no representation of the task graph has to be held available anywhere in the system. The proposed self-scheduling scheme leads to self-organizing task graph execution, no matter whether the task graph is mapped to a single processor or to a processor array. Besides the intrinsic nap and sleep commands of the Virtualization Layer, no additional modules are required in order to establish the self-scheduling scheme. This mechanism will be exploited for the Agile Processing scheme detailed in Section 3.4.

2.4.5 Intermediate Conclusions

Scheduling tasks, i.e., resolving dependencies, accounting for timing budgets and execution times, can be a fairly complex problem. When it comes to scheduling for multi-processor systems, existing problems are further hardened. An evaluation of scheduling schemes for a MPSoC as well as an algorithm to map tasks to processors in a multi-processor environment is given in the work of [Ventroux 2005]. When details about the floorplan of the design are taken into consideration, even the minimization of a system's energy consumption at various execution phases may be included into the scheduling [Momtazpour 2011].

When having decided, which task to map on which processor, the virtualization concept offers several techniques for task scheduling, such as simple autonomous budget-based time multiplexing or advanced techniques, such as the autonomous self-scheduling scheme. As the virtualizable MPSoC allows for a transparent variation of the number of processor instances employed, a further level of complexity is added to the problem of scheduling. Here, the self-scheduling automatically maintains a correct execution order at the expense of a slight timing overhead caused by unsuccessful invocation and subsequent deactivation of tasks. However, for most scenarios, this overhead, which is in the range of 100 clock cycles for each unsuccessful task invocation, should be negligible. In consequence, the virtualizable MPSoC intrinsically supports a variety of scheduling options, which allows designing systems featuring cooperative and preemptive multi-tasking schemes.

For the self-scheduling scheme, it is assumed that tasks, which feature data dependencies among each other, may transfer data. However, data transfer in a virtualized environment has to undergo a special treatment. Thus, a task communication scheme for a virtualizable system will be highlighted in the following section.

2.5 Virtualized Task-to-Task Communication

Apart from the self-scheduling scheme, tasks were regarded as isolated modules by now, which do not interfere with each other. In real-world applications, however, tasks of course interact. At first sight, a solution might be to just exploit communication schemes, which are already provided by the specific processor type employed, i. e., existing bus or point-to-point interfaces. The virtualization properties, however, render this approach unfeasible. In the virtualized system, a task has no knowledge about on which processor it is currently being executed. Moreover, if a task needs to send data to another task, also the processor instance on which the targeted task is being executed is unknown. Even worse, the sending task does not even know, whether the targeted task is currently being active or not. Possibly another task is currently occupying the processor of the receiving task. This occupying task may even be the sending task. Besides tasks, the processors of the virtualizable processor array also lack of knowledge, which task they are currently executing.

In order to solve these issues, a communication concept is required, which not only overcomes the problem of transparent task placement, but also handles data transfer in case that the receiving communication participant is not active at the time of a sending event. Besides these fundamental requirements, another constraint is that such a communication concept may not pose a significant overhead in terms of latency.

The following section discusses in short several communication alternatives and their individual characteristics. From this starting point a suited communication scheme for the virtualizable system is then derived.

2.5.1 Communication Alternatives

For the communication paradigm four common techniques come into consideration. The first solution would be the usage of shared memory, cf. Figure 2.47a. Here, all tasks have access to a common memory space. This space has dedicated regions of which each corresponds to a certain task. Other tasks may send messages to this task

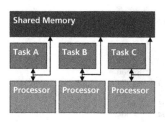

(a) A Multi-Processor System with a Shared-Memory.

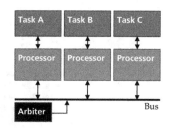

(b) A Multi-Processor System with a Data Bus.

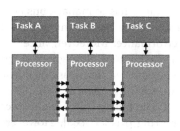

(c) A Multi-Processor System with Point-to-Point Interfaces.

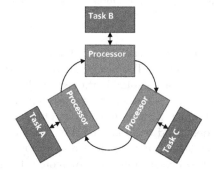

(d) A Multi-Processor System interconnected by a Data Ring.

Figure 2.47: Illustration of different Communication Alternatives.

by writing into this memory region. If a lot of data has to be transferred between tasks, instead of copying these values to the shared memory, a task may just receive a pointer to the memory region containing this data. At first sight, shared memory seems as a well-suited communication scheme for the virtualizable MPSoC as this solution does not require knowledge on which processor a task is currently being executed. However, this concept has several drawbacks. There has to be some access management provided in order to prevent write/read conflicts. Furthermore, globally addressable memories as described in the case where pointers are used, are a potential security risk. It has to be ensured that a task may not harmfully access or corrupt data stored in memory regions reserved for other tasks. Moreover, for the FPGA-based prototype of the virtualizable MPSoC, large shared memories are hard to synthesize efficiently due to the on-chip memory primitives that usually just feature two read ports and a common write port. The usage of an off-chip shared memory, however, would increase the latency and, therefore, significantly slows down the system performance.

Another alternative for task communication is bus transfer, cf. Figure 2.47b. Here, all tasks have access to a common communication interface. They may communicate by writing the receiver address and the payload data to this interface. Since all tasks are

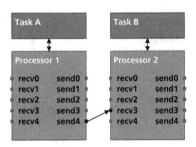

Figure 2.48: In conventional Designs, Point-to-Point Interfaces are hard-wired among Processors.

assumed to eventually send data, a bus arbiter instance has to manage bus accesses among tasks. The more participants are connected to the bus, the more the arbiter becomes a potential bottleneck of the system performance. Moreover, since the bus may only be accessed by one writing instance at a point in time, throughput of the bus is limited. As a solution, several busses might be instantiated. Each task then features a dedicated bus that just this task may access in a writing manner. The IBM Cell architecture, e. g., exploits a set of four ring-based data busses. Here, eight so-called SPU processor units are interconnected by a data ring [Kistler 2006]. However, this causes a tremendous overhead in terms of both resources and wiring complexity.

The last communication alternative to address is point-to-point connection. Here, communication participants are usually hardwired together, cf. Figure 2.47c. This allows for very fast data transfer; however, with an increasing number of participants, the wiring complexity dramatically increases since each participant has to be connected to each other participant in the system. As an alternative, a chain or ring of connected participants may be established, cf. Figure 2.47d. For ring-based communication, the saving in terms of resources and wiring complexity are paid for by a significantly higher latency, as data may have to pass several processors before reaching the designated one. Furthermore, other tasks have to interrupt their execution in order to forward data meant for other tasks.

Obviously, none of these techniques may directly be exploited for the virtualizable system. Therefore, a suited communication scheme has to be derived from the communication alternatives described above. As the performance of task communication will directly affect the system's overall performance, a solution with low latency, even at the expense of a higher resource consumption, is favored. Here, point-to-point communication outperforms shared memories as well as bus-based solutions. To overcome the communication issues arising from transparent task migration, the advantage of shared memories, which feature task-based addressing instead of relying on hard-wired processor point-to-point communication interfaces, is exploited. The following section will, thus, detail the merging of a conventional point-to-point communication scheme with a shared memory approach to form a hybrid communication scheme tailored to the needs of the virtualizable system.

2.5.2 Conventional Point-to-Point Transfer in non-Virtualized Systems

As described above, point-to-point communication usually relies on hard-wired processor interfaces. In conventional designs, which feature static task-processor bindings, the designer initially defines on which processor a task will be executed. We assume task A being statically bound to processor 1 and task B to processor 2. If task A has to send data to B, the designer connects one of the sending point-to-point interfaces of processor 1, in this example *send4* with one of the receiving point-to-point interfaces of processor 2, in this example *receive3*, cf. Figure 2.48.

In the software code of task A, the designer addresses the point-to-point interfaces of the processor by dedicated commands, which are provided in the processor application programming interface (API) . These commands usually feature the number of the specific interface to be addressed as well as the variable, which is about to be sent or received. Sometimes, parameters about the communication format and semantics are additionally entered. In the given example, a transfer might look as follows:

```
//Code for Task A (sender)
myVariable = 1234;
sendP2P(myVariable, 4);
```

Here, sendP2P is the specific command provided by the processor API to address the communication interface. 4 denotes sending interface 4 to be addressed. The payload data to be sent is the content of myVariable.

On the receiving side, the corresponding reception of the transferred data might look as follows:

```
//Code for Task B (receiver)
int newVar;
recvP2P(newVar, 3);
```

Here, by addressing receive interface 3 of processor 2, the value sent by task A via send interface 4 of processor 1 is stored into the variable newVar.

Many processors feature a set of such point-to-point interfaces. For the Xilinx MicroBlaze, which is employed for the prototyped architecture, e. g., the Fast Simplex Link (FSL) [Xilinx, Inc. 2011] and a point-to-point variant of the Advanced eXtensible Interface Bus (AXI) [ARM 2010] are provided. The prototype exploits FSL. It is, however, neither reliant nor restricted to this specific interface type. With appropriate customization of the design, other point-to-point interfaces on other processor types may be exploited as well. The MicroBlaze offers up to 16 FSL send and 16 FSL receiving interfaces. This limits the maximum number of point-to-point communication partners via conventional FSL to 16.

Addressing interfaces may either be static or dynamic. In the static case, the interface identifier is written statically into the software code, whereas in dynamic addressing, the identifier is the result of a computation, which takes place at runtime. Dynamic addressing will be, e. g., exploited for the Agile Processing scheme detailed in Section 3.4. As each variant is translated to different machine code representation and, later on, will undergo special treatments in order to enable virtualized task communication, it is necessary to discuss both variants in short.

Static Interface Addressing

For FSL, the send command of the example above reads as:

```
//Code for Task A (sender)
myVariable = 1234;
putfslx(myVariable, 4, FSL_DEFAULT);
```

Here, the default parameter `FSL_DEFAULT` sets the communication semantics to be blocking. If the interface identifier is static, `putfslx` is translated to the following machine code representation according to the MicroBlaze datasheet [Xilinx, Inc. 2012]:

0 1 1 0 1 1	0 0 0 0 0	rA	1 n c t a 0 0 0 0 0 0 0	FSLx	put
0	6	11	16	28	

The first six bits indicate the opcode of the instruction. Bit 16 distinguishes between a send and a receive instruction. `rA` from bits 11 to 15 addresses the register, which contains the content to be sent. `n, c, t,` and `a` are optional flags, which indicate non-blocking semantics, sending of a control word instead of a data word, atomic instruction sequences, and a simulated test write. For the prototype implementation, the flags to indicate non-blocking semantics and control words are considered. The four bits `FSLx` from bit position 28 to 31 indicate, which of the 16 FSL interfaces of the Microblaze is addressed.

In the example above, the value of variable `myVariable` of task A is assumed to be stored in register 11 of the MicroBlaze. Consequently, the machine code for the `putfslx` instruction of task A is:

0 1 1 0 1 1	0 0 0 0 0	0 1 0 1 1	1 0 0 0 0 0 0 0 0 0 0 0	0 1 0 0	put
0	6	11	16	28	

On the receiving side, the corresponding code is:

```
//Code for Task B (receiver)
int newVar;
getfslx(newVar, 3, FSL_DEFAULT);
```

Accordingly, the machine code representation of `getfslx` is as follows:

0 1 1 0 1 1	rD	0 0 0 0 0	0 n c t a e 0 0 0 0 0	FSLx	get
0	6	11	16	28	

putfslx and getfslx share the same opcode and bit 16 defines the selected instruction. Here, rD designates the address of the register, in which the received data word is written. Again, the FSL interface is explicitly addressed by the four bits of FSLx. As only addition to the optional parameters, e may indicate an exception in case of a control bit mismatch. As exception handling is not considered for the prototype implementation, the usage of this parameter is restricted. For the sake of completeness, the machine code representation of task B's getfslx is as follows, if variable newVar is assumed to be stored into register 19 of the receiving processor:

0 1 1 0 1 1	1 0 0 1 1	0 0 0 0 0	0 0 0 0 0 0 0 0 0 0 0 0	0 0 1 1	get
0	6	11	16	28	

Dynamic Interface Adressing

In case the interface identifier is computed at runtime, the dedicated instructions putdfslx and getdfslx are translated to the following machine code representation, where the interface identifier is given indirectly by the last four bits of rB. The opcode is different compared to the commands with static addressing.

0 1 0 0 1 1	0 0 0 0 0	rA	rB	1 n c t a 0 0 0 0 1 1	putd
0	6	11	16	21	

0 1 0 0 1 1	rD	0 0 0 0 0	rB	0 n c t a e 0 0 0 1 1	getd
0	6	11	16	21	

As much code employed in today's designs is based on legacy code, the envisaged communication scheme should require just slight adaptions of existing software code. Therefore, the advocated solution aims at relying on the communication commands as already provided by the processor's API. Thus, the instructions introduced above are reused for the virtualizable task communication scheme. The underlying architecture, however, is essentially modified as follows.

2.5.3 Architectural Enhancements and Code Changes

The first step to enable virtualized task communication is to leave the processors' point-to-point interfaces completely unconnected. The usage of these interfaces is discarded. As a next step, the designer assigns a static ID to each task in the design. This ID will be used to address a task regardless of the processor instance on which it is being executed. So, instead of denoting a processor's interface identifier in a point-to-point communication command, the designer sets the ID of a task at the position of the interface identifier. In the example above, the designer arbitrarily defines task A to have ID 0, task B to have ID 1. The corresponding code is then changed to:

```
//Code for Task A (sender)
myVariable = 1234;
putfslx(myVariable, 1, FSL_DEFAULT);
```

0 1 1 0 1 1	0 0 0 0 0	0 1 0 1 1	1 0 0 0 0 0 0 0 0 0 0 0	0 0 0 1	put
0	6	11	16	28	

```
//Code for Task B (receiver)
int newVar;
getfslx(newVar, 0, FSL_DEFAULT);
```

0 1 1 0 1 1	1 0 0 1 1	0 0 0 0 0	0 0 0 0 0 0 0 0 0 0 0 0	0 0 0 0	get
0	6	11	16	28	

For software, which dynamically computes the designated communication partner, i. e., features dynamic addressing, the designer has to make sure to compute the ID of a task and not a specific point-to-point interface identifier of the processor.

In contrast to the conventional solution of the previous Section, the sending task now directly addresses the receiving task by its ID as well as the receiver explicitly denotes the ID of the sender. Obviously, executing this code in a processor design, where, additionally, the processors' point-to-point interfaces remain unconnected would lead to an erratic system behavior. Thus, the architecture has to be further modified in order to be able to correctly accomplish data transfers.

Inside the Virtualization Layer, a so-called Message Hub is instantiated. It consists of a *Task Data Matrix* (TDM) and a *Message Memory*. The TDM features a send row and a receive column for each task active in the design, cf. Figure 2.49. In Figure 2.49, the highlighted cell contains the data value 1234, which is about to be sent from the task with ID 0 to the task with ID 1. Each cell in the TDM features a width of $32 + 1$ bit, corresponding to the width of the processors' data memory interface and point-to-point interfaces[20] plus a control bit. The write and read logic corresponding to each task is connected to the multiplexer on the tasks' data memory interface as depicted in Figure 2.51. Here, the multiplexer on the right hand side may be configured at runtime in a way that the processor will access the TDM either for reading or writing. Additionally, the designer may define communication ports for external modules, cf. Section 2.5.6.

The Message Memory is a memory block, which will store data sent to tasks, which are currently not configured into one of the task memories in the system. As discussed in Section 2.3.5, tasks may be replaced at runtime as their corresponding task memory is overwritten by the content of another task. For FPGA-based implementations, this

---

[20]In most processor architectures, the width of point-to-point interfaces is of the same or a smaller width as the data memory interface. In the unusual case that it is larger, the communication scheme will have to be slightly modified.

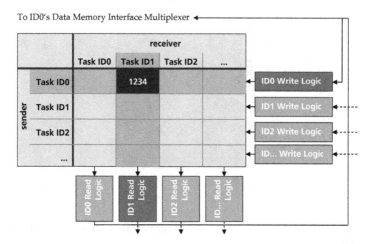

Figure 2.49: The Task Data Matrix with a Send Row and a Receive Column for each Task currently mapped into a Task Memory. The Write and Read Logic of a Task is routed to its Data Memory Interface Multiplexer as depicted in Figure 2.51.

can be achieved, e.g., by partial reconfiguration. Each task, which is currently not mapped into a memory, features a dedicated memory region in the Message Memory. Each address is assigned to another task in the system, cf. Figure 2.50.

The *Instruction Stream Monitor* (ISM) will be exploited to detect send and receive commands and passes this information to the Code Injection Logic (CIL), cf. Figure 2.51.

The actual task communication scheme may be divided into three distinct steps. The runtime code modification for sending, the Message Hub transfer, and the runtime code modification for receiving data. These three steps are detailed in the following sections. At first, a basic communication scheme is introduced, which is then expanded in order to support dynamic addressing as well as transfers to tasks currently not being mapped into a task memory.

2.5.4 Basic Communication Scheme

The basic communication scheme enables communication in the virtualizable MPSoC with no additional timing overhead caused by the dynamic code modification compared to a non-virtualized point-to-point communication and a one word-sized buffer. For the basic communication scheme it is assumed that every communication partner is mapped into a task memory, i.e., is directly addressable within the TDM. Only static addressing and blocking semantics are allowed here. Furthermore it is assumed that every send and receive passed from the instruction memory to the processor will be executed.[21].

---

[21]The enhanced scheme in the following section will highlight, why this is not always the case.

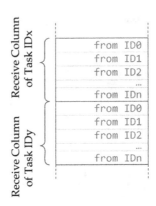

Figure 2.50: The Message Memory is a Communication Matrix sequentialized into a Memory Block.

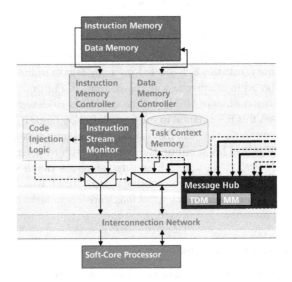

Figure 2.51: A Section of the Virtualization Layer displaying the Connection of the Message Hub to a Task's Data Memory Interface Multiplexer.

Runtime Code Modification for Sending

As mentioned in Section 2.2.5, the Virtualization Layer is able to monitor the instructions sent from a task's instruction memory to its corresponding processor. Moreover, the

CIL can be routed to the processor's instruction interface in order to force instructions into the processor. The virtualization logic is now extended to monitor the occurrence of communication commands such as the machine code representation of putfslx in the instruction stream via the ISM. A command is identified by its opcode. As soon as a putfslx instruction is detected, this instruction is withheld by the Virtualization Layer and the CIL is routed to the processors' instruction interface to inject a dedicated instruction sequence. The CIL replaces at runtime the original putfslx command by a store word immediate instruction. This instruction is part of the default instruction set of common processors. It is designed to write contents of a processor register into the data memory. For the prototyped implementation on Xilinx MicroBlazes, according to its datasheet [Xilinx, Inc. 2012], the store word immediate command has the following format:

```
swi rD, rA, IMM
```

rD designates a register address of one of the 32 general purpose registers of the MicroBlaze. Its content will be output on the processor's data memory interface, which is usually connected to a task's data memory. To address the memory, the sum of the content of register rA and the value of IMM is taken. IMM is a so-called immediate value, which is directly passed as an argument in the command. The bit pattern of the store word immediate instruction is as follows:

1 1 1 1 1 0	rD	rA	IMM		swi
0	6	11	16		

The CIL now sets rD to the value of rA, which was denoted in the original putfslx command, cf. Section 2.5.2. rA of the store word immediate instruction is set to 0, thus addressing general purpose register 0, which statically contains the value 0. IMM is filled with the task ID of the receiver, which was commited in the FSLx section of the putfslx command, cf. Section 2.5.2. Revisting the example of Section 2.5.2, the following machine code is injected into the processor:

1 1 1 1 1 0	0 1 0 1 1	0 0 0 0 0	0 0 0 0 0 0 0 0 0 0 0 0 0 1 0 0	swi
0	6	11	16	

This will output the value of myVariable, which is stored in register 11, on the processor's data memory interface. As a memory address, 1 is being output, which is the ID of the receiving task, cf. Figure 2.52. The value being consequently output by the processor is, however, not forwarded to the data memory. Instead, the Message Hub catches this value.

Message Hub Transfer

As soon as the processor executes an instruction, which was modified by the CIL, the task's data memory is detached and the Message Hub is routed to the processor's data

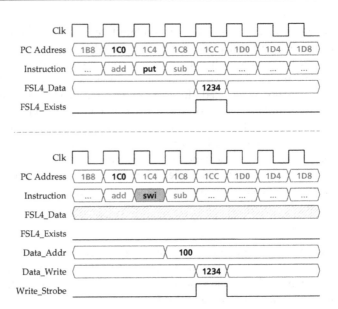

Figure 2.52: The upper Part illustrates a conventional Instruction Sequence. In the lower Part, the CIL alters a putfslx to a store word immediate, thus, addressing the receiving Task by its ID.

memory interface.[22] In the example, the value of myVariable being the output on the processor's data memory interface is written into the TDM by the corresponding write column of the sending task. The cell of this row is addressed by the task ID of the receiver. For commands with static addressing, the ID is passed on the Data_Addr lane, cf. Figure 2.52. If a new value is written into a cell of the TDM, the TDM cell indicates this by a flag. This flag will be reset during the following read process. After successfully accessing the TDM, the task's data memory is reattached to the processor. By withholding the injection of the store word immediate instruction in case a TDM cell is already occupied when trying to write in a blocking manner, the task's execution stalls in accordance with blocking semantics. However, the task remains interruptible by the virtualization procedure as the processor itself is not in a blocking condition. Algorithm 15 denotes the steps for sending commands with static addressing via the virtualizable communication scheme.

As each task features a dedicated write logic and read logic, all tasks in the system may write or read in parallel. This prevents the TDM from becoming a bottleneck for task communication. The newly written data is now ready for being received by another task.

---

[22]Depending on the processor type, the time between instruction fetch and the actual execution of the command may vary. The time depends of the pipeline depth of the employed processor type.

Algorithm 15 Sending with static Addressing.

Require: A processor p_i, which executes task t_j, the Virtualization Layer featuring a TDM and for each task an ISM and a CIL.

Ensure: Sending Data from t_j via the TDM in blocking manner.

 1: **while** ISM detects no "send" instruction with static addressing in instruction stream from t_j's instruction memory to p_i **do**
 2: **end while**
 3: ISM reads target address in instruction
 4: CIL replaces "send" instruction by `store word immediate`
 5: CIL checks flag of corresponding TDM cell for availability
 6: **while** TDM cell is not free (indicated by '1') **do**
 7:     CIL withholds `store word immediate` instruction   ▷ processor stalls at instruction fetch. Guarantees interruptibility by virtualization procedure despite blocking semantics.
 8: **end while**
 9: CIL forwards `store word immediate` to p_i
 10: Detach t_j's data memory
 11: Attach TDM to p_i's data memory interface
 12: TDM writes value being sent out on p_i's data memory interface into corresponding TDM cell
 13: TDM sets flag of TDM cell to '1' indicate that it is full
 14: TDM acknowledges write to p_i
 15: Detach TDM, reattach t_j's data memory to p_i's data memory interface

---

Receiving Command with Static Addressing

In analogy to the code modification for sending, a receiving point-to-point instruction is also modified by the CIL. The original machine code representation of `getfslx` is substituted by a `load word immediate` instruction, which normally loads a data word from the task's data memory. The machine code format is similar to that of a `store word immediate`. For the virtualizable communication scheme, instead of denoting an address of the data memory, the identifier of the sending task is set in the IMM section of the `load word immediate` command, cf. Figure 2.53.

Before injecting the `load word immediate` into the processor when replacing a receive command featuring blocking semantics, it is checked whether the corresponding TDM cell contains data. If not, the injection of the `load word immediate` is withhold. In doing so, the receiving task stalls until data is available. In case that a virtualization procedure deactivates the receiving task, it will resume its execution after its next reactivation at the point waiting for data. In case the TDM cell contains data, the data memory interface of the receiving task's processor is routed to the TDM and the `load word immediate` instruction is injected. The TDM cell containing the value to be received is addressed by the read logic of the receiving task. The value written in the cell is read into the processor. The read logic of the receiving task furthermore sets the flag in the TDM cell, which indicates a new data in the cell, back to 0. Algorithm 16 denotes the steps performed in order to accomplish a read.

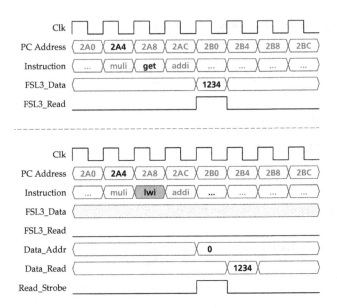

Figure 2.53: A conventional Instruction Stream is modified at Runtime to receive Data of a Point-to-Point Transfer via the Data Memory Interface.

Algorithm 16 Receiving with static Addressing.

Require: A processor p_i, which executes task t_j, the Virtualization Layer featuring a TDM and for each task an ISM and a CIL.

Ensure: t_j receiving Data via the TDM in a blocking manner.

1: **while** ISM detects no "receive" instruction with static addressing in instruction stream from t_j's instruction memory to p_i **do**
2: **end while**
3: ISM reads target address in instruction
4: CIL replaces "receive" instruction by load word immediate
5: CIL checks flag of corresponding TDM cell for a new value
6: **while** TDM cell does not contain new value (indicated by '0') **do**
7:     CIL withholds load word immediate instruction   ▷ Processor stalls at instruction fetch. Guarantees interruptibility by virtualization procedure despite blocking semantics.
8: **end while**
9: CIL forwards load word immediate to p_i
10: Detach t_j's data memory
11: Attach TDM to p_i's data memory interface
12: p_i loads value from corresponding TDM cell
13: TDM acknowledges read by p_i
14: TDM sets flag of TDM cell to '0' indicate that the value has been read out
15: Detach TDM, reattach t_j's data memory to p_i's data memory interface

Benefits and Disadvantages of the basic Communication Scheme

The basic communication scheme replaces one original send or receive instruction by one dedicated store or load instruction. Thus, the sequence of the instruction stream remains in order and no correction of the program counter address is necessary. Consequently, there is no timing overhead introduced to the execution of the tasks. A communication is completed within one clock cycle. The interruption of the tasks' execution by the virtualization procedure at any point in time is still guaranteed even when applying blocking semantics, which may stall a task's execution. The basic communication scheme is, thus, a reliable and fast method to provide communication in a virtualized environment.

This basic scheme, however, also features some drawbacks. It is assumed that a instruction sent to the processor is eventually being executed. However, depending on the code, a send or receive instruction may immediately follow a conditional branch. In case a branch is taken, the send or receive instruction or rather their dynamic replacement is already read into the processor's pipeline but will not be executed. In this case, the TDM will already be configured to receive or provide data. The actual read or write access, however, will not happen. As an alleged solution, a compiler might be modified in order to prevent the placement of communication commands close behind branch instructions.

In order to provide dynamic addressing, not only information on the actual data, but also details about the actual sender or receiver have to be passed to the Message Hub. In order to obtain this information, the original send or receive command has to be replaced by a sequence of instructions. The replacement of one instruction by a sequence enforces a subsequent correction of the program counter of the task. Moreover, the basic scheme does not consider that some tasks are not configured into a task memory at runtime. A solution might be to scale the TDM to a size of $n \times n$, where n is the number of all tasks in the system. However, this would lead to very inefficient synthesis results. Thus, in order to cope with all these issues, an enhanced communication scheme is built on top of the basic communication method.

2.5.5 Enhanced Communication Scheme

The Enhanced Communication Scheme is structured into the code modification sequence and the behavior of the Message Hub.

Code Modification Sequence for Enhanced Communication Scheme

For the enhanced communication scheme, send or receive commands are replaced by a dedicated sequence of operations. This sequence is structured in the following way:

1. Detection, whether static or dynamic addressing is present and detection, whether the original send or receive instruction would be executed by the processor.

2. Detection, which would be next instruction to be actually executed by the processor, saving of this address as return address.

3. Injection of `load` or `store` command, optionally preceded by a chain of nop instructions in case of blocking behavior.

4. Optionally setting processor's status register accordingly (e. g., error bit).

5. Unconditional jump to return address saved in Step 2.

In Step 1, it is identified, whether the original send or receive command would be executed by the processor. If the command would be fed into the processor while, e. g., a branch target calculation is ongoing, the command will not be executed. This circumstance is detected by replacing the original send or receive command by a `store word` command. The address of this `store word` is set, e. g., to `0xFFFFFF`. In case of a dynamically addressed send or receive command, the `store word` command is exploited to read out register containing the dynamic target address at once. If subsequently an output is detected on the processor's data memory interface with the corresponding address, this proves that this instruction has been executed. Consequently, the original send or receive command would have been executed as well. For dynamic addressed send or receive commands, the dynamic address has been output by the `store word` as well. In case that no output on the processor's data memory interface to this address has been detected, the corresponding send or receive command would not have been executed. Thus, the communication sequence is terminated by executing Steps 2 and 5 under skip of the actual transfer performed in Steps 3 and 4.

In Step 2, it is defined, at which program counter address the task shall continue its execution, if no sequence would have been injected into the processor. It is important to detect the instruction address, at which an instruction is actually being executed by the processor. Figure 2.54 highlights several cases, which may occur. The correct address is identified by injecting a sequence of `store word` instructions with designer-defined addresses, such as `0x11111111`, `0x22222222`, and `0x33333333` and keeping track of the program counter addresses corresponding to these commands. The first of these memory addresses in combination with a write detected on the processor's memory interface indicates the address, which is the next to be executed by the processors. The corresponding program counter address is, thus, saved as return address. The length of this sequence is dependent on the actual processor architecture, e. g., by the longest delay caused by branch commands. For the prototype implementation on top of MicroBlaze processors, this sequence consists of three `store word` commands.

After these arrangements, in Step 3, the actual `store word` or `load word`, respectively, is injected into the processor as for the basic communication scheme. In case of blocking semantics, this command is preceded by a sequence of nop instructions, until the corresponding cell in the message hub either provides data or is free for write access. In doing so, the interruptibility by the virtualization procedure is ensured.

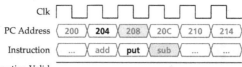

(a) The Communication Command is valid as well as the Instruction immediately following.

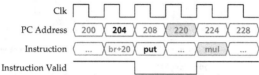

(b) The Communication Command is invalid as a Branch Target Calculations is ongoing. The next Instruction is executed after the Branch Target Calculation has been completed.

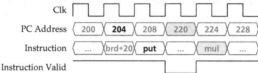

(c) The Communication Command is valid as it lays in the Delay Slot of a Branch Command. The Instruction following directly is invalid due to the Branch Target Calculation.

Figure 2.54: The highlighted Instructions mark the first Instructions to be executed after Occurrence of a Communication Command.

Depending on the original send or receive instruction and its semantics, bits in the processor's status register are modified. In the optional Step 4, these modifications in the status register are handled. This is the case, e. g., when expecting receiving data marked by a control bit[23], but receiving data without this bit being set. This is indicated in the processor's status registers.

At last, in Step 5, an unconditional jump to the return address saved in Step 2 is performed. After having completed this sequence, the task resumes its normal operation. As soon as another communication command is detected, the sequence is triggered again. The behavior of the Message Hub and the TDM is modified as well.

Behavior of the Message Hub and TDM

For the basic communication scheme, only the TDM of the Message Hub was exploited. In doing so, all tasks mapped to task memories could communicate with each other. Now, a task may also send data to a task, which is currently not mapped into a task memory. Therefore, the TDM is accompanied by the Message Memory. While the TDM contains rows and columns for each task currently being mapped into a task

---

[23]A status bit to indicate, whether user data or control data are being transmitted.

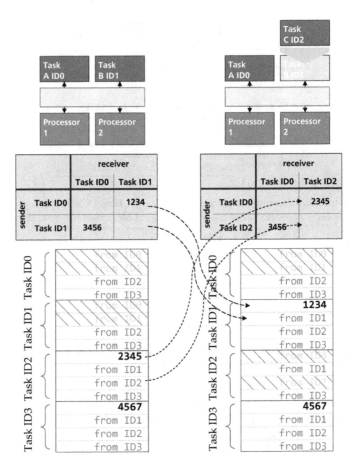

Figure 2.55: Replacing the Content of the Task Memory leads to an Update of the TDM Configuration.

memory, the Message Memory is a sequential memory space consisting of a matrix of all tasks. As soon as a task is mapped into the task memory, a part of its communication content, which covers the active tasks in the system, is transferred from the Message Memory into the TDM, cf Figure 2.55. The communication content of the task, which is overwritten, is consequently written into the Message Memory. In doing so, active tasks may communicate fast and efficiently without the need for a large-scaled cross matrix. Communication with tasks currently not mapped into a task memory is slower due to the sequential access to the Message Memory. The amount of communication with these tasks is, however, considered to be lower than that with active tasks. As replacing the content of a task memory, e. g., by partial reconfiguration takes a fair amount of

Table 2.3: Averaged Latency of conventional Communication compared to virtualized Communication.

	Conventional Point-to-Point	Virtualized Point-to-Point
Unidirectional Transfer	3 clock cyc.	18 clock cyc.
Bidirectional Transfer	10 clock cyc.	47 clock cyc.

time, swapping of TDM and Message Memory contents can be done in parallel without adding additional timing overhead.

2.5.6 Properties and Advanced Features

The virtualizable task communication scheme features several characteristics, which are now discussed in short.

Timing Behavior

In comparison to point-to-point data transfers via interfaces, which are natively provided by the processor core, the virtualizable solution via the TDM features a slight latency overhead. For the reference implementation of the communication architecture, which was done by Boris Dreyer [Dreyer 2014], a latency as denoted in Table 2.3 was measured. All timing values are averaged from 50 subsequent transfers. In the unidirectional case, the latency is the average time, until a receiver has received a value from the sender. In the bidirectional case, the latency denotes the average time needed to send a value to a communication partner and to subsequently receive a value from this partner. For large bursts of data, the enhanced scheme may thus reduce the performance of the system. Nevertheless, as any point-to-point communication scheme, this scheme is very efficient for few, fast data transfers. For applications requiring a huge amount of memory transfers in a MPSoC, globally addressable memories are presumably a better choice, however, at the expense of their disadvantages, which have already been addressed earlier.

Data Broadcasts and Non-Blocking Semantics

A feature, which is enabled by the virtualized data transfer and that is usually not available for common point-to-point data transfer is the option for data broadcasts. A designer may define an ID, which acts a broadcast address. If the Virtualization Layer detects this target ID address by a send command, the corresponding data word is written in a non-blocking manner into the entire write row of the sending task in the TDM. As this happens concurrently, the broadcast expansion does not add any latency. Therefore, existing values in the TDM, which have not yet been read out, are overwritten. The automotive application example in Section 4.1 will exploit this feature to continuously distribute sensor data to a set of driver assistance tasks.

TDM Buffer

Routing data transfers via the Message Hub has the significant advantage that a receiving task does not necessarily have to be executed at the time the sending task outputs its data word. The Message Memory buffers this data word until the receiving task is activated and reaches the receive instructions. In doing so, even tasks may communicate with each other that share the same processor instance in a time division scheme.

An extension to the advocated communication scheme can be made by adding a third dimension to the TDM. In this case, each cell of the TDM could buffer several data words. Depending on the specific application scenario, this could prevent stalls and improve the system's throughput. The communication scheme itself, however, does not gain any advantage or level of complexity in doing so. As discussed for the task-processor interconnection network in Section 2.3.5, the expected structure of a TDM with larger buffer depth is not well-suited to be efficiently mapped to the inherent structure of an FPGA. Therefore, the implementation of a larger buffer depth of the TDM was skipped for the prototype implementations.

Guaranteed Task Interruption despite blocking Semantics

The communication scheme may either be adjusted to feature either blocking or non-blocking semantics. However, in order to prevent deadlocks, the Virtualization Layer has to maintain the ability to disable a task at any time, e. g., due to a scheduling event, even if the task is currently stalling because of a blocking send or receive. Blocking is realized by consecutively feeding nop instructions into the processor. Therefore, in case a task currently stalling due to a blocking send or receive has to be deactivated, the processor itself is not in a blocking condition and the CIL may inject the virtualization machine code to disable the task. Upon the task's next activation, task execution is resumed at the point of interruption within this sequence.

Communication with external Modules

The tasks in the virtualizable system may also communicate with external modules via the task communication scheme. Therefore, each external module receives a static ID, just as the tasks in the system. For each external module, the Message Hub transparently acts as glue logic between virtualized tasks and external components. The automotive application scenario in Section 4.1 demonstrates the usage of external modules in combination with the virtualizable task communication scheme.

The Virtualization Layer provides a safe execution environment due to its disjoint task memory design. However, for systems relevant to security, communication may pose a potential thread. The designer may want to restrict or at least control communication between tasks of the virtualizable processor array and external modules. In this case, approaches as proposed in [Cotret 2012] may be exploited. Here, for FPGA-based MPSoC, an additional local firewall can be added for each communication participant, which manages and controls data transfers. While this was presented for bus-based systems, the concept of local firewalls might be transferrable to the virtualizable communication scheme.

Intermediate Conclusions

For the design of virtualizable systems, an advantage of the advocated communication scheme is that a designer may continue to use existing software commands to establish data transfers, as these instructions are modified during runtime. As only change, the original address of the dedicated processor interface is replaced by the task ID of the sender or receiver. As both, processor interface or task ID are later represented by numbers at a specific position in the machine code representation of the command, compilers do not need to be adapted in order to work with the present approach. This significantly eases writing software for the virtualizable system, as for the software workflow no changes are required.

As the virtualized data transfer keeps the strict disjuncture of the tasks' contexts, it avoids potential threads arising, e. g., from address space violations in common shared memories. The virtualizable communication scheme, thus, contributes to the safe and reliable execution of tasks in the system. Moreover, the virtualizable MPSoC may be configured to feature dedicated reliability modules as well.

2.6 Reliability Features of the Virtualization Layer

The Virtualization Layer's intrinsic features towards system safety are the fully transparent virtualization procedure and the strict task separation. In addition, the layer is now being expanded to feature generic modules which will enable task redundancy in order to meet Postulate 5 (*Mechanisms for fault detection and masking*). Redundancy is a mean to ensure system safety. Two of the most prominent redundancy concepts are Dual Modular Redundancy (DMR) and Triple Modular Redundancy (TMR), respectively.

In DMR, two instances of a task are executed in parallel. The results of both tasks are compared by a dedicated voter module. In case that the results coincide, a correct task behavior is assumed. As soon as a deviation in both results is detected, an error is denoted by the voter. However, it is not possible to determine, which task produced an erroneous result. To clarify this, several approaches exist. For example, predefined input data, whose corresponding output is known in advance, may be applied. Based on the results, the erroneous process may be identified. Other approaches may check

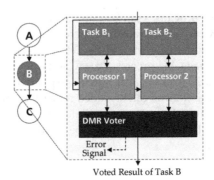

Voted Result of Task B

Figure 2.56: Task B of the Task Graph is executed in a Dual Modular Redundancy Scheme.

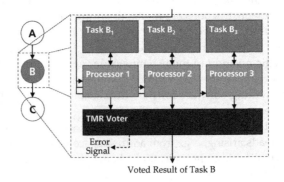

Voted Result of Task B

Figure 2.57: Task B of the Task Graph is executed in a Triple Modular Redundancy Scheme.

output data for being in a feasible range. Such monitoring has been presented, e. g., in [Biedermann 2011a]. A simple DMR system is depicted in Figure 2.56.

For TMR, three instances of a task are executed in parallel. Here, one faulty process may be identified if two processes output identical results and a third one deviates. In case that all results are different, the same issue as for DMR arises. Here, similar approaches may be applied to resolve this situation. A TMR system is depicted in Figure 2.57.

As depicted in Figures 2.56 and 2.57, in DMR- or TMR-voted systems, each task instance is usually statically bound to a processor. The voter module is connected to the processors. In the virtualized system, however, the task-processor binding may change during runtime. Moreover, a task may not be the sole user of a processor resource. These challenges have to be considered.

In order to support redundancy schemes, the Virtualization Layer features generic modules, the so-called Virtualized Module Redundancy (VMR) modules, which may

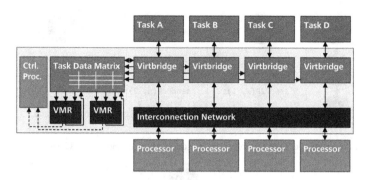

Figure 2.58: Virtualization Layer featuring the generic VMR Modules for Redundancy.

either act in DMR or in TMR mode. In a design with n task memories, $n/2$ VMR modules are instantiated, as for $n/2$ DMR-voted tasks, n task memories are necessary. A virtualizable MPSoC featuring 4 task memories and 4 processors expanded by VMR modules is depicted in Figure 2.58. Each of the VMR modules is connected to the TDM for data exchange. For this purpose, the designer defines a unique ID for each VMR module, which may not overlap with the IDs already assigned to tasks or to external modules.

Besides these voting modules, the behavior of the Virtualization Logic as well as the binding definitions have to be adapted in order to support the redundancy schemes. This is illustrated by means of an example. Given the task graph in Figure 2.59, left hand side, task A sends its result to task B, which passes its result further to task C. In order to enable virtualized task communication as detailed in Section 2.5.3, the designer has arbitrarily defined task A to feature ID 0, whereas task B has ID 1 and task C ID 2. The right hand side of Figure 2.59 depicts the corresponding software code. Now, a redundant execution of task B with subsequent result voting is desired. Accordingly, a second task instance of B as well as a voting module is added, cf. Figure 2.60. The original task B now acts as instance B_1. The second instance B_2 of B is treated just as a normal task in the system by the architecture, even if its software code may be an identical copy of original task B. Consequently, the designer has to define a unique ID to task B_2 in order to enable communication for this task. He arbitrarily choses ID 4.

Obviously, changes in the code of all tasks are now necessary. A has to be modified in order to provide data not only to B_1, i. e., the original B, but also to B_2. Both instances of B have to be revised in order to send their data not immediately to C, but to a voter module. Additionally, C has to be altered in order to receive B's data via this voter module. The simplest solution would be to burden the designer with the duty of adapting task communication to the redundancy scheme. The present approach will, however, automatically handle these issues and, therefore, enable the transparent transition between redundant and non-redundant task execution at runtime.

Figure 2.59: An example Task Graph with its corresponding Software Code.

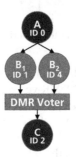

Figure 2.60: The Task Graph of Figure 2.59 with Task B being executed in a redundant Scheme.

At first, the Binding Vector has to be expanded not only to denote information about which tasks to execute in a redundancy scheme, but also in order to pass information about the data flow in the task graph. For the example in Figure 2.59, a corresponding Binding Vector might be:

$$BV_1 = (A \mapsto 1), (B \mapsto 2), (C \mapsto 3)$$

A is mapped to processor 1, B to processor 2, and C to processor 3. For the task graph in Figure 2.60 with a redundant execution of task B, the expanded Binding Vector is denoted as follows:

$$BV_2 = (A \mapsto 1), (B_1 \mapsto 2), (C \mapsto 3), (B_2 \mapsto 4); (A, (B_1(1), B_2(4)) \mapsto VMR(9))$$

Here a second instance of B is mapped to processor 4. Additionally, configuration information for a VMR module is passed in the Binding Vector. The configuration information has the following format:

$$(l_d, (b_1(ID_1), b_2(ID_2), [b_3(ID_3)]) \mapsto VMR(ID_{VMR}))$$

with l_d being a list of tasks, the redundant task depends of. b_1, b_2, and b_3 are the redundant task instances, which are to be voted. ID_1, ID_2, and ID_3 are their corres-

---

Algorithm 17 Applying Redundancy Schemes in a virtualizable MPSoC.

Require: A binding vector BV with VMR configuration information.
Ensure: Application of redundancy schemes as defined by VMR configuration information.
1: Virtualization Layer configures interconnection network according to BV, cf. Algorithm 6
2: VMR configuration information is passed to VMR modules
3: **for all** Tasks denoted in l_d in the VMR configuration information **do**
4:     Configure corresponding ISM to detect send commands addressed to either b_1, b_2, or b_3 in instruction stream
5: **end for**
6: **if** A task in l_d addresses b_1 by a send command **then**
7:     Distribute data to b_1, b_2, and, in case of TMR, to b_3 ▷ Handled by Message Hub
8: **end if**
9: **if** In instruction stream of b_1, b_2, or b_3 appears send command **then**
10:     CIL of the task's Virtbridge alters send command to send command to VMR module selected in BV
11:     **if** Current task is b_1 **then**
12:         CIL passes information about original destination address to VMR
13:     **end if**
14: **end if**
15: **if** VMR module has received data from b_1, b_2, and in case of TMR from b_3 within designer-defined time interval **then**
16:     VMR voter votes inputs
17:     **if** VMR voter detects deviation **then**
18:         VMR outputs error code to control processor
19:     **end if**
20: **else**
21:     VMR outputs Timeout Error to control processor
22: **end if**
23: VMR addresses subsequent tasks originally addressed by b_1 and sends voted result by exploiting b_1's TDM write column

---

ponding communication IDs. By denoting two task instances, DMR is selected. If three task instances are denoted, TMR is automatically selected in the corresponding VMR module. ID_{VMR} denotes a specific voter module in the system by its communication ID. In the example, l_d consists of task A. The tasks to be voted are task B_1 with ID 1 and task B_2 with ID 4. As voter, the VMR module with ID 9 is chosen.

From this point, the Virtualization Layer manages the corresponding data distribution to and from voter modules. Algorithm 17 denotes the behavior of dynamic communication rerouting when executing a redundancy scheme. For the example, Figure 2.61 details the resulting TDM transfers.

Note that for l_d the data distribution is not realized by means of inserting additional send commands as this would require a subsequent correction of l_d's program counter. Instead, the Message Hub is configured to distribute the data to the b parts. For all tasks in the system, the employment of voter modules is fully transparent. Therefore, there is no need to manually modify the software of tasks in order to apply a redundancy scheme. Furthermore, the system may switch at runtime between redundant and

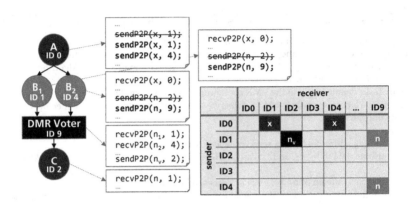

Figure 2.61: Runtime Code Manipulations and Data Transfers via the TDM when executing a Redundancy Scheme based on Algorithm 17. In the TDM, VMR sends the voted result n_v to Task C with ID 2 by exploiting B_1's Write Column.

non-redundant execution modes. By exploiting the dynamic task replacement detailed in Section 2.3.5, redundant instances of a task may be configured onto the FPGA on demand. Additionally, a redundant task instance might share its processor with another task via the virtualization procedure as the voter correlates with tasks, not with processors. However, in most designs, which require task redundancy, the designer will presumably refrain from binding other tasks with a redundant task instance to the same processor.

An implementation of the VMR modules was done in the scope of a master thesis by Andreas Rjasanow [Rjasanow 2013]. The initial configuration of the VMR modules when receiving a new Binding Vector takes 10 clock cycles, which is shorter than the setup needed for the interconnection network. Voting results are computed within one clock cycle. Summing up, the overall timing overhead of few clock cycles generated by the redundancy modules is negligible. The resource overhead caused by the VMR modules is also negligible. For the FPGA-based prototype, a VMR module occupies 51 flip-flops and 52 LUTs on a Xilinx Virtex-6 LX240T device.

By providing generic voting modules, which can cope with the transparent migration of tasks in the system, the reliability and safety achievable by exploiting the virtualizable MPSoC is significantly increased. Furthermore, means to detect faults during the system's execution in combination with the ability to shift the execution from faulty processors to other processor instances enable the design of systems, which feature self-healing properties. These properties will be detailed in Section 3.2. Besides reliability as relevant constraint in embedded system design, the often limited supply of energy renders energy awareness as another design requirement. The following section will highlight the energy awareness features provided by the Virtualization Layer.

2.7 Features for Energy Management

As more and more embedded computers are implemented in hand-held devices or at least wireless devices, such as smartphones or wireless sensor networks, sustaining power supply is a crucial issue. Despite progress in the field of battery research, modern smartphones require loading the battery at least once every two days.[24] As battery capacity is not expected to increase drastically in near future, an embedded architecture has to feature means of energy awareness in order to expand the time between two charge cycles. Besides, these means are also suited in order to cope with temporary deviations in the power supply. Such deviations may occur, e. g., for solar-powered devices which may, despite capacitors buffering energy, face a shortcoming of energy during shadowing.

The virtualizable multi-processor architecture exploits several approaches in order to optimize the overall power consumption of the processor array. It is assumed that the system has knowledge about the current battery capacity or energy supply in order to be able to react to shortcomings or deviations. Main principle to preserve energy is the deactivation of on-chip modules. This may be achieved, e. g., by clock gating, i. e., by disconnecting the clock signal from clocked modules. In doing so, the activity of a module is significantly reduced. A trivial solution might, therefore, be to simply deactivate processor resources of the system during a shortcoming of energy. However, in doing so, the tasks that were originally executed on these processors would terminate their execution and their current context would be lost.[25] In order to overcome these issues, the strengths of the Virtualization Layer come into play. The virtualizable MPSoC architecture features the following means to dynamically regulate the energy consumption.

As mentioned, the simplest way to reduce current energy consumption is the temporary deactivation of processors, cf. Figure 2.62. However, instead of just deactivating the clock input of a processor, the virtualization procedure is triggered for the task currently being executed on a processor that is to be deactivated. In doing so, the context of the task is preserved until the processor is reactivated. A positive side effect arising from resuming task execution at the point of its previous interruption instead of completely having to restart its execution is achieved. First, execution time for the task to finish is reduced and, second, no energy has to be spend to repeat the execution of sections of the task that have already been executed before the processor's temporary deactivation.

In consequence, during a shortcoming of energy supply or when running short of battery life, the virtualizable architecture allows to exclude less important tasks from being executed on the processor array. The system designer may either define several

---

[24]When being on standby most of the time, the battery of a smartphone may last for about a week. However, the author observed this to be a rare consumer behavior for smartphone users.

[25]Depending on the processor type employed, a processor may automatically induce a self-reset as soon as the clock input recovers from suspension.

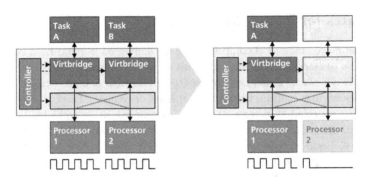

Figure 2.62: In order to reduce the Power Consumption of the System, a Task's Context is extracted by the Virtualization Procedure and the corresponding Processor Instance is disabled.

"low energy" profiles by hand or a system scheduling instance may decide at runtime about which tasks to exclude from execution. In the updated binding, the tasks to be deactivated are not assigned to a processor. The update of the task-processor binding may then free processor resources, which, in consequence, may be temporarily disabled as described above.

In the scope of a Bachelor Thesis of Antonio Gavino Casu [Casu 2013], the effect of deactivating clock inputs of processor cores was analyzed. Here, a Virtex-6 LX240T FPGA was equipped with a system monitor, which tracks the on-chip power consumption of Xilinx MicroBlaze processors. A dedicated processor instance is exploited for measurement management. Figure 2.63 depicts the effect on power consumption in a four processor system, when varying the number of active cores. All active processor cores run on 200 MHz. Despite a static power offset present in the system, which is, e. g., caused by the processor used for measure management, power consumption is linearly linked with the number of cores as visible from Figure 2.63.

Instead of completely deactivating a processor instance, the clock frequency or the supply voltage may be lowered in order to reduce the temporary energy consumption of the system. In these cases, the virtualization procedure is not needed, [Irwin 2004]. However, as processor and task memory are clocked modules, they need to feature a common clock signal in order to function properly. Consequently, when stepping down a processor's frequency, also the frequency of the tasks bound to the processor have to be stepped down accordingly, cf. Figure2.64. An analysis of the measurements of [Casu 2013] reveals a correlation between a MicroBlaze's frequency and the system's power consumption, cf. Figure 2.65.

The virtualizable architecture may also consider Task Groups for energy management. Instead of just suspending a task's execution, when the corresponding processor is being disbaled, the task originally bound to this processor may be scheduled in a Task Group together with other tasks on another processor in the array instead. This is depicted in

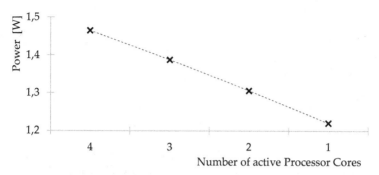

Figure 2.63: Power Consumption in a Multi-Processor System scales linearly with the Number of active Cores. All Cores employ the same Frequency.

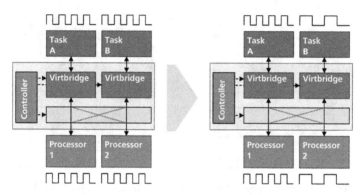

Figure 2.64: Stepping down a Processor's Clock Frequency may reduce the temporary Energy Consumption of the System. The Frequency of the Task Memory has to be stepped down accordingly.

Figure 2.66. Here, processor 2 is being disabled. Instead of also deactivating task 2, this task now shares access to processor 1 together with task 1. This feature is enabled by the transparent resource sharing provided by the Virtualization Layer, cf. Section 2.2.6. However, care has to be taken by the designer in order to not violate timing constraints of tasks thereby. The usage of such "low energy" profiles is demonstrated for the quadrocopter application example in Section 4.2.

The last mean to preserve energy discussed is the dynamic reduction of the parallelization degree. Section 3.4 will demonstrate that the virtualizable architecture may be tailored towards a data-flow multi-processor system featuring a dynamic degree of parallelism. As several processors execute parallelized sections of a task, by lowering the degree of parallelization at runtime, processor resources are freed and may be

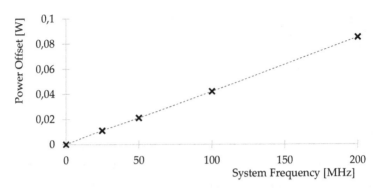

Figure 2.65: Power Consumption is directly affected by a Processor Core's Clock Frequency.

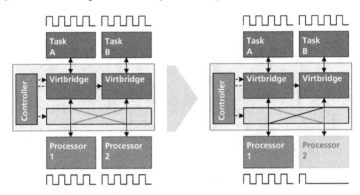

Figure 2.66: Tasks originally assigned to a Processor, which is being disabled, may share access to another Processor Resource by the Transparent Multi-Tasking provided by the Virtualization Layer.

deactivated as highlighted above. As a further step, the execution of the task may be shifted completely from a parallel to a pure sequential representation. In doing so, all but of one processor may be deactivated. This will also be demonstrated in Section 4.2.

In a nutshell, the virtualizable architecture features several techniques in order to cope with deviations in the energy supply. These methods include the processor instances, the tasks as well as corresponding Virtbridges. Measurements on the proto-type implementation for a Virtex-6 LX240T FPGA have proven that these methods are effective means to realize energy-aware systems.

2.8 Intermediate Conclusions

This chapter has introduced a Virtualization Layer between off-the-shelf embedded processors and task memories. As a result, a transparent task migration at arbitrary points in time is enabled. This allows for dynamic binding updates. A dynamically reconfigurable interconnection network provides intrinsic means for processor resource sharing between tasks. Task groups, i. e., tasks, which are assigned to the same processor resource, may be scheduled in a time division scheme or apply a self-scheduling scheme, which eliminates the need for a central scheduling instance. Fast task communication despite varying processor assignments is accomplished by the runtime modification of point-to-point communication commands. Data is thereby rerouted via a Message Hub. This hub expands common point-to-point protocols by features such as data broadcasts. Generic VMR voter modules enable the application of common redundancy strategies in order to increase the system's reliability. By exploiting the virtualizable task communication scheme, a fully transparent transition from non-redundant to redundant task execution is achieved. Features for energy management allow for dynamic reactions to deviations in power supply, e. g., by processor frequency stepping or processor deactivation. The feature to dynamically update task-processor updates assures the execution of tasks despite the deactivation of parts of the processor array.

The following Chapter will address the challenge of designing MPSoC systems, which may exploit the advocated virtualization properties.

3 The Virtualizable MPSoC: Requirements, Concepts, and Design Flows

The previous Chapter has introduced a hardware-based virtualization procedure for tasks running on embedded processors. This architecture enables task migration at runtime and, thus, provides a huge degree in execution dynamism. However, by now, the aspect of designing systems for this virtualizable architecture has not been considered.

This problem of efficiently exploiting the benefits provided by the virtualizable architecture for embedded designs may be divided into two parts. The first part of the problem is providing a suited design environment, which allows for a fast and safe instantiation of the underlying virtualizable architecture based on the needs of the designer. Therefore, the following section will discuss in short requirements for efficiently creating designs for the virtualizable architecture. Afterwards, common flaws and weaknesses in current design frameworks regarding the design of embedded multi-processor systems are outlined before highlighting a framework, which features support for the virtualizable architecture.

The second part of the problem is the establishment of adequate design flows, which make use of the execution dynamism of the architecture. These design flows, in turn, require the existence of design tools, as stated in the first problem, in order to map the designs onto the virtualizable architecture. The past has proven several times that promising, cutting-edge multi-processor architectures, such as the AmBrick chip, which in 2008 featured up to 336 streaming RISC processors on a single die [Ambric Inc. 2008], will eventually fail [Portland Business Journal 2008], if the aspect of providing corresponding paradigms is neglected. In case of Ambric these issues were discussed, e. g., in [Biedermann 2008]. Without either new, easy to adopt design flows or transition solutions, which allow for re-using legacy designs, even the most powerful new architecture will remain futile. Thus, the following sections will highlight a set of design flows tailored to recent trends in embedded system design, which may directly profit from the virtualization features. Figure 3.1 depicts some of the design optimization goals achievable with the virtualizable MPSoC. Foundation of the envisaged design flows is the ability for a dynamic reshaping of the system's (initial) configuration, i. e., task-processor binding. Initial configurations are being setup by executing either Algorithm 6, 11 or 13, depending on whether the binding vector contains task groups or not. Algorithm 18 denotes the general procedure for runtime system reshaping, which exploits the mechanisms introduced in the last chapter.

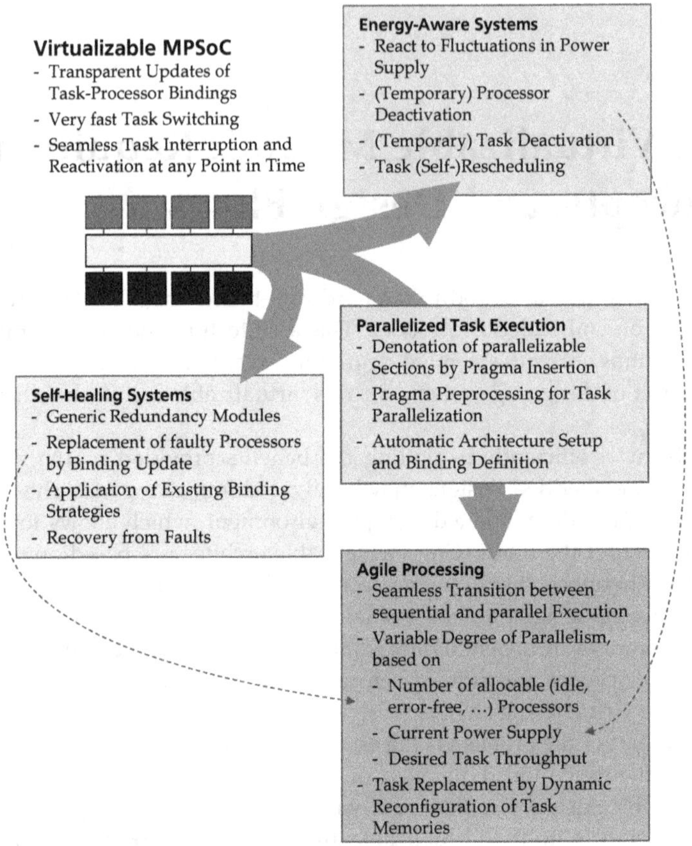

Virtualizable MPSoC
- Transparent Updates of
  Task-Processor Bindings
- Very fast Task Switching
- Seamless Task Interruption and
  Reactivation at any Point in Time

Energy-Aware Systems
- React to Fluctuations in Power
  Supply
- (Temporary) Processor
  Deactivation
- (Temporary) Task Deactivation
- Task (Self-)Rescheduling

Self-Healing Systems
- Generic Redundancy Modules
- Replacement of faulty Processors
  by Binding Update
- Application of Existing Binding
  Strategies
- Recovery from Faults

Parallelized Task Execution
- Denotation of parallelizable
  Sections by Pragma Insertion
- Pragma Preprocessing for Task
  Parallelization
- Automatic Architecture Setup
  and Binding Definition

Agile Processing
- Seamless Transition between
  sequential and parallel Execution
- Variable Degree of Parallelism,
  based on
  - Number of allocable (idle,
    error-free, ...) Processors
  - Current Power Supply
  - Desired Task Throughput
- Task Replacement by Dynamic
  Reconfiguration of Task
  Memories

Figure 3.1: Possible Design Goals achievable by means of the virtualizable MPSoC.

Algorithm 18 System Reshaping by Virtualization.

Require: A system realizing a binding vector BV_1, a trigger for the reshaping procedure.
Ensure: A reshaping of the system to realize binding vector BV_2.

1: **if** Trigger requests a reshaping of the system's configuration **then**   ▷ application-specific
2:   Control processor (cf. Figure 2.12) fetches new binding vector BV_2 ▷ storage location of BV_2 is
3:   application-specific
4:   Control processor forwards BV_2 into Virtualization Layer
5:   Suspend all tasks of BV_1 currently being executed on a processor by executing Algorithm 3
6:   **for all** Tasks t_i denoted in BV_2, where t_i is either the first task listed in a task group or is not part of
     a task group **do**
7:     Activate t_i by executing Algorithm 4
8:   **end for**
9: **end if**

3.1 Requirements for Designing on Top of the virtualizable Architecture

The virtualizable architecture has resolved the static binding between tasks and processors. This binding resolution, therefore, has to be represented in the modeling process. Thus, the notation of sets of Binding Vectors, which may be activated at runtime, has to be supported. Section 3.2.1 will then handle the question about how to derive suited sets of Binding Vectors in the design process. As a consequence, the design process shifts from a processor-centric view towards task-based modeling.

The following section will discuss in short, why existing design tool frameworks are not suited for designing on top of the virtualizable architecture.

3.1.1 Weaknesses of Existing Design Tools

An extensive overview over existing tools for electronic system level (ESL) design used both in industry and academic is given in [Densmore 2006]. Unfortunately, besides providing a rough classification of tools and a notation of their employed level of abstraction, quantifiers about usability and workflow efficiency are missing. For FPGA-based designs, most prominent design frameworks are provided by the leading FPGA device vendors Xilinx, Inc. and Altera. Xilinx, Inc., e. g., features Xilinx ISE, a framework mainly aimed at low-level instantiation of modules provided in hardware description languages such as VHDL or Verilog. In order to accomplish the design of processor-centric designs, Xilinx, Inc. furthermore provides Xilinx EDK. Similar in various ways is Altera's product Quartus. Both design frameworks rely on the processor/co-processor view, which was the predominant design paradigm in the previous decades. As a consequence, the workflow focusses on adding co-processing modules via buses or point-to-point interfaces to a central processor unit. The addition of extra processor instances is supported as well. However, the designer is burdened with performing a long sequence of tedious and error-prone steps, which have to be repeated for each processor instance added to a design. Consequently, the design of multi-processor systems is not only significantly slowed down. Moreover, the design tools lack of a visual representation, which clearly aids the structure of the design. Figure 3.2 depicts the fraction of a screenshot of a design in Xilinx EDK. Here, five processor instances called "blue", "filter", "green", "reassemble", and "red" are displayed with their corresponding interconnects on the left hand side. Obviously, it is not possible to intuitively derive the system's structure based on this representation. While the design tools perform well for the mentioned single-processor-centric view, they are not suited in terms of multi-processor designs. Xilinx, Inc. has reacted to the recent trend by the introduction of the Vivado tool suite, which focuses more on a system-centric view [Xilinx, Inc. 2013c]. However, clear visual representation of the design and explicit support for the smooth instantiation of multi-processor architectures are not listed as key features.

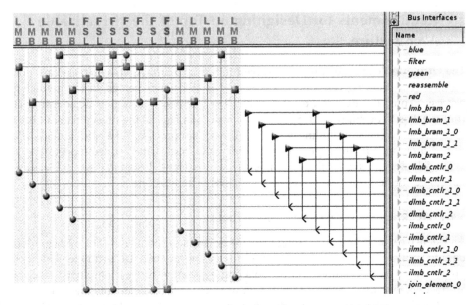

Figure 3.2: Xilinx EDK features a confusing visual Representation of Multi-Processor Designs.

Unsurprisingly the design tools, such as Xilinx EDK only feature a strict binding of tasks to processors. Therefore, their application in combination with the virtualization solution is not considered further. Instead, a new, dedicated design framework is introduced, which not only resolves the most hindering issues when designing embedded multi-processor systems, but also keeps a mutual compatibility to existing design frameworks, such as Xilinx EDK. In doing so, the advantages of established workflows, as the seamless link to other tools in the tool chain, e.g., to system simulators, is maintained.

The following section will introduce this design framework and highlight the extensions made in order to support the application of the virtualizable architecture.

3.1.2 The FripGa Design Framework

In order to overcome the weaknesses of existing design tool regarding the design of embedded multi-processor designs, a dedicated design framework called FripGa [Biedermann 2012a] is provided, cf. Figure 3.3. FripGa is a design tool set aimed at a fast and smooth instantiation of a large set of soft-core processor and hardware IP-core instances. Repetitive and error-prone steps, which, in other design tools, have to be performed by hand in order to setup multi-processor designs, are fully automated. Thus, the creation of such multi-processor designs is significantly accelerated.

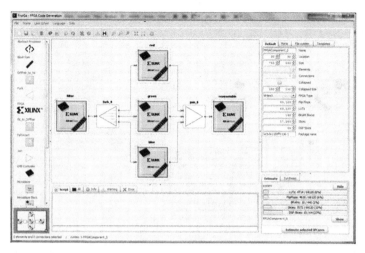

Figure 3.3: Work Environment in FripGa Tool with clear visual Representation.

For reference, the instantiation of a MicroBlaze soft-core processor takes in Xilinx EDK approximately 50 mouse clicks in different workspace windows. A skilled designer is able to perform this tedious sequence in about two and a half minute. FripGa accepts input either by exploiting a visual paradigm or in terms of scripting commands based on the language Tcl [Tcl Developer Xchange 2013]. Thus, in comparison, in FripGa the instantiation of the same processor type is performed either by simply dragging an processor instance into the design window or by executing a single Tcl command. Both alternatives take less than 10 seconds. Figure 3.4 depicts a design, which is automatically setup if the designer executes a corresponding Tcl script. In consequence, processor instances, communication links, software projects as well as processor-task bindings are automatically created. The resulting design is ready for synthesis.

FripGa features a mutual compatibility to existing design tools. As a consequence, an already existing design flow and tool chain may be exploited. For the prototype implementation, FripGa exploits the Xilinx Design Flow, which targets FPGAs, cf. Figure 3.5. Thus, designs created in FripGa may be exported into Xilinx EDK. In Xilinx EDK, modules and interconnects, which are not natively supported by FripGa, may be added and configured. The ability to refine a design in existing design tools unburdens FripGa from the need to replicate the full functionality of these design tools. Moreover, the re-import of a design, which was altered in EDK, into FripGa is possible. Despite not displaying modules unsupported by FripGa, FripGa keeps them in the design description. In doing so, maintenance of designs, which were created in FripGa and were then further altered in EDK is enabled. The design depicted in Figure 3.3 in FripGa is the same as in EDK in Figure 3.2, which features a confusing visual representation. The yield in terms of a clear representation is obvious.

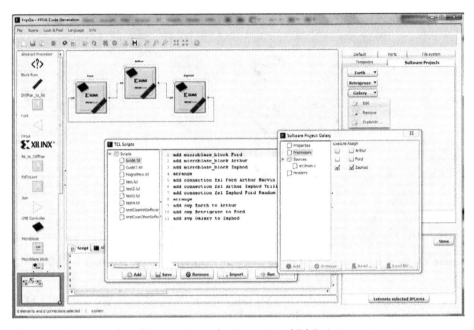

Figure 3.4: Automated Architecture Setup by Execution of Tcl Scripts.

As a second consequence of this compatibility to existing design flows, designs created in FripGa may be directly evaluated and tested, e. g., by system simulators such as ModelSim [Mentor Graphics 2013]. After successful testing, the assembly of a device configuration file, the so-called bitstream, may be triggered directly in FripGa. Since FripGa allows the smooth creation of complex designs consisting of dozens of processors, this increasing level of complexity is accompanied by a growing computing effort in order provide cycle-accurate simulations. Thus, in [Meloni 2010], an FPGA-based simulator for embedded multi-processor systems is introduced. There, an FPGA is exploited in order to provide a more efficient simulation of complex MPSoC in comparison to common software-based simulators. Such approaches might be suited in future to validate complex designs created in tools such as FripGa.

The initial implementation of FripGa was done by Maik Görtz in the scope of a master thesis [Görtz 2011]. The functionality of FripGa was successively expanded by several student groups [Glöckner 2011, Koch 2011, Casu 2011, Koch 2012, Rückelt 2012] in the scope of practical courses. Meanwhile, the FripGa source code consists of about 50.000 lines of Java code.

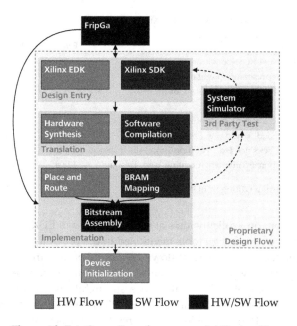

HW Flow **SW Flow** **HW/SW Flow**

Figure 3.5: Design Flow with FripGa on Top of a commercial Design Flow, e. g., for Xilinx FPGAs.

Conventional Workflow in FripGa

By exploiting FripGa, conventional multi-processor designs, i. e., designs featuring a static binding between tasks and processor instances, may easily be established. Besides the set of processor instances and hardware IP cores, the designer may add a set of software tasks. A software task consists of the source code files, corresponding header files and linker scripts for the structure of data and instruction memory. In contrast to common design tools, such as Xilinx EDK, in FripGa a software task may be bound to more than one processor instance, thus easing the creation of single instruction, multiple data (SIMD) architectures. Here, multiple instances perform the same set of operations, however, each instance on a dedicated set of data. As a demonstration, a parallelized version of a FIR-filter for image downscaling was implemented with the help of FripGa by Jan Post in the scope of a bachelor thesis [Post 2011]. Here, up to 18 soft-core processors form a data-flow-oriented architecture with different parallel filter stages, which exploit the SIMD paradigm. Within few minutes, the design may be restructured to feature a higher or lower degree of parallelism. In contrast in, e. g., Xilinx EDK, the maintenance of such a design is not feasible. Performance of the design tool is significantly slowed down in such a way that each mouse click took about twenty seconds to respond. Moreover, the visual representation of the design in EDK is – as expected – completely unsuited to recognize the structure of the architecture. While

Table 3.1: Comparison between FripGa and Xilinx EDK.

Feature	FripGa	Xilinx EDK
Clear Visual Representation	✓	–
Visual Representation editable by Designer	✓	–
Smooth Scaling of Processor Count	✓	–
Scripted Input	✓	(✓)[1]
Copy and Paste of Parts of the Design	✓	–
Time needed to add one Processor Instance	~2 s.	~150 s.
Mouse Clicks needed to add on Processor Instance	~2	~50
Tool Response Time when editing large Designs	fast	slow

[1] Not during editing in EDK.

this application scenario explicitly aims at the weaknesses of EDK, these disadvantages hold true for most of the design tools mentioned in the previous Section. Design tools commonly exploited in commercial flows are complex, feature-heavy tools, whose functional range has grown over years, but which currently lack decent support for the design and editing of embedded multi-processor architectures. Table 3.1 provides a side-by-side comparison of FripGa and Xilinx EDK. Besides these advantages, FripGa supports the design of virtualizable MPSoC architectures as well.

Workflow for Virtualizable Designs in FripGa

Aside from facilitating the smooth design of conventional multi-processor designs, FripGa is furthermore dedicated to support the virtualizable architecture introduced in Chapter 2. Since the task-processor assignment is dynamic when employing the virtualizable architecture, the workflow in FripGa is shifted to a task-based flow. As a first step, a virtualization element is added to the design, cf. Figure 3.6. Into this virtualization element, tasks are placed as depicted in Figure 3.7. As for the conventional workflow, a software project, i.e., a task, consists of software code, header files and linker scripts.

In Figure 3.7, four tasks are added to the Virtualization Element. The number of processors for this component is set to 2, cf. the red rectangle in Figure 3.7. After having placed tasks, a binding editor allows entering sets of Binding Vectors. It is application-specific and up to the designer, to define why and when to apply a specific Binding Vector. At runtime, a dedicated processor will manage the update of task-processor bindings. Thus, the binding sets are automatically translated into C code, which is automatically assigned to this control processor. The C code containing the binding commands automatically created by the binding editor are depicted in the lower right half of Figure 3.7. When synthesizing a virtualizable design created in FripGa, all components, such as task memories, processor instances, and an interconnection network of the corresponding size are instantiated. By adding a second or third

Figure 3.6: Virtualization Element in FripGa.

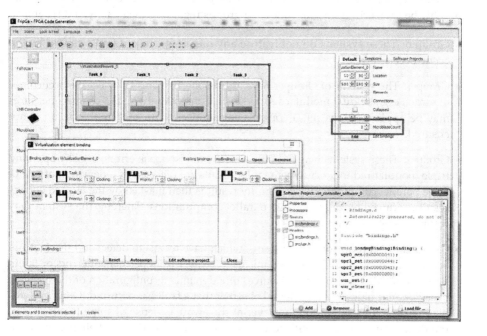

Figure 3.7: Workflow for virtualizable Designs: Tasks are added to the Virtualization Element, the Number of Processors as well as sets of Task-Processor Bindings are defined.

Virtualization Element to FripGa, clustered designs, as detailed in Section 2.3.5 may be established. Designs containing one or more virtualization elements may be simulated in common simulators, such as ModelSim, just as conventional designs.

With FripGa, a design tool is provided, which not only covers the smooth setup of multi-processor architectures, but which also exploits the features enabled by the Virtualization Layer. The following sections highlight design concepts, which rely on the virtualization properties and which rely on FripGa in order to implement a corresponding virtualizable MPSoC design.

3.2 Design Concepts for Reliable, Self-Healing Systems

Unlike for most personal computer systems, ensuring safety is a crucial factor in many embedded designs. Embedded systems employed, e. g., in satellites, avionics, or even in automotive environments, as the case study in Section 4.1 will highlight, need to rely on a guaranteed, fail-safe task execution. Otherwise, erroneous computations may lead to an unsafe system state, which may cause the loss of control of the entire system, i. e., the satellite, plane, or car, and may eventually lead to a severe accident. Systems may roughly be categorized into the following groups regarding their safety and reliability:

- Group 0: These systems do not feature any means to prevent faults caused by the occurrence of errors.

- Group 1: The systems of Group 1 have at least mechanisms to detect the occurrence of errors, e. g., by dual modular redundancy. Consequently, suited counter-measures may be applied. However, a correct continuation of the system execution is not ensured.

- Group 2: These systems may not only detect, but also mask errors, e. g., by applying triple modular redundancy, where faulty results are detected as a deviation of one of three parallel computations. This faulty result is then masked by the alleged correct result produced by the other two parallel computations. Thereby, the system may resume its execution.

- Group 3: This group contains systems, which have means to detect and mask errors and may, additionally, apply mechanisms to recover from permanent errors or faults. Systems, which provide spare resources or a dynamic reconfiguration of the system's behavior, may hide from an external observer that a fault has occurred. Other systems may resume their operation, however at the aware expense of some features, e. g., the deactivation of tasks with lower priority or a reduction of their performance due to the disabling of defunct processor resources. Systems in Group 3 are called *Self-Healing* systems within this work.

In literature, a plethora of self-healing strategies for embedded systems exist. While some rely on fairly common system architectures accompanied by redundancy modules and dynamic reconfiguration of affected areas at the event of errors as, e. g., in [Gericota 2005], others propose dedicated architectures tailored for self-healing purposes. E. g., in [Zhang 2003, Lala 2003] grids of computing cells are introduced. In both approaches, at the occurrence of faults, a defective cell in the grid is deactivated and its functionality is shifted along the interconnections of the grid to the next spare cell. An overview about cell-based self-healing systems is given in [Seffrin 2010]. However, the more self-healing architectures differ from common system design, the less likely is their feasibility to actual system design problems.

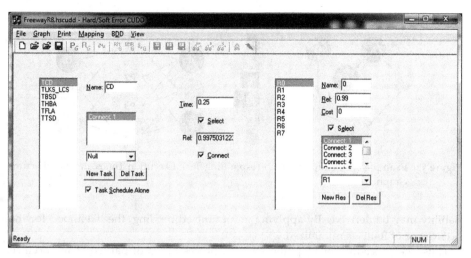

Figure 3.8: Hard/Soft Error CUDD Tool introduced in [Israr 2012], which derives optimal Bindings.

A self-repair approach for an MPSoC was presented in [Muller 2013]. Here, an array of Very Long Instruction Word (VLIW) processors provide means of self-healing at the event of errors. Due to the VLIW architecture of the processor cores, each instruction word consists of several slots, which may be filled with operations. In case that a part of the circuitry, which executes a certain slot, is detected as being defective, a re-scheduling of the task takes place so that the corresponding slot is not used anymore. In case that the entire resource is faulty, tasks may be bound to another processor. However, in contrast to the virtualizable MPSoC, a dedicated VLIW architecture has to be exploited, while in the virtualizable MPSoC, any embedded general-purpose processor architecture may be employed. Moreover, in [Muller 2013] a binding update is performed by means of memory transfers. Instead, the binding update via a network reconfiguration takes no additional memory access overhead. Furthermore, as the network configuration is computed in parallel with the task context extraction, it outperforms a solution, which relies on memory transfers.

The execution dynamism achievable with the runtime binding updates of the virtualizable MPSoC in combination with the redundancy modules detailed in Section 2.6 enable self-healing features of the virtualizable MPSoC. The following section will highlight some strategies tailored to the virtualization features. The actual application of these measures is application-specific.

3.2.1 Dynamic Binding Strategies

Based on the current system state, which includes the number of active processors and tasks as well as the redundancy techniques employed, optimal bindings in terms of re-

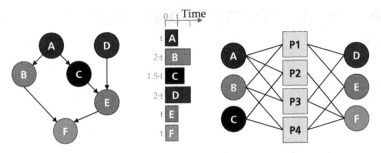

Figure 3.9: Example Task Graph with corresponding Task Execution Times and Architecture Graph.

liability may be derived. By applying an optimized binding, the likelihood for the occurrence of faults is minimized.

Thus, the procedure of mapping tasks to processors is of particular importance. In general, a plethora of mapping strategies with various optimization goals for multi-core architectures has been proposed. An overview is provided in [Singh 2013] and [Marwedel 2011].

The work in [Israr 2012] details an approach to optimize task-processor bindings regarding reliability and power consumption as two main optimization goals. As input values, a task graph and an architecture mapping as depicted in Figure 3.9, as well as reliability values for the processors employed are taken. The designer is hereby aided by a frontend with graphical user interface in order to input the design specification, cf. Figure 3.8. Output is a set of task-processor bindings, which are optimal in terms of reliability and power consumption. For each processor constellation, an optimal binding is given, cf. Table 3.2. The resulting bindings may directly be exploited as input for the control processor in the virtualizable MPSoC. If processor instances fail at runtime, the virtualization procedure allows switching to another optimal binding by a reshaping, cf. Algorithm 18.

While conventional embedded systems with static task-processor bindings may indeed be tailored to feature an initial binding, which has been optimized, e. g., by the procedures given in [Israr 2012], in the case of failing processor resources, a switch to another task-processor binding is not possible. The virtualizable MPSoC, however, may establish a new binding by exploiting the virtualization procedure introduced in Section 2.2.5 within approximately 90 clock cycles. Figure 3.10 depicts the binding update after errors have been detected in the results of tasks, e. g., by means of redundancy techniques or self-tests. By exploiting the self-scheduling scheme of Section 2.4.4, no additional scheduling procedures are necessary in order to facilitate the execution of the tasks in the new mapping. In the given example, the execution cycle of the task graph is repeated at the detection of an error. This behavior is, however, application-specific. The following section will propose several schemes in order to

Table 3.2: Example Binding Set optimized for Reliability.

Processors	Binding Sets			
P1 P2 P3 P4	$(A,B) \mapsto 1$	$(C,F) \mapsto 2$	$(D) \mapsto 3$	$(E) \mapsto 4$
P1 P2 P3 P4	$(A,B,E) \mapsto 1$	$(C,F) \mapsto 2$	$(D) \mapsto 3$	
P1 P2 P3 P4	$(A,B,D) \mapsto 1$	$(C,F) \mapsto 2$		$(E) \mapsto 4$
P1 P2 P3 P4	$(A,B,E) \mapsto 1$		$(D) \mapsto 3$	$(C,F) \mapsto 4$
P1 P2 P3 P4		$(C,F) \mapsto 2$	$(A,D) \mapsto 3$	$(B,E) \mapsto 4$
P1 P2 P3 P4	$(A,B,D,E) \mapsto 1$	$(C,F) \mapsto 2$		
P1 P2 P3 P4	no valid binding as C can only be mapped to P2 or P4			
P1 P2 P3 P4	$(A,B,D,E) \mapsto 1$			$(C,F) \mapsto 4$
P1 P2 P3 P4	no valid binding as E can only be mapped to P1 or P4			
P1 P2 P3 P4	no valid binding as D can only be mapped to P1 or P3			
P1 P2 P3 P4			$(A,D) \mapsto 3$	$(B,C,E,F) \mapsto 4$
...	no valid bindings for a single processor			

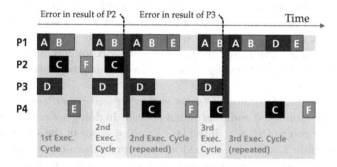

Figure 3.10: The dynamic Binding Update at the Detection of Errors based on the System defined in Figure 3.9 and the Bindings denoted in Table 3.2.

provide self-healing capabilities. The application example in Section 4.1 will then demonstrate the combination of a binding optimization process and fault-detection mechanisms in the virtualizable MPSoC under consideration of Quality of Service aspects.

3.2.2 Self-Healing Strategies in the virtualizable MPSoC

Foundation of self-healing strategies is the ability to detect errors and faults in the first place. As detailed in Section 2.6, the virtualizable MPSoC supports dual and triple modular redundancy by its generic VMR modules.

The VMR modules realize redundancy on a task-based level, i. e., they take the output of a task, which is sent to subsequent tasks in the task graph, into consideration. In contrast, many schemes for redundancy on a lower abstraction exist, e. g., in [Koal 2013]. There, virtual TMR is performed on flip-flop level. In this scope, the term virtual applies to the on-demand activation of redundancy schemes for different function inputs. In the context of MPSoC with large processor arrays, n Modular Redundancy (NMR) may be applied. Here, a redundant execution is spread between n parallel instances of a task. However, determining the optimal degree of redundancy is not trivial, [Runge 2012].

DMR modules may hint to an error in a task's execution, however, a distinct assignment to one of the two redundant task instances is not possible. In a TMR scenario, however, it is fairly easy to identify an error, as a task is being executed on three instances. Consequently, three results are produced, which are then compared to each other. In case that just one result deviates from the other two, with a high probability, this deviation is an indication for an error.[1] In case that all three task instances produce results, which deviate from another, a TMR module may not identify any correctly working task.

Thus, another solution to identify faulty tasks is the execution of predefined code portions, whose results are previously known. In doing so, the actual results can be compared to the expected, pre-calculated results in order to identify faulty tasks. In doing so, the task instances voted by a TMR module, which shows deviations for all three results, may be checked by such a code routine. As module redundancy significantly increases device costs, the procedure of periodically running such self-tests is a cost-saving alternative. However, unlike module redundancy, this procedure is not able to mask errors.

Instead of running dedicated self-tests and interpreting their results, actual task outputs may be monitored and interpreted as well. In doing so, erroneous behavior of tasks may be concluded, e. g., if the task's output is out of the scope of probable or even reasonable results. For embedded soft-core processors as well as HW IP cores a monitoring solution was proposed in [Biedermann 2011a]. The designer adds customizable wrappers around processors or HW IP cores and configures dedicated monitoring modules, which observe, e. g., the range of the output value, the gradient of subsequent task results or the time interval between task results. Based on the intended purpose of the task, suited boundary values for the monitoring modules are defined by the designer. For example, a module inside a car, which outputs the car's velocity, could be identified as faulty, if it outputs a velocity of 600 km/h. A module, which keeps track of the mileage, is assumed to be erroneous, if the mileage is not monotonically increasing. As the monitoring approach of [Biedermann 2011a] was prototypically implemented and evaluated for MicroBlaze processors in the work of [Rjasanow 2012, Rückelt 2011], its features may be transferrable to the prototype implementation of the virtualizable MPSoC, which employs MicroBlaze processors as well. A related approach is presented in [Seebach 2010]. Here, in the concept of Organic Design Pattern (ODP) , properties of modules as well as design constraints are specified in a top-down design flow. Tasks may be (re-)allocated to modules depending on

---

[1] With lower probability, the two matching results, however, may be wrong as well. Furthermore, the matching results may be wrong with the one causing the alleged deviation being correct.

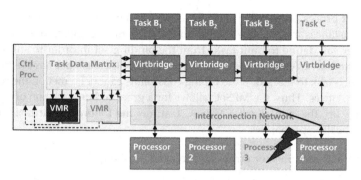

Figure 3.11: Shift of Processor Assignment after TMR Error Detection.

whether the modules provide the required properties. As for the monitoring approach, defects are assumed, if some system properties are out of the bounds of a corridor of valid states.

After having identified an error or a fault, e. g., by exploiting one or several of the means mentioned above, the virtualizable MPSoC may trigger corresponding countermeasures. As the virtualizable MPSoC enables dynamic updates of task-processor bindings, a task's execution may be shifted at runtime to another processor resource, e. g., to a dedicated spare resource held ready for the event of errors, cf. Figure 3.11. In doing so, the processor instance, on which an error was detected, may either be reset or be completely deactivated. If the system does not feature any spare resources, two tasks may swap their processor assignment as a first measurement before completely abandoning the faulty processor resource. Possibly, this new task-processor assignment does not produce errors, e. g., if a bit is permanently stuck in a register of the faulty processor, which is not read or written by the newly assigned task. Other approaches, such as in [Bolchini 2007, Paulsson 2006a] apply a partial dynamic reconfiguration at the event of permanent errors detected by TMR in order to recover to a correct system state. When reconfiguring the affected area with the same functionality but another mapping, the defunct cell is potentially not part of the new mapping. As the exact identification of a defunct cell is, however, a complex task and the success when applying a new mapping is not predictable, this approach is not considered for the proposed self-healing concepts.

In conventional embedded systems, deactivating a processor instance also automatically implies the deactivation of the tasks, which are mapped to this processor instance. The binding dynamism of the virtualizable MPSoC, however, allows for disabling the faulty processor instance and for the rescheduling of its tasks to other processor instances in the array as depicted in Figure 3.10. By exploiting the self-scheduling mechanism detailed in Section 2.4.4, apart from defining a new binding, which omits the faulty processor instance, this task rescheduling procedure is completely self-organizing. Depending on the actual system, scheduling of the tasks, which were assigned to a now defunct processor, together with the other tasks in the system on the remaining processor instances may violate application-specific timing constraints. In this case, the designer can define to omit tasks from the binding set in order to still fulfill the timing constraints. In contrast to conventional systems, the designer has the freedom to choose, which task to discard, if the timing constraints cannot be met on the remaining processor instances. Thus, the MPSoC allows for a gracefuld degradation of the system.

Summing up, the virtualizable MPSoC features the following, intrinsic means to enable self-healing properties:

- Generic **VMR modules** for error detection and masking

- **Update of task-processor bindings** at runtime, e. g., to exclude defunct processor resources

- Compensation for defunct processor resources by **transparent migration to spare processor resources** by reshaping

- Application of results of **binding optimization strategies** in order to determine the optimal binding to apply when the number of processor resources changes

- **Self-organized re-scheduling of tasks** when exploiting the self-scheduling scheme, cf. Section 2.4.4

- **Graceful degradation** by selective deactivation of tasks in case a system cannot meet constraints anymore due to failures of one or more processor resources

By combining these features, embedded MPSoC can be designed, which may cope with multiple defects without having to forfeit executing the most crucial tasks in the system. The application example in Section 4.1 will highlight these self-healing abilities.

3.3 Design Flow for Parallelized Execution

After having highlighted the employment of a virtualizable MPSoC for systems with high constraints in terms of reliability and safety, another design goal achievable by the virtualization properties is now detailed: The ability for dynamic parallel execution.

3.3.1 Problem Motivation

With the advent of multi-processor architectures, the problem of efficiently exploiting these architectures became immanent. The majority of existing legacy code was written and compiled in order to run sequentially on a single-core processor. Neither most program paradigms nor most compilers were originally designed to cope with parallelism. Several solutions were proposed in order to make use of parallel processor resources.

One approach is to tailor existing programming languages as well as programming paradigms towards parallel execution. This may include dedicated libraries and special statements, which will later be executed in parallel. In doing so, the software code already contains intrinsic parallelism before being compiled. A disadvantage of this approach is the fact that legacy code has to be re-written in order to feature these new statements. Moreover, the designer has to take data dependencies, which may occur during runtime, into consideration. For complex program structures is difficult to manually decide, whether several program parts may be executed in parallel and fully independent of each other. Examples of this approach are Cilk++ [Leiserson 2010], CUDA [Nvidia 2011] or OpenCL [Khronos OpenCL Working Group 2008].

Other approaches rely on sequential legacy code, but exploit dedicated pre-compiler statements and/or compilers, which identify sections that may be executed in parallel. Here, data dependencies are either resolved or avoided. The biggest advantage of this approach is that legacy code may be re-used without any alteration. However, by fully automating the parallelization process, the designer has little influence over the outcome of this parallelization process. However, these concepts have been around for a long time, such as OpenMP [Dagum 1998].

The work of [Cordes 2013] proposes a parallelization approach tailored for embedded MPSoC based on Integer Linear Programming (ILP) . This approach is able to expose parallelism inherent in a task's sequential structure. Parallelism can be derived from constructing dependency graphs, as demonstrated, e. g., in [Ottoni 2005]. Gaining parallel representations by unrolling loop statements was demonstrated, e. g., in [Chandra 1997, Franke 2003].

For the virtualizable architecture, parallel execution of software is based on sequential legacy code, which is expanded by dedicated pre-compiler statements to denote parallelism. This is conform to Postulate 8 (*Minor or no modification of existing software code of tasks*) from Chapter 2. The actual procedure is oriented on OpenMP. By a precompilation, the sequential software is split into several parallel portions, which are then assigned to dedicated processor instances. The precompiler resolves static as well as dynamic data dependencies. As an advantage, existing software needs not to be adapted except for the precompiler statements, which are added at suited points in the software code. As this procedure is a semi-automated with the designer defining not only the sections to be parallelized, but also the desired degree of parallelism, the outcome may be tailored exactly to fit on the underlying virtualizable architecture as proposed in [Biedermann 2012d].

3.3.2 Parallelization Topologies

Not every part of software code contains inherent parallelism. A sequence of instructions, e. g., of which each instruction relies on the result of the preceding operation, cannot be parallelized. Thus, in order to transform sequential software code into a parallel representation, some parts of the original software code will remain sequential.

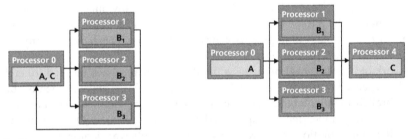

```
main {
    ...
    a = b + c;
    ...                                                        A

    for (i=0; i<3; i++) {
        my_arr[i] = 2 * i;
    }                                                          B

    ...
    d = a + my_arr[1] + my_arr[2] + my_arr[3];
    ...                                                        C
}
```

(a) Co-Processor Scheme.

(b) Data Flow Scheme.

Figure 3.12: A parallelizable Code Section B may be executed in a Co-Processor Scheme (a) or a Data Flow Scheme with higher Throughput (b).

When assuming that a given sequential software code contains parts, which may be parallelized, it may be divided into three parts A, B, and C. This is depicted in the upper half of Figure 3.12. Parts A and C are portions, which cannot be parallelized, whereas part B can be executed in parallel. As an embedded multi-processor architecture is targeted, each parallel thread in B is planned to be executed on a dedicated processor instance.

The lower half of Figure 3.12 depicts two design alternatives for the resulting structure. In the left hand side, a processor/co-processor scheme is applied. Processor 0 starts the execution of part A. The parallelizable sections B_i may be seen as tasks, which are outsourced to a set of co-processors, which send their results back to the original processor. Processor 0 then executes part C. In this scheme, the B tasks are fed by processor 0 with all data they need in order to be executed. Resolution of data dependencies is, therefore, easy. However, this scheme has a significant disadvantage, e. g., if the software is executed in a cyclic way, as it is not uncommon for tasks in embedded systems. Here, processor 0 has to finish the execution of part C before it

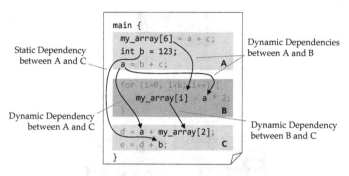

Figure 3.13: Several static and dynamic Dependencies between Code Sections A, B, and C.

may start another execution cycle. During this time, the processors, which execute the B_i tasks remain unused.

Thus, a data flow scheme as depicted in Figure 3.12, right hand side, is advocated. In contrast to the co-processor scheme, part C is assigned to a dedicated processor. Consequently, the processor, which executes part A, feeds the processors executing the B_i tasks. These processors send their results further to processor 4, which executes C. Meanwhile, processor 0 may already start the next execution cycle of A. In doing so, a pipelined structure is established, which delivers a higher throughput than the co-processor scheme. As visible from the code depicted in Figure 3.12, part C relies on variables computed in part A, e.g., variable a. When dividing code into several disjoint sections, these dependencies between part A and C have also to be considered.

3.3.3 Data Dependencies

As mentioned above, the highlighted approach has to resolve data dependencies. They may occur during parallel execution of software on different processor instances. For sequential code, dependencies are resolved by the compiler [Kuck 1981]. For parallel systems, however, a code section C, which is being executed, e.g., on processor 4 may need a value being stored in the code section A, which is currently being executed on processor 0. In Figure 3.13 this applies, e.g., for variables a and b. Thus, this value needs to be transferred somehow from A to C. Depending on the type of the data dependency, which may either be static or dynamic, two different techniques are applied. These techniques are detailed in short before discussing the actual design flow.

Static Dependencies

For static dependencies, the value, which is needed by C and that is stored in A, is not altered by A at runtime, i.e., remains static. In Figure 3.13, this applies to variable b. Thus, once transferred from A to C, C may re-use this value for each of its execution cycles. A compiler may identify static variables, e.g., by the fact that they are read-only

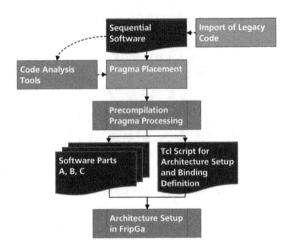

Figure 3.14: Design Flow for parallelizing Software by exploiting Pragmas.

values, which are never overwritten. As such variables may already be detected during the compilation phase, instead of transferring this value once at runtime, they may be copied to C at the compilation phase. In doing so, a data transfer at runtime is avoided, which reduces execution time.

Dynamic Dependencies

For dynamic dependencies, the value stored in A, which is needed by C, may be overwritten by A at runtime, e. g., if it is the result of A's computations. In Figure 3.13, this applies to variable a. Between sections B and C, the variable stored in my_array[2] also causes a dynamic dependency. In this case, copying the original value to C at the compilation phase will cause erratic behavior, as the value in A will vary at runtime. As a solution, a dynamic transfer of this value is established. For each execution cycle of C, the value, which is stored and processed in A, will be sent from A to C. The performance as well as the amount of dynamic data transfers will significantly affect the overall performance of the parallelized system, as the following sections will outline.

3.3.4 Design Flow

Figure 3.14 depicts the design flow for parallelizing software tailored to the virtualizable MPSoC. The following sections will detail the steps of this design flow. At the end, a parallelized implementation for a multi-processor design is created in FripGa. The design may then be further processed according to the FripGa design flow as detailed in Section 3.1.2, cf. Figure 3.5.

Denoting Parallel Sections by Pragmas

Starting point of the parallelization process is sequential software code. In order to create a parallel executable version, sections, which are planned to be executed in parallel, are marked by precompiler statements, so-called *pragmas*. A pragma is indicated by a # following the parallelization information, e. g.,

```
#pragma fp_parallel for numProcessors(4)
for(i = 0; i < n; i++) {
...
}
```

The type of the pragma is defined by the keyword pragma following fp parallel after which the actual pragma type is denoted. The approach is designed to support the types for, which covers loops, section, which partitions the code into disjoint sections that may be executed in parallel and pipeline, which splits the code into a chain of sequential sections. In the bachelor thesis of Matthias Zöllner [Zöllner 2012], the for pragma was implemented and evaluated. The expansion towards the other to pragma statements remains future work. With the numProcessors parameter, the designer may define the maximum number of parallel processor instances. If not, the loop counter will be taken as number of parallel B parts.

Other approaches, which cope with the problem of code parallelization, such as OpenMP [Dagum 1998], also make use of pragmas. OpenMP, however, focuses mainly on thread-based parallelism for workstations and personal computers, while this approach explicitly targets embedded architectures on the basis of the virtualizable MPSoC.

It may be difficult for the designer to decide, which part of the software may be suited to be executed in parallel. Therefore, existing code analysis tools, such as [Vector Fabrics 2013] may be exploited. Other analysis approaches are explicitly targeted for embedded MPSoC, such as in [Ceng 2008]. The hints given by these analysis tools aid the designer to set pragmas. After having placed pragmas into the code, the precompiler will handle the interpretation of pragmas. As a result, independent code sections ready for their parallel execution are created.

Precompilation and AST Creation

After the software code has been complemented by pragmas, a pre-compilation is triggered. The precompiler is based on the ROSE compiler framework [Quinlan 2011], which is focused on the creation of abstract syntax trees (AST) out of code. The AST is then cut in order to produce several independent code files. The cutting process reveals data dependencies. Static dependencies are resolved by copying the corresponding values to the places, where they are needed, cf. Section 3.3.3. For dynamic dependencies, send and receive routines are automatically inserted into the software. This is depicted in Figure 3.15. There are dedicated routines for distributing arrays to a set of parallel B

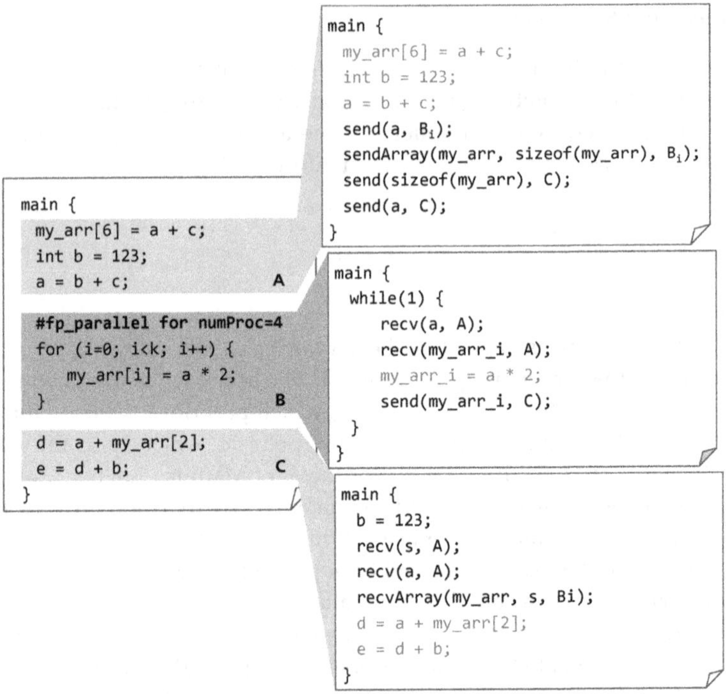

```
main {
    my_arr[6] = a + c;
    int b = 123;
    a = b + c;
    send(a, B_i);
    sendArray(my_arr, sizeof(my_arr), B_i);
    send(sizeof(my_arr), C);
    send(a, C);
}
```

```
main {
    my_arr[6] = a + c;
    int b = 123;
    a = b + c;                    A

    #fp_parallel for numProc=4
    for (i=0; i<k; i++) {
        my_arr[i] = a * 2;
    }                             B

    d = a + my_arr[2];
    e = d + b;                    C
}
```

```
main {
    while(1) {
        recv(a, A);
        recv(my_arr_i, A);
        my_arr_i = a * 2;
        send(my_arr_i, C);
    }
}
```

```
main {
    b = 123;
    recv(s, A);
    recv(a, A);
    recvArray(my_arr, s, Bi);
    d = a + my_arr[2];
    e = d + b;
}
```

Figure 3.15: Processing a Pragma splits the sequential Software into three Parts A, B, and C. Communication Commands resolve dynamic Data Dependencies.

parts. The B parts are fed sequentially with array elements. After having processed the array, the C part reassembles the elements into an array. For this purpose, A transmits the size of the array to C, cf. Figure 3.15. The send and receive routines exploit the virtualizable task-to-task communication scheme, which was detailed in Section 2.5.

In the precompiler, the communication IDs of code sections A, B, and C as well as the ID of the control processor of the Virtualization Layer are denoted. An example invocation of the precompiler may look as follows:

```
ParallelPreprocessor -IexternSource --output-dir Output
example.c --CMB=0 --A=1 --C=2 --B=3, 4, 5, 6
```

CMB denotes the ID of the control MicroBlaze, A, B, and C the IDs of the corresponding code sections. The list of IDs denoted for the B sections must match the actual number of B parts created, either defined by the loop counter of the encapsulated for-loop or by the numProc parameter.

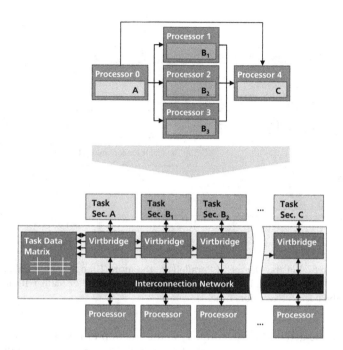

Figure 3.16: Architecture resulting from Pragma Processing.

Automated Architecture Setup

After having split the sequential software into the A, B, and C parts, a Tcl script is created by the pre-compilation process. This Tcl script contains commands, which will setup the architecture, i. e., the processor instances, as well as the corresponding software-processor bindings in FripGa. When executing this script in FripGa, the A and C part, as well as the number of B parts as defined in the pragma are bound to a corresponding number of processor instances. The designer may now either further elaborate the design in FripGa, simulate the design on a system simulator or he may trigger the bitstream generation phase. The resulting structure of the MPSoC design is depicted in Figure 3.16.

3.3.5 Discussion

The speedup achievable by parallelizing a task can be estimated by Amdahl's Law [Amdahl 1967]. It may be denoted as

$$S = \frac{1}{r_s + \frac{r_p}{n}}$$

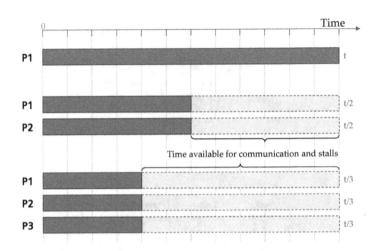

Figure 3.17: The higher the Degree of Parallelism, the more Time in each parallel Processor Instance P_i is available for Communication Overhead or Stalls without increasing the overall Execution Time.

with S being the achievable speedup. r_s is the fraction of a task, which is executed sequentially, r_p denotes the fraction, which is executed in parallel on n parallel modules. Thus, $r_s + r_p = 1$. By following this law, the sequential portion limits the potential speedup. The smaller the parallelizable fraction r_p is, the less effective is increasing the degree of parallelism. Thus, in an ideal case, the B parts of the proposed solution account for most of the computational effort, while the A and C part just distribute and accumulate data.

Figure 3.17 depicts a theoretical consideration of communication overhead for parallelizing tasks. When dividing a task into parallel instances assigned to dedicated processor instances P_i each, the theoretical execution time t of the task is reduced to t/n with n being the number of parallel instances. However, time for resolving data dependencies and stalls caused by waiting for receiving these data will occur in real world. Waiting for data and transferring these data may take up to $t - t/n$ for each instance without increasing the overall execution time. This is the theoretical border which defines the efficiency of a parallelization solution. In Figure 3.18 the execution time of the task consisting of the Sections A, B, and C is higher for a parallelized version of the task (a) than for the sequential implementation running on a single processor. This is due to the resolution of dynamic data dependencies, i. e., the delay caused by data transfers as detailed beforehand. In this example, the communication overhead – depicted as s and r for send and receive – is very high in comparison to the computation time spent in the parallelized sections of B. For this example, no dynamic dependencies between A and C are assumed. By delivering the parallel instances in a

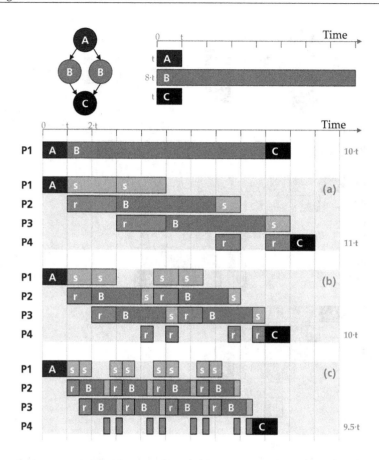

Figure 3.18: Increase in Execution Time despite Parallelization due to the Overhead for resolving Data Dependencies (a). Increased Throughput and reduced Execution Time by Pipelining (b and c).

pipelined fashion (b), the execution time may be reduced, as the parallel instances may start earlier with their computations in comparison to (a). However, the execution time is equal to the sequential implementation despite the fact that now four processors instead of one are executing the task. Further pipelining the data transfers (c) eventually shows a reduction of the execution time.

When talking about parallel architectures, the most obvious step to further reduce the execution time is to increase the degree of parallelism. Figure 3.19 depicts the same task as above, but now being executed on six processors, i. e., with four parallel instances. Timing overhead is assumed to be the same as in the example above. Now,

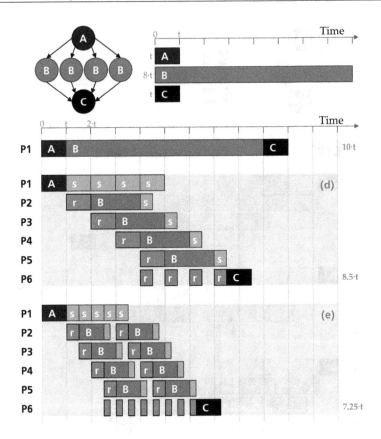

Figure 3.19: Lowered Execution Time by higher Parallelization Degree (d). Further Decrease by Pipelining; Stalls between two Execution Cycles, e. g., in P_2, indicate that an additional parallel Instance will not further reduce the Execution Time. (e)

the timing overhead for resolving the dynamic data dependencies carries less weight due to the higher number of parallel instances (d). The overall execution time is lower than for the sequential implementation. By applying the pipelining scheme (e), the execution time may further be reduced. Therefore, the code parallelization by pragma insertion exploits the pipelining scheme to reduce the execution time. Thus, each parallel instance is fed with the smallest fraction of data possible in each turn. As visible from the small gaps, e. g., in (e) at P_2 between its two execution cycles of B, further increasing the number of parallel instances would not lead to a further reduction of the execution time. As P_2 stalls until receiving the data for its second execution cycle of B, a theoretical fifth parallel instance would have to wait the same time until beginning its first execution cycle of B.

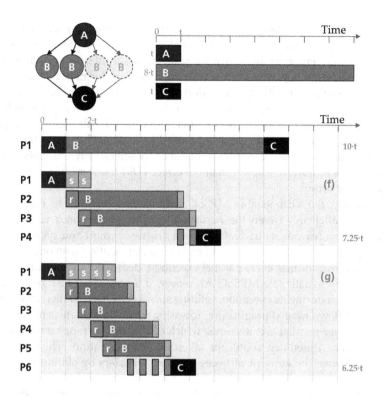

Figure 3.20: Less Communication Overhead in Comparison to the Execution Time of B Sections reduces Execution Time considerably.

The overhead for stalls and transferring data is the main bottleneck for parallelizing tasks. Figure 3.20 depicts the same task parallelization as before in a non-pipelined manner with two (f) and four (g) parallel instances, respectively. Now, the delay for sending and receiving is assumed to be lower, e. g., due to less data needed for the computations in B or a faster communication infrastructure. As visible, the execution time is now already lower than the sequential implantation for the version with two parallel instances (f). This time is further reduced by the version with four parallel instances (g). Due to the reduction of the communication overhead, a fifth parallel instance would lead to a further reduction of the execution time, as it could immediately be delivered right after P_5 is fed. Thus, the efficiency of a parallelization solution is not only defined by the number of parallel instances, but likewise by the overhead caused by resolving data dependencies. For the virtualizable MPSoC, the virtualizable task-to-task communication scheme detailed in Section 2.5 provides fast data transfers with low latency and therefore contributes to efficient parallelization solutions.

Higher degrees of parallelization require a higher number of processor instances. Thus, the virtualizable MPSoC has to be scaled accordingly. As the size of the virtualizable MPSoC also enlarges the size of the task-processor interconnection network, a higher parallelization degree leads to a drop in system performance, cf. Section 2.3.4. While for conventional multi-processor designs with pure sequential execution, clustering of smaller virtualizable MPSoCs, cf. Section 2.3.5, may be a suited solution to avoid the drop of the system frequency, this may pose a bottleneck for the parallelized execution of tasks. Parallelized tasks need to transfer data in order to resolve dynamic data dependencies. The transfer of data between clustered virtualizable multi-processor arrays is, however, slower than the direct TDM transfer inside a virtualizable multi-processor array.

Consequently, the virtualizable MPSoC is indeed well-suited to realize smaller degrees of parallelism. Given the performance data of Section 2.3.4, up to eight processors pose a reasonable tradeoff between processor count and system frequency. Accordingly, up to six B parts may run in parallel in combination with one A and one C part. Nevertheless, for massively parallel execution, dedicated architectures are better suited than the virtualizable MPSoC. Moreover, if a sequential task requires heavy memory transfers during its execution, splitting such a code into parallel representations given the data flow-oriented pragma preprocessing may lead to inefficient performance. In this case, other parallel architectures, which enable fast memory transfers, i. e., by means of a shared memory, should be taken into consideration. The designer may, however, influence the amount of necessary data transfers by skillful placement of pragmas.

The advocated approach for parallelized task execution on the virtualizable MPSoC, however, does not exploit one of the key features of this architecture, i. e., the dynamic update of task-processor bindings.[2] Given the reliability features of the virtualizable MPSoC detailed in Section 3.2, upon detection of a fault in a processor instance, the execution of a B section of a parallelized task could be, e. g., seamlessly shifted to another processor instance at runtime. In case of a permanent processor fault or shortcomings in energy supply, which require the deactivation of one or more processor instances, the parallelized task could lack enough processor resources to execute the A, C and all the B sections. Therefore, by combining the feature to update task-processor bindings with the parallelization abilities of the pragma approach, a new execution scheme may be derived. In the so-called *Agile Processing* scheme, a dynamic and transparent transition between sequential and parallel execution in various degrees of parallelization is deployed.

---

[2]The pragma preprocessor has indeed a second configuration mode, in which a multi-processor system may be set up without the Virtualization Layer between tasks and processors.

3.4 Design Flow for Agile Processing

3.4.1 Motivation and Challenge

For most embedded designs, the decision, whether a task is being executed sequentially or in parallel, is a static one. Transitions between sequential and parallel execution are avoided because, on the one hand, such a shift of the execution scheme is complicated and, on the other hand, suited multi-core processors or multi-processor architectures, respectively, are lacking. Moreover, if a parallel execution is chosen, the degree of parallelism is most often fixed, because the dynamic allocation of processor instances or processor cores as well as the dynamic distribution of data to the varying number of parallel instances is complex.

Nevertheless, the ability to switch between a sequential and several parallel implementations of a task at runtime offers a plethora of advantages. In a multi-processor system with a large set of tasks, a parallelized task may reduce its degree of parallelism in order to free processor resources for other tasks. If the supply of energy is not ensured for all processor instances anymore, e. g., due to a weakened battery, a parallelized task may shift from parallel to sequential implementation on a single processor so that the system may deactivate the now unused processors in order to save energy. For a sensor-based system, the throughput of a task, i. e., its degree of parallelism, may be tailored to cope with the amount of data currently being detected by the sensors. The feature to dynamically alter the execution scheme of tasks in a multi-processor system between sequential and parallel execution is called *Agile Processing* in this work.

Agile Processing emerges from a concept known as *Invasive Programming* [Teich 2008]. Invasing Programming covers a design methodology, which allows for a switch of the degree of parallelism in a multi-processor system.[3] Currently unused processors may be *invaded* by parallelized code portions [Teich 2012, Henkel 2012, Biedermann 2013b]. Agile Processing, however, takes a step further. Here, a smooth transition between sequential and parallel execution behavior is possible. As for Invasive Programming, the degree of parallelism may be tailored dynamically. Agile Processing – not to be confused with the software development method Agile Programming [Beck 2001], which covers the dynamic evolvement of design requirements in teams of software programmers – may be defined as:

Definition 5 (Agile Processing). *A methodology, which provides a parallelization concept for sequential software as well as an underlying hardware architecture, which is able to toggle transparently between sequential and parallel execution modes of this software, is called Agile Processing in this work.*

In contrast to Invasive Programming, which requires a resource-aware programming style, the software written for the Agile Processing has no statements dedicated to the

---

[3]In contrast to the name suggesting to be just a programming paradigm, Invasive Programming covers also the aspect of hardware architectures capable of tailoring the degree of parallelism at runtime.

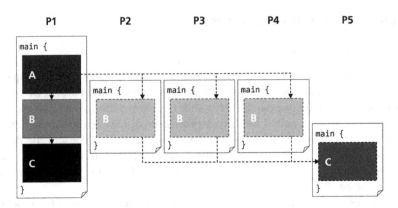

Figure 3.21: Instead of a sequential Execution, parallel Instances of the Task may be evoked.

underlying architecture apart from the instructions to self-activate a virtualization procedure, cf. Section 2.4.4. The following sections will demonstrate that the virtualizable MPSoC provides fundamental prerequisites in order to support Agile Processing.

3.4.2 Prerequisites

With the Agile Processing scheme, sequential and parallel execution cycles of a task may take turns. Consequently, it is assumed, that after a task has finished its execution, it will be executed again, either immediately or at least eventually in the future. This holds true for most tasks in embedded systems. Many tasks run permanently, i. e., nested in a unconditioned loop. For each execution cycle of a task, the execution scheme, i. e., sequentially or in parallel, may be selected.

Figure 3.21 depicts a task with three sections A, B, and C. As in Section 3.3, the code in section B can parallelized, e. g., by means of pragma preprocessing. In the Agile Processing scheme, a task's execution may either be sequential or in parallel. In the latter case, parallel instances of the B section are mapped to processor instances by means of a binding update via the virtualization procedure. Results of the parallel instances are sent to section C, which in case of the parallel execution is also executed on a dedicated processor. In order to obtain the desired structure, the procedure of pragma preprocessing is now being upgraded.

3.4.3 Design Flow Modification

In order to support the Agile Processing Scheme, the design flow for parallelized execution on the virtualizable MPSoC, which was highlighted in Section 3.3 is now being modified. Figure 3.22 depicts the new design flow. The following sections detail the adaptions towards the Agile Processing Scheme.

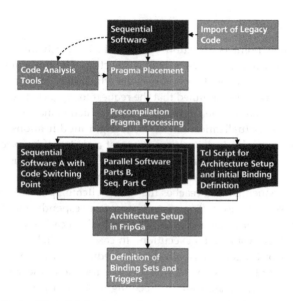

Figure 3.22: The Design Flow for the Setup of a Design supporting Agile Processing.

Modifications in Pragma Preprocessing

By now, the result of pragma preprocessing was a task, which has been split into three disjoint parts A, B, and C. A distributes data to the parallel instances of B, while C accumulates the results computed by B. This representation is now being merged with the pure sequential representation of the task in order to match the structure with Figure 3.21. Consequently, the preprocessor for pragma evaluation is modified so that the result of the procedure is again three disjoint parts of the task. However, instead of section A, an instance of the sequential task with dedicated code portions for data distribution to the instances of B is created. Depending on the desired execution scheme for the current execution cycle, the task either resumes its sequential implementation or enters the code portion, which acts as section A of the original procedure, cf. Figure 3.23.

In the Agile Processing scheme, the number of parallel instances of the B section is variable. Therefore, the routines, which resolve dynamic data dependencies, have to be modified as well. This minor change is implemented by replacing the fixed variable in send and receive routines, which denote the number of parallel instances into a dynamic parameter, which will be passed by the control processor at runtime to the code switching point. Additionally, the designer defines in the preprocessor the communication IDs of the sequential section, the B sections, and the C section. It is required that the IDs of the B sections are assigned as a continuous sequence. Changes in the preprocessing have been implemented by Matthias Zöllner in [Zöllner 2014].

Code Switching Point

The code switching point is a section of the task, in which the execution scheme for the current execution cycle of the task is selected. The motivation for the Agile Processing scheme has denoted several reasons which may trigger the switch of the execution mode. By now it is assumed that the request to toggle between sequential and parallel execution is sent by the control processor, which manages the task-processor bindings inside the Virtualization Layer. With slight modifications in the following communication protocol, a task itself may request a switch of its execution mode. In the latter case, a task, e. g., in a sensor system, which detects an unusual high number of incoming sensor events might, therefore, temporarily switch to a parallel execution.

As soon as the sequential task reaches the code switching point, it requests information about the execution mode. The control processor responds with the information, whether as sequential or parallel execution is desired. In case a sequential execution is indicated, the task resumes its execution. In case a parallel execution is selected, the control processor triggers a virtualization procedure in order to activate the corresponding instances of the B section as well as the C section in the system. If required, these task sections may dynamically be reconfigured into the system as detailed in Section 2.3.5. Accordingly, the control processor passes information about the number of the B sections as well as the ID of the ResultMux to the sequential task. The duty of the ResultMux module is detailed in the following section. Consequently, the send routines to automatically resolve dynamic data dependencies start distributing data to the allocated B instances starting with the B instance with the lowest ID. If there are dynamic data dependencies between the sequential and the C section, these are resolved as well, cf. Figure 3.23. The C section is provided with the ID of the ResultMux module. After accumulating the results generated in the parallel stages of the instances of the B section, the C section sends these results further to the ResultMux. Figure 3.24 depicts the communication between the participants of the Agile Processing Scheme.

Result Aggregation

As a consequence of the structure of a parallelized task as depicted in Figure 3.21, results of a task's execution may either be generated in the sequential section or in section C, if a parallel execution scheme was selected. As the execution scheme may vary over runtime, valid results are, thus, being output at two different points in the system. A subsequent task cannot decide, from which point to obtain new data. Informing every subsequent task about the current producer of output data would cause a communication overhead. Therefore, the accumulation of results is necessary. For this purpose, so-called ResultMux modules, cf. Figure 3.25, are added into the virtualizable MPSoC. They feature a connection to the control processor, which may configure the ResultMux to sort the values delivered by its two inputs – one is connected to the sequential task, the other to the C section of the parallelized task – and output them in the correct order to the subsequent tasks.

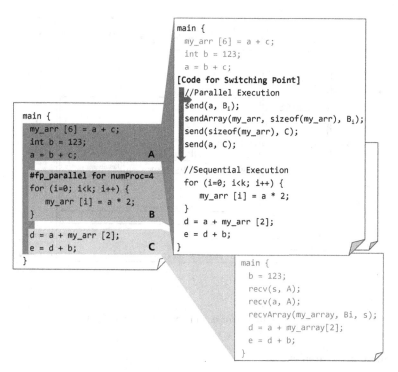

Figure 3.23: Data Dependency Resolution.

Beneath sorting result values, the ResultMux has the duty to provide the results for subsequent tasks in the task graph. A sequential task implementation as well as each B and C section of its parallelized implementation feature a Task ID, cf. Section 2.5 in order to enable virtualized task communication, cf. Figure 3.26. The ResultMux disguises itself as being the sequential implementation of the task. This is depicted in Figure 3.27. In doing so, the designer may build the communication among tasks in the task graph based upon a pure sequential representation of all tasks. If tasks are being executed at runtime in a parallelized version, the ResultMux ensures the correct addressing of tasks. In order to mimic the sequential representation of a task, a ResultMux is able to access the write column of this task in the TDM. For subsequent tasks it is, therefore, transparent whether they are accessing data delivered by the sequential representation or by the ResultMux.

Definition of IDs, Bindings, and Triggers

In contrast to the conventional parallelization approach detailed in Section 3.3, the precompiler statement is expanded to feature the ID of the corresponding ResultMux.

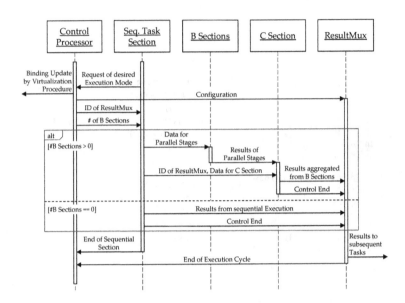

Figure 3.24: Communication Sequence for each Execution Cycle of a Task.

An example invocation is:

```
ParallelPreprocessor -IexternSource --output-dir Output
example.c --CMB=0 --R=9 --A=1 --C=2 --B=3, 4, 5, 6
```

Here, R denotes the ID of the ResultMux.

As visible from Figure 3.22, the modified Pragma preprocessing outputs a Tcl script, which may be executed in FripGa in order to set up the corresponding architecture accordingly. The resulting design contains an initial binding, which maps all of the task sections to a dedicated processor. As it is highly application-specific to define triggers to toggle the execution mode as well as defining the degree of parallelism for a certain situation, it is up to the designer to define corresponding binding sets. For this duty, the binding editor in FripGa, which is depicted in Figure 3.7 is provided. It is required that when less than maximum number of B parts is instantiated, the B sections with the lowest communication IDs are instantiated. This is because the sequential section of a task, which provides data for the parallel stages, addresses the B section with the lowest communication ID at first before sequentially addressing the next B instances, until the desired number of parallel instances is fed with data.

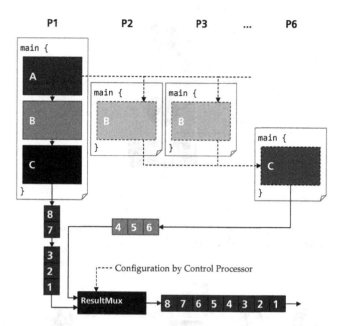

Figure 3.25: The ResultMux Module aggregates and sorts Results generated in sequential and parallel Stages.

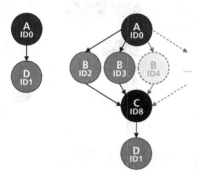

Figure 3.26: Based on the Execution Scheme, a subsequent Task may receive Results either from the A or the C Part of the preceeding Task.

3.4.4 Scheduling Schemes for Agile Processing Designs

Basic Scheduling Scheme

While the transition between sequential and parallel execution of a task is now enabled, the scheduling of a task graph, which contains parallelizable tasks is challenging. Figure 3.28 depicts a task graph and corresponding task execution times. Task B is

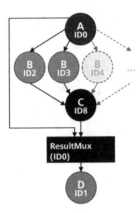

Figure 3.27: The ResultMux mimics the sequential Implementation of a Task in order to provide Results for subsequent Tasks.

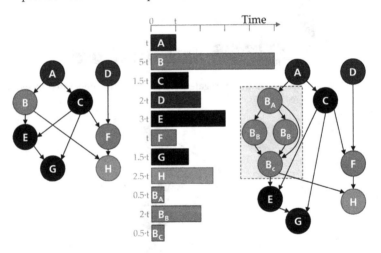

Figure 3.28: A Task Graph and corresponding Task Execution Times with B being an Agile Processing Task.

an Agile Processing task, i. e., it may be executed either in a sequential or a parallel fashion. For a parallel version featuring a parallelization degree of 2, the task execution times for the parts B_A, B_{Bi}, and B_C are given as well. The corresponding task graph with a parallelized version of B is also depicted in Figure 3.28. When employing the self-scheduling scheme of Section 2.4.4 with an arbitrary binding, the pure sequential execution of the task graph is self-organizing as depicted in Figure 3.29 (a). Here, the binding

$$BV = ((G,E) \mapsto 1), ((F,A) \mapsto 2), ((H,C) \mapsto 3), ((B,D) \mapsto 4)$$

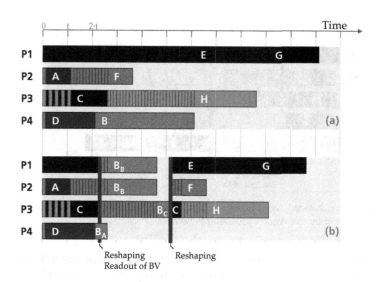

Figure 3.29: A normal self-scheduled Scheme (a) in comparison to the Agile Processing Scheduling Scheme (b).

Algorithm 19 Scheduling of a Task Graph in case of parallel Execution of an Agile Processing Task.

Require: A (random) binding vector BV, which contains an Agile Processing task t_{AP}, the control processor indicating a parallel execution of t_{AP}, which will occupy every processor in the system.
Ensure: An execution scheme for the task graph with parallel execution of t_{AP}.
1: Setup tasks and processors of the virtualizable MPSoC according to BV   ▷ cf. Algoritm 13
2: **if** Control processor indicates parallel execution of t_{AP} **then**   ▷ cf. protocol in Figure 3.24
3:    Control processor reads-out current state of BV from Virtualization Layer ▷ tasks already having
     finished their execution have removed themselves via sleep instruction from the BV
4:    Control processor removes t_{AP} from this BV and stores the result as BV_2
5:    Control processor reshapes the MPSoC by entering binding vector BV_{AP}, which maps the A part,
     the B parts, and the C part of t_{AP} to processors exclusively
6:    **while** Awaiting End of t_{AP}'s execution cycle **do**   ▷ indicated by a ResultMux, cf. Figure 3.24
7:    **end while**
8:    Control processor reshapes the system by entering BV_2 ▷ system resumes with normal
9:   eradication of remaining task
10:   graph at the point of
11:   interruption
12: **end if**

---

was randomly chosen. Task B passes its results via a ResultMux to E and H not depicted here. In each invocation, a task checks whether it can start its execution. If not, it suspends itself via the nap instruction. If it has eventually finished its actual execution, it removes itself from the task group via a sleep instruction.

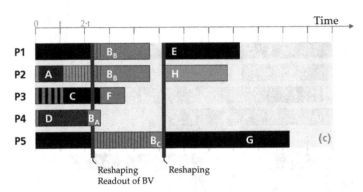

Figure 3.30: The enhanced Agile Processing Scheduling Scheme: Tasks C and F are not interrupted by the Agile Processing Scheme.

For scheduling a parallelized version of B, the following consideration is taken: B only takes advantage from a parallel execution, if its parts B_A, B_{Bi}, and B_C are allocated on processor resources at the same time. Only then it is assured that the B_B parts may immediately accept data sent from the B_A part to start with their computation. Moreover, it is assumed that resolving dynamic data dependencies requires a fair amount of data being transferred between the parallelized parts. If this amount exceeds the buffers of the communication interface, the sending task would stall until the receiving part would become active. Therefore, the task graph must not be executed in the conventional scheme, if a parallelized execution of an Agile Processing task is required. Instead, the virtualization concept is exploited as denoted in Algorithm 19. In doing so, as soon as a parallel execution of the Agile Processing task is indicated, all other tasks in the system are suspended by the virtualization procedure. Consequently, only B_A, B_{Bi}, and B_C are allocated to processors. As soon as their corresponding ResultMux indicates the end of this execution cycle, the remaining tasks of the task graph are mapped to the processor array. Due to the virtualization procedure, they may resume their execution at the point of their interruption. According to Algorithm 19, the bindings applied during this procedure are

$$BV_2 = ((G, E) \mapsto 1), (F \mapsto 2), ((H, C) \mapsto 3)$$
$$BV_{AP} = (B_{B1} \mapsto 1), (B_{B2} \mapsto 2), (B_C \mapsto 3), (B_A \mapsto 4)$$

The resulting execution scheme is depicted in Figure 3.29 (b).

Enhanced Scheduling Scheme

In case that the control processor choses the parallelization degree to apply to be lower than the number of processors present in the system, some tasks may resume their execution despite an ongoing Agile Processing phase. The question about which tasks to

---

Algorithm 20 Scheduling of a Task Graph in case of parallel Execution of an Agile Processing Task with ongoing Execution of other Tasks.

Require: A (random) binding vector BV, which contains an Agile Processing task t_{AP}, the control processor indicating a parallel execution of t_{AP} and a set T_s of tasks, which should not be interrupted by parallel execution of t_{AP}.

Ensure: An execution scheme for the task graph with parallel execution of t_{AP} and simultaneous mapping of T_s.

1:   Setup tasks and processors of the virtualizable MPSoC according to BV   ▷ cf. Algorithm 13
2:   **if** Control processor indicates parallel execution of t_{AP} **then**   ▷ cf. protocol in Figure 3.24
3:      Control processor reads-out current state of BV from Virtualization Layer
4:      Control processor removes t_{AP} from this BV and stores the result as BV_2
5:      Control processor stores mappings of tasks from BV_2, which are in T_s in BV_{AP}
6:      **if** Number of processors in the system, which are currently not included in BV_{AP} is $<$ 4 **then** ▷ at least four processors are needed for a reasonable parallelization (one A part, two B parts, one C part)
7:         Indicate sequential execution to t_{AP}
8:      **else**
9:         Control processor maps A part, the B parts, and the C part of t_{AP} to individual processors not yet covered in BV_{AP}
10:        Control processor reshapes MPSoC by applying BV_{AP}
11:        **while** Awaiting End of t_{AP}'s execution cycle **do**   ▷ indicated by a ResultMux, cf. Figure 3.24
12:        **end while**
13:        Control processor reads-out BV_{AP} and removes all parts of t_{AP}
14:        Control processor merges BV_2 and BV_{AP} to BV_3 ▷ in case some tasks of T_s are not finished yet
15:        Control processor reshapes the system by entering BV_3 ▷ system resumes with normal
16:   eradication of remaining task
17:   graph at the point of
18:   interruption
19:      **end if**
20: **end if**

---

deactivate in favor of the parallel execution of another task is highly application-specific. Task priorities may be considered here. E. g., if a task X, which is currently being executed, while a parallel execution of task Y is about to be triggered, features a higher priority than Y, then X and, hence, its corresponding processor are not interrupted by the Agile Processing scheme. Algorithm 20 handles this case. Figure 3.30 demonstrates this behavior for the binding:

$$BV = (E \mapsto 1), ((H, A) \mapsto 2), ((F, C) \mapsto 3), ((B, D) \mapsto 4), (G \mapsto 5)$$

Tasks C and F are assumed to feature a higher priority than task B. Thus, in case an Agile Processing phase for task B is requested, the execution of tasks C and F is not suspended by the parallel invocation of B. During the eradication of Algorithm 20, the following bindings are computed:

$$BV_2 = (E \mapsto 1), (H \mapsto 2), ((F,C) \mapsto 3), (G \mapsto 5)$$
$$BV_{AP} = (B_{B1} \mapsto 1), (B_{B2} \mapsto 2), ((C,F) \mapsto 3), (B_A \mapsto 4), (B_C \mapsto 5)$$
$$BV_3 = (E \mapsto 1), (H \mapsto 2), (G \mapsto 5)$$

Preservation of Contexts

In order to fully profit from this approach, the task memories of the MPSoC are initially filled with normal, i. e., sequential tasks. Only in case of a parallel execution, the corresponding code sections are mapped into task memories, e. g., by means of a partial dynamic reconfiguration. However, as discussed in Section 2.3.5 overwriting a task memory also erases the TCM of the task which previously was active. In case of the Agile Processing Scheme, thus, an interrupted task could not resume from the point of its interruption after its re-activation, when the parallelized task has finished its computation. As Section 2.3.5 has detailed, performing a TCM read-out before overwriting the task memory with another task or providing dedicated TCMs for each task are solutions to this issue. Alternatively, the Virtualization Layer could be modified so that the B parts and the C part, which are mapped into task memories at runtime, do not access the TCM of the previously active tasks. As the B parts and the C part they start from scratch, they do not need to restore any of their contexts. Consequently, the Virtualization Layer would have to be adjusted to not erase the TCM context in case of a partial reconfiguration. While this is a safety feature, which enforces Postulate 4 (*Strict encapsulation and isolation of tasks*), this may be disabled for the Agile Processing scheme.

3.4.5 Discussion

By applying the Agile Processing scheme, the execution behavior of tasks may be tailored to dynamic factors, such as temporarily increased need for throughput, defective processor resources, or variations in energy supply. In combining the pragma parallelization approach, which splits sequential code into data flow-oriented code sections, with the virtualization features, a high degree of execution dynamism is achieved. The virtualization procedure guarantees a smooth and fast transition between the execution modes. As for other tasks in the task graph the current execution mode of a task is fully transparent, there is no need for the designer to modify the original task graph and the addressing of task-to-task communication.

By now, just one parallelized task was considered. However, the design flow depicted in Figure 3.22 may be executed for each task to be parallelized before the step of the automatic architecture generation. Afterwards, the architecture generation phase may be triggered once in order to set up the design. The designer may then define the corresponding triggers for each task.

Each parallelized task occupies four or more processors.[4] As discussed in Section 3.3.5, the interconnection network of the virtualizable MPSoC performs well for a processor count up to eight processors but may lead to a drop in throughput for larger network sized. Thus, only a subset of tasks can efficiently be run in parallel at one point in time. E. g., by denoting task priorities in the software of the control processor, the rivaling behavior of several tasks, which request a parallel execution, may be handled.

3.5 Conclusions

This Chapter has demonstrated how to exploit the virtualization properties in order to create architectures with distinct optimization goals. Reliable architectures may be set up as well as architectures, which feature the parallelized execution of tasks. The design of such architectures is supported by a dedicated design framework, which is seamlessly integrated into existing design flows. Consequently, a designer may rely on a comprehensive workflow in order to set up his desired system. The following Chapter highlights application examples, which will demonstrate the actual system behavior when employing a virtualizable processor array.

---

[4]One for the A and the C section each as well as at least two instances of the B section. One B section is regarded a pathological case.

4 Application Scenarios

This chapter demonstrates some selected use cases, which highlight the diversity of a virtualizable MPSoC. The proposed virtualization concept, e. g., enables the design of reliable, energy-constraint, real-time, or parallelized architectures. The first application example is an automotive use case, where the virtualization features provide functional reshaping in order to adapt a car's assistance systems to the current road type under the consideration of reliability and harsh timing constraints.

Afterwards, energy awareness features and Agile Processing schemes are exploited for a simulated energy-constrained quadrocopter, which is assumed to be equipped with several sensors and analysis tasks. Based on the available power supply, the quadrocopter facilitates processing either in a parallelized fashion or sequentially.

4.1 Reshaping in an Automotive Assistance System

Today's cars are equipped with a variety of driver assistance systems, which may guide the driver in difficult scenarios, autonomously react to threats, or which may just raise the driver's comfort. In addition to the embedded circuitry necessary for the elementary driving functions, such as motor control, these assistance systems add a further degree of complexity to the system. Moreover, as part of these assistance systems may directly influence the driving behavior, e. g., by inducing a braking maneuver in order to prevent a collision, a highly reliable execution has to be ensured at any time.

In the following scenario, a virtualizable MPSoC handles the driver assistance tasks. The virtualization features enable runtime reshaping of the active set of assistance tasks. In doing so, the tasks currently being active in the car are tailored to the actual driving environment, such as freeways or rural roads. This process is called *functional reshaping*. In the event of processor defects, a so-called *reliability reshaping* is applied, which exploits the outcomes from a binding optimization procedure as detailed in Section 3.2.1. In doing so, a self-healing procedure is triggered, which may restore the system's functionality despite the fact, that parts of processor array are defunct.

The subsequent sections will outline the automotive assistance architecture, as well as the supported road types and driver assistance tasks. Afterwards, the dynamic behavior of the virtualizable MPSoC regarding the reshaping processes is demonstrated and detailed.

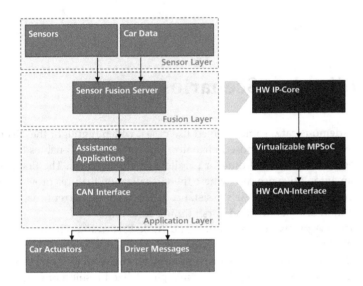

Figure 4.1: Layers of the Automotive Assistance Systems [Darms 2006]. Modules implemented for this Case Study are depicted on the right hand side.

4.1.1 System Architecture

Foundation of the case study is the Proreta project [Darms 2006]. Here, a car is equipped with a set of sensors. Raw sensor data are accumulated by a so-called "Sensor Fusion Server" and passed to an application layer. In the application layer, several independent tasks analyze sensor data in order to facilitate, e. g., collision detection or parking assistance. The results are then sent further via the Controller Area Network (CAN) Bus either to steer corresponding actuators in the car or to display assistance messages on the driver's cockpit interface. This architecture is depicted in Figure 4.1.

For the prototype implementation, assistance applications are mapped to the virtualizable MPSoC, which was proposed in Chapter 2. The evaluation setup is based on the "Hardware-in-the-Loop" concept. A dedicated HW IP-core acts as the Sensor Fusion Server, which forwards sensor data to the application layer. Here, the broadcasting expansion of the virtualized point-to-point communication scheme as highlighted in Section 2.5.6 is exploited to deliver all tasks in the application layer in parallel with sensor data. Results of tasks are passed to another HW IP-core, which acts as a CAN bridge and simulates communication with car actuators or the driver's interface.

4.1.2 Driver Assistance Tasks

The following set of safety-critical applications as well as comfort functions are considered for the case study:

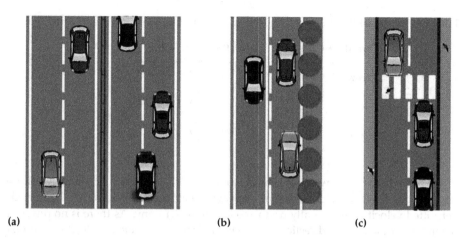

(a)   (b)   (c)

Figure 4.2: Freeway, rural Road, and Town Profile.

- **Collision Detection (CD)** decelerates the car in case of an imminent collision

- **Blind Spot Detection (BS)** warns the driver, if another car is currently present in the mirror's blind spot

- **Lane Change Support (LCS)** recognizes envisaged lane changes, prevents collision with cars in the blind spot

- **Lane Keeping Support (LKS)** monitors lane markings to keep the car on track

- **High Beam Assistance (HBA)** deactivates high beam to prevent dazzling of oncoming traffic participants

- **Fog Light Assistant (FLA)** activates fog light, if fog is detected

- **Traffic Sign Detection (TSD)** warns the driver in case a passed traffic sign is assumed to be not correctly interpreted by the driver

- **Parking Assistant (PA)** highlights parking spots and aids backing into a parking spot.

4.1.3 Road Types

The case study assumes three road types. In the freeway profile, the car regularly moves at velocities above 100 km/h. There is more than one lane per direction, cf. Figure 4.2a. Both driving directions are separated by a central reserve. Challenges in this profile are articulated differences in the cars' velocities as well as constant overtaking or being overtaken, respectively.

Table 4.1: Functional Profiles, i. e., active Driver Assistance Tasks depending on Road Type.

Profile	CD	LCS	LKS	BS	TSD	HBA	FLA	PA
Freeway	0	1	1	2	2	3	4	
Road	0		1		2	3	4	
Town	0	1	1	2	2			4

The second road type, which is considered, is rural road. These roads usually feature one lane per direction with no distinct separation besides a center line, cf. Figure 4.2b. Permitted velocities are usually up to 100 km/h in Germany. As there is no physical separation of the driving directions, accidentally leaving the lane may lead to a frontal collision.

The third road type to be considered is roads in towns, cf. Figure 4.2c. Here, despite the quite low velocity of below 50 km/h, an additional risk is added by pedestrians crossing the street as well as by frequent lane changes necessary in front of large crossroads. Finding a fitting parking spot is a further challenge.

4.1.4 Functional Profiles

Out of the set of applications and road types listed above, three driving profiles are derived: Freeway, Road, and Town. In each profile, a subset of the tasks listed above is considered, cf. Table 4.1. These profiles have been defined in the final thesis of Kevin Luck [Luck 2013]. The numbers in the cells of Table 4.1 denote the tasks' priority value. The lower the value, the higher the task priority is.

4.1.5 Timing Constraints

Task Execution Times

Information about actual execution times of driver assistance tasks vary widely depending on the underlying processor architecture. As the prototype implementation of the advocated virtualization scheme exploits Xilinx MicroBlaze soft-core processors with fairly limited performance, explicit task execution times are not given. Instead, task execution times are denoted by means of abstracted time units. Based on execution times available in literature, such as in [Chen 2009, Leu 2011, Cerone 2009, Wu 2009, Jung 2005], and confidential data provided by commercial manufacturers, execution times of assistance tasks are scaled to be comparable. The times denoted in Figure 4.3 are assumed for the assistance tasks to be the worst case execution time to interpret sensor data and to deliver a result.

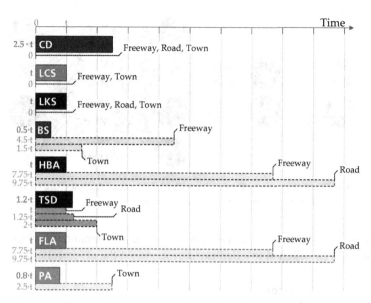

Figure 4.3: Execution Times of the Assistance Tasks. The Reactivation Times for each Road Type are indicated by dashed Bars.

The usage of LKS and LCS is mutually exclusive. As soon as a planned lane change is detected, e. g. by the activation of the direction indicator, LKS has to be deactivated in favor of LCS. Otherwise, LKS would interfere with the driver's aim to change the lane. Therefore, LKS and LCS may be both bound to the same processor.

Task Reactivation Times

Besides the task execution times, another time constraint needs to be considered. As sets of tasks will be scheduled on a processor instance, it has to be ensured that each task will be reactivated soon enough to fulfill its duty. A blind spot detection, e. g., which could only check every 20 seconds for another car in the blind spot due to scheduling would be meaningless as for most of the time, the driver would not receive up-to-date information of potential cars in the blind spot. Thus, the so-called *reactivation time* is defined as the time between the deactivation of a task and its next reactivation, cf. Figure 4.3. Based on the assumed velocity of the car, the individual properties of the task and the task's worst case execution time, a reactivation time for each task is derived. Only if a task is suspended for less than the reactivation time, it can support the driver reasonably. As for the execution times, abstract time values are derived from a set of actual timing values found in literature or provided confidentially by manufacturers. CD, LKS, and LCS feature harsh timing constraints, their reactivation time is given as 0. Thus, scheduling one of these tasks with any other task on the same

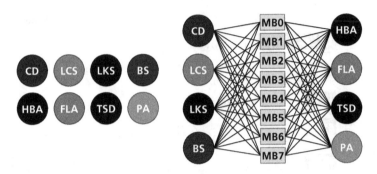

Figure 4.4: Task Graph featuring eight independent Tasks and Architecture Graph for the Automotive Application Example.

processor resource will lead to a violation of its timing constraints. Therefore, each of these tasks will be assigned to a dedicated processor in the processor array.

4.1.6 Binding Derivation

Generating Reliability-optimal Bindings

In order to find suited mappings of the driver assistance tasks to the virtualizable processor array, the binding optimization methodology of [Israr 2012], whose exploitation for the virtualization approach was detailed in Section 3.2.1, is employed. Input is an unconnected Task Graph and a fully connected Architecture Graph as depicted in Figure 4.4. As reliability value for the employed MicroBlaze processors, 0.99 is assumed. After a Design Space Exploration, the output of this optimization process are bindings, which are optimal in terms of reliability. For each functional profile and possible combination of processors in the system, an optimal binding is generated. According to [Israr 2012], in case that there are several bindings with the same level of reliability for a given set of tasks and processors, the one producing the shortest execution time is chosen. However, this procedure does not take the reactivation times introduced above into consideration. Thus, the procedure may output bindigs, which violate some timing constraints.

Therefore, the design flow is expanded to an iterative procedure, which, as first step, outputs bindings with optimal reliability for a task graph and its corresponding architecture graph. Subsequently, these bindings are checked whether they meet the timing constraints arising from reactivation times. If not, two alternatives exist. One the one hand, another binding might be chosen by hand, which complies with timing constraints, but which in return abandons the property of optimal reliability. On the other hand, instead of trading reliability, tasks with low priority may subsequently be discarded before calculating new bindings by the optimization procedure with the remaining task graph until a binding is derived, which meets the timing constraints. As

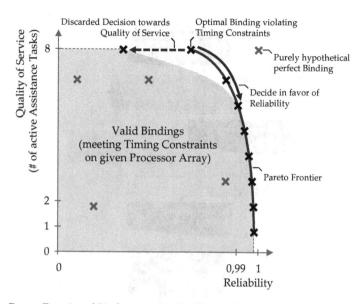

Figure 4.5: Pareto Frontier of Bindings optimal in Terms of Quality of Service and Reliability.

reliability and the quality of service, i. e., the number of active driver assistance tasks, represent Pareto optima, it is up to the designer to decide, which optimization goal to favor.

Considering the fact that some of the driver assistance tasks, such as Collision Detection, directly account for the driver's safety and his probability of survival at the event of an accident, their highly reliable operation outweigh the deactivation of less important tasks, such as the Fog Light Assistant. In Figure 4.5, the corresponding Pareto frontier is depicted. In case the binding optimization process outputs a binding, which violates the timing constraints, instead of choosing a binding with lower reliability (arrow with dashed line), the number of tasks is reduced, until a binding optimal in terms of reliability is found, which holds the timing constraints.

Based on this deliberation, a design flow as depicted in Figure 4.6 is derived.

Timing Validation

Depending on the execution behavior of the underlying virtualizable processor array, the timing validation procedure differs. In the original Task Group Scheduling proced-ure detailed in Section 2.4.1, all tasks being in a Task Group are sequentially executed in turns. As the tasks are activated in turn, there is no control overhead in managing the task order. When applying this scheme to the automotive application example, however, the following binding would violate the timing constraints:

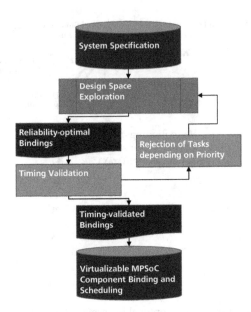

Figure 4.6: Iterative Design Flow to obtain Timing-validated Bindings which are optimal in Terms of Reliability.

$$BV_{Town_1} = ((BS, TSD, PA) \mapsto 1)$$

This is depicted in Figure 4.7. Below the tasks' execution times and their corresponding reactivation times for the town profile, a sequence of the conventional Task Group Scheduling is given. As BS is activated not until TSD and PA have been activated, the reactivation time of BS is violated. This is validated by Algorithm 21. If it is assumed that this binding was generated by the binding optimization procedure of [Israr 2012] and is optimal in terms of reliability, as a next step, one of these tasks would now be discarded in order to generate a new binding with the remaining tasks as detailed in the previous Section.

However, below the conventional Task Group Scheduling in Figure 4.7, another execution sequence for the tasks BS, TSD, and PA is given, which does not violate the timing constraints. By evoking BS each time after either TSD or PA have completed one execution cycle, all reactivation times are met. Thus, the designer may apply the enhanced task scheduling scheme, cf. Algorithm 10 of Section 2.4.1, by denoting an explicit task execution sequence. This sequence is derived by the timing validation algorithm denoted in Algorithm 22. Here, not only a binding, but also a scheduling sequence is being output. The procedure denoted in Algorithm 22 is depicted in Figure 4.8. Both scheduling mechanisms unburden the central control instance, which manages the update of task-processor bindings, as scheduling events are intrinsically

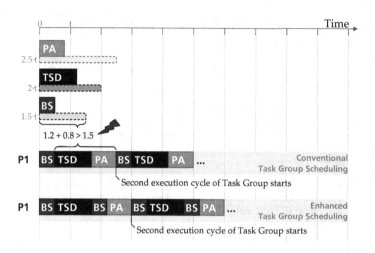

Figure 4.7: The conventional Task Group Scheduling leads to a Violation of Timing Constraints. With an enhanced Scheme, the Tasks meet the Timing Constraints.

Algorithm 21 Timing Validation of a Binding for the conventional Scheduling Scheme.

Require: A reliability-optimal binding $B : T \to P, t \mapsto p$, with each task t_i featuring an execution time $t_{i_{et}}$, and a reactivation time $t_{i_{rt}}$.
Ensure: A validation whether B meets the timing constraints.
1: **for all** Processors $p_i \in P$ **do**
2:    $NS_i \subseteq T$ is the set of tasks mapped to processor p_i by B
3:    **for all** Tasks $t_x \in NS_i$ **do**
4:       **if** The sum of all task execution times $\sum t_{y_{et}} \forall t_y \in NS_i \setminus t_x > t_{x_{rt}}$ **then**
5:          **return** B violates timing constraints
6:       **end if**
7:    **end for**
8: **end for**
9: **return** B fulfills timing

---

managed inside the Virtualization Layer by interpreting the self-scheduling instructions inserted into the tasks' software code.

4.1.7 Task Scheduling

For the conventional Task Group Scheduling as above, the software code of the driver assistance tasks is equipped with a nap instruction, cf. Section 2.4.4 after the last instruction of the actual assistance task, cf. Figure 4.9. In doing so, the task will be deactivated by the virtualization procedure and the next task of the task group, which is denoted in the execution sequence, will be activated on the processor. As the driver

---

Algorithm 22 Timing Validation of a Binding for an enhanced Scheduling Scheme.

Require: A reliability-optimal binding $B : T \rightarrow P, t \mapsto p$, task execution times T_{et}, and task reactivation times T_{rt}.

Ensure: A validation whether B meets the timing constraints and, in case they are met, a schedule S.

1: **for all** Processors $p_i \in P$ **do**
2:    $T_i \subseteq T$ is the set of tasks mapped to processor p_i by B
3:    $NS_i = T_i$ is the set of tasks not yet scheduled on p_i
4:    $S_i = \varnothing$ is a vector of the scheduling sequence of tasks mapped to p_i
5:    $RT[j]_i = t_{j_{rt}} \forall t_j \in T_i$, list of remaining reactivation time for each task mapped to p_i
6:    end_flag= 0
7:    **while** end_flag $\neq 1$ **do**
8:       end_flag= 1
9:       **while** There is a non-empty subset of Tasks $t_x \in T_{i_{S1}} \subseteq NS_i$, with $t_{x_{et}} \leq RT_i[j] \forall t_j \in T_i \setminus t_x$ **do**
10:              $\triangleright$ execution time of each element in $T_{i_{S1}}$ lower than reactivation time of every other task
11:       Select $t_x \in T_{i_{S1}}$ with $RT_i[x] = \min(RT_i[k]) \forall t_k \in T_{i_{S1}}$
12:       Remove t_x from NS_i
13:       Append t_x to S_i
14:       $RT_i[x] = t_{x_{rt}}$ $\triangleright$ reset t_x's reactivation time
15:       $RT_i[j] = RT_i[j] - t_{x_{et}} \forall t_j \in T_i \setminus t_x$ $\triangleright$ reduce reactivation time of all other tasks by $t_{x_{et}}$
16:       **end while**
17:       **if** $NS_i \neq \varnothing$ **then**
18:          **while** There is a set of Tasks $t_x \in T_{i_{S2}}$, whose elements are in S_i and with $t_{x_{et}} \leq RT_i[j] \forall t_j \in T_i \setminus t_x$ **do**
19:          Select $t_x \in T_{i_{S2}}$ with $RT_i[x] = \min(RT_i[k]) \forall t_k \in T_{i_{S2}}$
20:          Append t_x to S_i
21:          $RT_i[x] = t_{x_{rt}}$ $\triangleright$ reset t_x's reactivation time
22:          $RT_i[j] = RT_i[j] - t_{x_{et}} \forall t_j \in T_i \setminus t_x$ $\triangleright$ reduce reactivation time of all other tasks by $t_{x_{et}}$
23:          end_flag= 0
24:       **end while**
25:       **end if**
26:    **end while**
27: **end for**
28: **if** $NS_i \neq \varnothing$ for one or more NS_i **then**
29:    **return** B violates timing constraints
30: **else**
31:    **return** B fulfills timing when applying the set of schedules S
32: **end if**

---

assistance tasks are assumed to run within a `while(true)` loop, a new execution cycle will start as soon as the task is reactivated at the position of the nap instruction. In doing so, no external scheduling management is necessary.

4.1.8 Setup of the MPSoC and Binding Storage

After the timing of the bindings being output by the optimization procedure has been validated either for the conventional scheduling scheme or for an advanced one, the resulting bindings are stored in a dedicated storage accessible by the control processor of the virtualizable MPSoC. For each road type profile, there is a set of bindings, which

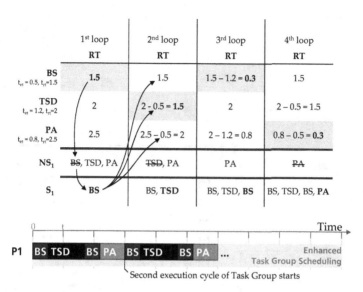

	1st loop	2nd loop	3rd loop	4th loop
	RT	RT	RT	RT
BS $t_{et}=0.5$, $t_{rt}=1.5$	1.5	1.5	1.5 − 1.2 = 0.3	1.5
TSD $t_{et}=1.2$, $t_{rt}=2$	2	2 − 0.5 = 1.5	2	2 − 0.5 = 1.5
PA $t_{et}=0.8$, $t_{rt}=2.5$	2.5	2.5 − 0.5 = 2	2 − 1.2 = 0.8	0.8 − 0.5 = 0.3
NS_1	~~BS~~, TSD, PA	~~TSD~~, PA	PA	~~PA~~
S_1	BS	BS, TSD	BS, TSD, BS	BS, TSD, BS, PA

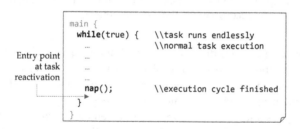

Second execution cycle of Task Group starts

Figure 4.8: Within four Cycles in the outer Loop of Algorithm 22, the Scheduling Sequence S is derived for the Binding $BV_{Town_1} = ((BS, TSD, PA) \mapsto 1)$.

```
main {
    while(true) {      \\task runs endlessly
        ...            \\normal task execution
Entry point   ...
at task       ...
reactivation  ...
        nap();         \\execution cycle finished
    }
}
```

Figure 4.9: Adding a *nap* Instruction to Driver Assistance Tasks enables Task Group (Self-)Scheduling without Need for explicit Scheduling Management.

correspond to the number of processors active in the system.[1] For the Application Example, bindings are stored on a personal computer, which is connected via an UART interface to the prototyped implementation on a Virtex-6 FPGA. For the test runs, fetching bindings via UART is the slowest part in the reshaping procedure. The time of the UART communication is not considered in the evaluation, as an external memory module in a real-world application would deliver bindings within a range of few clock cycles.

---

[1]The maximum number of stored bindings for each profile is $2^n - 1$, where n is the number of processors in the system.

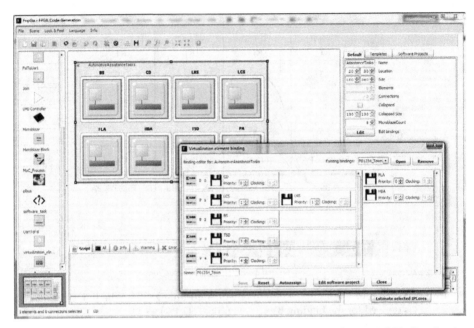

Figure 4.10: The Setup of the Driver Assistance Tasks in FripGa and an initial Binding for the Town Profile occupying five Processor Resources.

The corresponding setup is done in FripGa, cf. Figure 4.10 and is finalized in Xilinx EDK. Afterwards, the design is synthesized. The architecture, whose structure is depicted in Figure 4.11 is now ready for runtime operation. For the test runs, the underlying virtualizable MPSoC is scaled to feature a set of eight processors. As there are eight driver assistance tasks to be mapped, the employment of all eight processors at the same time leads to a trivial scenario. Hence, the test runs are performed for a subset of the processors in order to harden scheduling for demonstration purposes. The test runs highlighting the functional reshaping functionalities start with a processor set of six processors. The reliability reshaping will demonstrate exploiting the spare resources in the processor array for self-healing procedures at the event of failing processor resources.

4.1.9 Functional Reshaping

At first, a functional reshaping is demonstrated. Here, the car leaves a road type and enters another. Accordingly, the set of active driver assistance tasks is changed according to Table 4.1. As soon as a change of the road type is detected, an update of the task-processor binding is triggered. Consequently, a virtualization procedure is triggered for all active tasks in the system. Based on the new binding, which is fetched

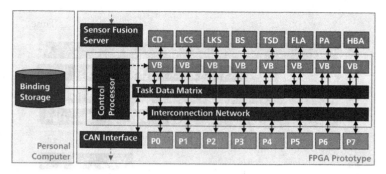

Figure 4.11: Architecture of the prototyped Automotive Assistance System.

via UART by the control processor from the central binding storage, a new network configuration is computed. Afterwards, the virtualization procedure enables the tasks as defined by the new binding.

Six Active Processors

For an architecture featuring six processors $P0$ to $P5$, the following bindings have been derived by the iterative Design Flow, which is depicted in Figure 4.6:

$$\begin{aligned}
BV_{Town_{012345}} &= (CD \mapsto 0), ((LCS, LKS) \mapsto 1), (BS \mapsto 2), (TSD \mapsto 3), (PA \mapsto 4) \\
BV_{Freeway_{012345}} &= (CD \mapsto 0), ((LCS, LKS) \mapsto 1), (BS \mapsto 2), (HBA \mapsto 3), \\
&\quad (FLA \mapsto 4), (TSD \mapsto 5)
\end{aligned}$$

The indices of bindings denote the processor instances active in the system. For the Town binding, processor resource $P5$ remains unused. In the simulation run, binding $BV_{Town_{012345}}$ is the system's initial configuration. The task-processor network is set according to Algorithm 13. As soon as a change of the road type is detected, processor $P5$ is activated by executing Algorithm 18, which setups the new binding $BV_{Freeway_{012345}}$. Figure 4.12 depicts the resulting task execution sequence. Besides the tasks LCS, which replaces LKS in case a lane change is indicated by the driver by activating the direction indicator, no task scheduling is required in this scenario. While fetching a new binding in by the UART interface was in the scope of milliseconds, as discussed in Section 4.1.8, the actual reshaping process by an update of the task-processor bindings and the interconnection network was accomplished in about 90 clock cycles.

Four Active Processors

Now, the system is designed to feature a set of four processors. The following bindings have been output by the binding optimization algorithm.

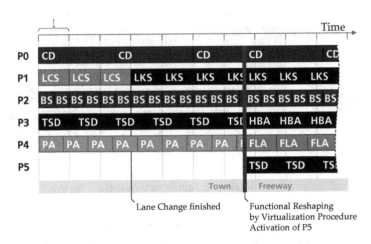

Figure 4.12: A functional Reshaping Process during the Transition between Road and Freeway for six Processors.

$$BV_{Freeway_{0123}} = (CD \mapsto 0), ((LCS, LKS) \mapsto 1), ((BS, FLA) \mapsto 2),$$
$$((HBA, TSD) \mapsto 3)$$
$$BV_{Road_{0123}} = (CD \mapsto 0), (LKS \mapsto 1), ((HBA, TSD) \mapsto 2), (FLA \mapsto 3)$$
$$BV_{Town_{0123}} = (CD \mapsto 0), ((LCS, LKS) \mapsto 1), ((BS, PA) \mapsto 2), (TSD \mapsto 3)$$

The timing of these three binding vectors has been validated by Algorithm 21.[2] Figure 4.13 depicts the execution sequence of the driver assistance tasks at runtime, where a car leaves freeway to enter a rural road, from where it enters a town.

The functional reshaping process is analogous to the one performed for six processors, cf. Algorithm 18. Here, however, all four processor resources are busy at any time, while in the scenario with six processors, one processor could be disabled, e. g., in the town profile. Scheduling of tasks is done by the self-scheduling feature of the Virtualization Layer. After each execution cycle, a task outputs a nap instruction. Consequently, the next task in the task group is being activated on the processor. Functional reshaping by the virtualization features provides a smooth transition between different execution profiles, i. e., road types in the scope of this application example.

4.1.10 Reliability Reshaping

Besides the ability for functionality reshaping, the virtualization features enable self-healing structures, which will allow the system to recover from erroneous states caused

---

[2]Generating better results with the enhanced scheduling scheme by executing timing validation Algorithm 22 eases the problem too much.

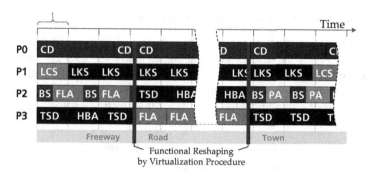

Figure 4.13: A functional Reshaping Process during the Transition between Road and Freeway for four Processors.

by defective processor resources. In the following, these features are highlighted for the automotive application example.

Detection of Faults by Runtime Tests

At first, the question arises about how to detect failing processor resources.[3] Here, several approaches exist. One might encapsulate a processor instance into a wrapper, which monitors the inputs and outputs handled by the processor resource. Out of an analysis of the input-output relations and the behavior of a set of output values, it can be assumed with a certain probability that the task running on a processor instance is working correctly. Such an approach was demonstrated for a MicroBlaze soft-core processor in [Biedermann 2011a]. Another possibility to detect errors in processor resources is a periodic execution of a short, dedicated self-test program, which e. g., consecutively reads and writes every process register and whose output value is known in advance. If the result differs from the expected value, it may be assumed that the processor resource is faulty, e. g., by a stuck bit value. In the following test runs, the presence of this fault detection mechanism is assumed. The dedicated self-test might for example be activated by the control processor in designer-defined intervals by the virtualization processor. For the simulation test runs, the occurrence of faults is manually indicated to the control processor.

---

[3]Errors may also occur in task memories or the TCM as a result, e. g., of bit flips caused by radiation effects. They may also become manifest in erroneous system behavior. In systems with high safety constraints, usually memory error correction mechanisms such as Error-Correcting Code (ECC) are exploited. Thus, this kind of errors is not considered in the scope of this example. Without dedicated memory error detection, if such an error is not due to a permanent defect of the circuitry, it may be treated, however, by overwriting the task memory with its initial configuration, clearing the TCM and restarting the task.

Self-Healing Strategy: Exploiting Spare Resources

For the first test case, a processor system consisting of eight processors is exploited, cf. Figure 4.11. As for the functional reshaping, an active set of six processors $P0$ to $P5$ is assumed at first. Two of the eight processor resources, $P6$ and $P7$ will act as spare resources. For six processors, the initial binding for the freeway road type, which is optimal in terms of reliability, is the same as for the functional reshaping process:

$$BV_{Freeway_{012345}} = (CD \mapsto 0), ((LCS, LKS) \mapsto 1), (BS \mapsto 2), (HBA \mapsto 3),$$
$$(FLA \mapsto 4), (TSD \mapsto 5)$$

Now, the detection of a defect of processor resource $P2$ is assumed. As there are spare processor resources left in the system, the system may compensate for the defunct processor instance by activating $P6$ or $P7$. Hence, the Binding $BV_{Freeway_{013456}}$ is fetched by the central processor and entered into the system, cf. Algorithm 18. As this new binding has been generated by the binding optimization process, it is also optimal in terms of reliability. The binding is as follows:

$$BV_{Freeway_{013456}} = (CD \mapsto 0), ((LCS, LKS) \mapsto 1), (BS \mapsto 3), (HBA \mapsto 4),$$
$$(FLA \mapsto 5), (TSD \mapsto 6)$$

As visible from Figure 4.14, after the reliability reshaping process, all tasks continue their work with the highest reliability value possible. Seen from the outside, the system resumes its operation as before the occurrence of the fault. This continues, when another processor resource, e. g., $P4$ fails. In this case, the left spare resource $P7$ is exploited to further assure a correct system operation. The new binding

$$BV_{Freeway_{013567}} = (CD \mapsto 0), ((LCS, LKS) \mapsto 1), (BS \mapsto 3), (HBA \mapsto 5),$$
$$(FLA \mapsto 6), (TSD \mapsto 7)$$

is also depicted in Figure 4.14. Until now, the systems functionality could be maintained even with two failing processor resources. In case another processor fails, a rescheduling will become necessary.

After the fails of $P2$ and $P4$, processor $P0$ fails. The binding

$$BV_{Freeway_{13567}} = (CD \mapsto 1), ((LCS, LKS) \mapsto 3), (BS, TSD \mapsto 5), (HBA \mapsto 6),$$
$$(FLA \mapsto 7)$$

now matches BS with TSD on the same processor resource. The timing validation for this binding given the task execution and reactivation times as depicted in Figure 4.3

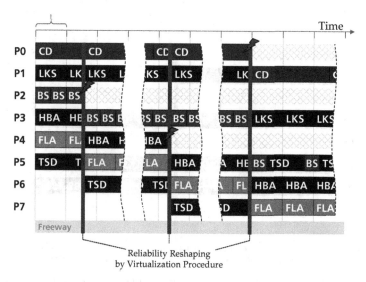

Reliability Reshaping
by Virtualization Procedure

Figure 4.14: Reliability Reshaping Procedures after the Detection of faulty Processor Resources.

was successful. Still, all tasks remain active in the system; the selected binding is optimal in terms of reliability. The execution sequence of this test run is depicted on the right hand side of Figure 4.14.

Self-Healing Strategy: Iterative Rescheduling

Finally, the unlikely event of a simultaneous fail of processor instances $P1$ and $P7$ is assumed. Thus, the system has to cope with the remaining processor instances $P3$, $P5$, and $P6$. The binding, which is optimal in terms of reliability and was initially generated by the reliability optimization process, is:

$$BV_{Freeway_{356/raw}} = (CD \mapsto 3), ((LCS, LKS) \mapsto 5), (BS, TSD, HBA, FLA \mapsto 6)$$

However, the timing validation reveals that in this case, the reactivation time of task TSD is violated. Thus, in order to both meet the timing constraints as well as to apply a binding optimal in terms of reliability, the task with the least priority in the system is discarded. As visible from Table 4.1, this is task FLA. After having removed FLA

$$BV_{Freeway_{356/val1}} = (CD \mapsto 3), ((LCS, LKS) \mapsto 5), (BS, TSD, HBA \mapsto 6)$$

TSD still violates timing constraints. Thus, according to Table 4.1, HBA is deactivated next. The resulting binding

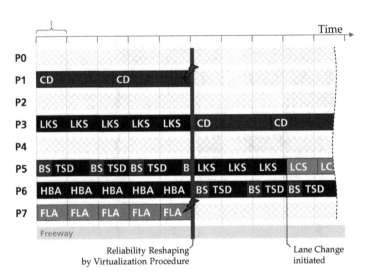

Figure 4.15: Reliability Reshaping after Tasks HBA and FLA have been discarded in order to meet Timing Constraints.

$$BV_{Freeway_{356}} = (CD \mapsto 3), ((LCS, LKS) \mapsto 5), (BS, TSD \mapsto 6)$$

finally meets the timing constraints. As detailed above, the validation and iterative re-computation of bindings under refusal of tasks has been performed already in the system design phase. The central processor may, thus, directly fetch and apply binding $BV_{Freeway_{356}}$. As this binding relies on the output of the binding optimization theory it is, despite the degradation of its scope of operation, still optimal in terms of reliability.[4] Figure 4.15 depicts the execution sequence during the simultaneous fail of $P1$ and $P7$.

While five failing processor instances out of a set of eight processors is a highly unlikely case, this application set has demonstrated that the reliability reshaping procedure is able to maintain the most important driver assistance tasks even at the event of a series of errors. Unlike for systems with static bindings, a failing processor resource not automatically affects the tasks currently being executed on this resource. Instead, in case the full operation cannot be restored, e. g., due to timing constraints in the remaining processor array, the least important tasks may be selected to be discarded first. Thus, the system's reliability and, last but not least, the driver's safety may profit significantly from the execution dynamism introduced by the Virtualization Layer.

---

[4]In fact, the overall reliability increases from 0.99283 over 0.99392 to 0.99481 when subsequently removing FLA and HBA. As there are less tasks in the system, the probability for a task having a fault is reduced.

Detection of Faults by Redundant Task Execution

Another method to detect or even cover faults is module redundancy. For FPGA-based automotive systems, a redundant hardware task exeuction scheme was presented in [Paulsson 2006b]. Here, reconfigurable slots of the FPGA are filled with redundant instances of the tasks and a TMR voter. In case the TMR voter detects a deviation, a partial reconfiguration of the affected slot is initiated or the task is moved to another slot. The virtualizable MPSoC takes a similar approach as the slot-based technique for hardware tasks. Detected deviations will cause a shift of the task to another "slot", i. e., to another processor. As detailed in Section 2.6, the Virtualization Layer features dedicated VMR modules to enable redundancy features. However, redundancy has to be paid by a significant overhead in terms of processor resources and task memory. In the following an example test run is shown for a subset of tasks, which is executed in different redundancy schemes.

The employment of Triple Modular Redundancy occupies three processor instances as well as three task memories for each task. Thus, in a virtualizable MPSoC with an 8×8 task-processor interconnection network only two tasks may be executed in a TMR scheme at one point in time. As six processors are occupied by redundant task execution, the remaining two processors may either be held ready as spare resources or they might be exploited to execute other tasks without a redundancy scheme. Usually, if a processor resource fails in a TMR scheme, the results produced by the faulty resource are masked by the TMR voting module. The subsequent computations rely, therefore, on the remaining two processor instances. The reshaping capabilities of the virtualizable MPSoC allow, however, replacing the processor instance, which has been identified as faulty. In doing so, not only faults are masked, but the original redundancy scheme with three, parallel executing task instances may be restored.

A binding for a TMR scheme and the most important tasks, CD and LKS for the freeway profile may appear as:

$$BV_{Freeway_{01234567T012T345}} = (CD_1 \mapsto 0), (CD_2 \mapsto 1), (CD_3 \mapsto 2), (LKS_1 \mapsto 3),$$
$$(LKS_2 \mapsto 4), (LKS_3 \mapsto 5); (ext_1, (CD_1(1), CD_2(2), CD_3(3)) \mapsto VMR(9)),$$
$$(ext_1, (LKS_1(4), LKS_2(5), LKS_3(6)) \mapsto VMR(10))$$

In order to allow for a correct voting procedure as detailed in Section 2.6, the task IDs of the redundant task instances are given as well as the source, which feeds the parallel instances. In this case, ext_1 refers to the simulated Sensor Fusion Server, which is connected as an external module via the TDM, cf. Algorithm 17. In case an error is detected in the TMR voter, a binding may be requested, which employs another, recently unused processor resource of the system. For the case that processor instance $P5$ fails, a new binding, in which the TMR assignment is renewed, is applied by application of Algorithm 18:

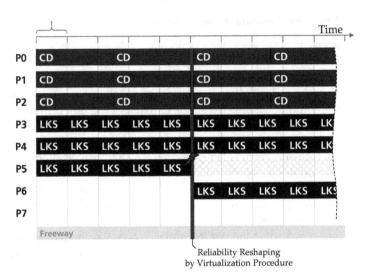

Figure 4.16: A TMR Execution Scheme: The Virtualization Procedure may replace and deactivate Processor Resources identified as faulty by TMR Voting Modules.

$$BV_{Freeway_{0123467T012T346}} = (CD_1 \mapsto 0), (CD_2 \mapsto 1), (CD_3 \mapsto 2), (LKS_1 \mapsto 3),$$
$$(LKS_2 \mapsto 4), (LKS_3 \mapsto 6); (ext1, (CD_1(1), CD_2(2), CD_3(3))) \mapsto VMR(9)),$$
$$(ext1, (LKS_1(4), LKS_2(5), LKS_3(6))) \mapsto VMR(10))$$

At runtime, an execution sequence like the one depicted in Figure 4.16 is obtained. In a DMR scenario, errors are masked. However, it is not able to identify, which of the processor resources produced an erroneous result. The Virtualization Layer allows to perform a "sequential TMR" out of a DMR scheme. In case a deviation is detected by a voter, the processors employed subsequently exchanged as denoted in Algorithm 23. This procedure is depicted in Figure 4.17. In doing so, a faulty processor resource may be identified and excluded from the current binding.

4.1.11 Synthesis Evaluation

An on-chip placement of the synthesized system for a Virtex-6 LX240T is depicted in Figure 4.18. The processor instances of the processor array are indicated by numbers. In grey, the central control processor is highlighted in the top left corner. By letters, the Block RAM columns storing the actual Machine Code Representation of the Driver Assistance Tasks are denoted. The light grey background depicts the widely distributed structure of the interconnection network. The connectivity of the interconnection

---

Algorithm 23 Identifying faulty Processors in a DMR Scenario.

Require: A binding, which features at least one task being executed as t_1 and t_2 on processors p_i and p_j in a DMR scheme, one spare processor resource p_k.
Ensure: An identification and deactivation of a faulty processor resource.

1: **if** DMR voter detects deviation in the results delivered by p_i and p_j **then**
2:   Control processor enters new binding, where t_1 is mapped to p_k instead of p_i
3:   **if** Deviation persists during next execution cycle **then**
4:     Control processor enters new binding, where t_1 is mapped to p_i and t_2 to p_k
5:     **if** Deviation persists during next execution cycle **then**
6:       Deviation is not allocable to one processor resource
7:       Control processor restores original binding, which maps t_1 to p_i and t_2 to p_j
8:     **else**
9:       Identify p_j as faulty processor resource
10:       Deactivate p_j
11:     **end if**
12:   **else**
13:     Identify p_i as faulty processor resource
14:     Deactivate p_i
15:   **end if**
16: **end if**

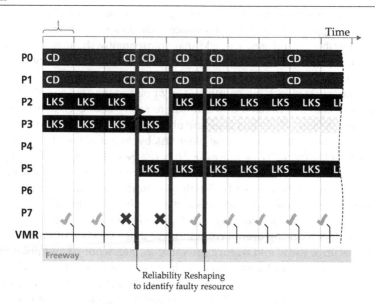

Figure 4.17: A DMR Execution Scheme: A faulty Processor Resource may be identifed by a ßequential TMR"Procedure.

network is depicted as a dark grey overlay. Figure 4.19 depicts the resource consumption of the synthesized system. While the overhead introduced by the Virtualization Layer seems to be significant at first sight, it has to be considered that just about 10% of the entire registers of the FPGA are occupied and the employed MicroBlaze processor types are designed to be mapped very efficiently to the underlying FPGA. Thus, the contribution of the Virtualization Layer appears to be significant, but only in comparison to the tiny MicroBlaze processors, not to the entire device. In terms of Lookup-Tables, however, the Virtualization Layer indeed introduces a fair overhead. As discussed in Section 2.3.5, this is due to the inefficient placement of the crossbar switches of the interconnection network, which also leads to the drop in system frequency when targeting an FPGA. The choice of another target chip architecture, however, will resolve this issue. The overall memory consumption is very moderate.

4.1.12 Outcome and Outlook

The automotive example has demonstrated the application of a virtualizable MPSoC in an environment, which faces harsh timing and reliability constraints. A dynamic adaption of the automotive assistance tasks is facilitated by the virtualization procedure. Moreover, the virtualization properties enable the compensation for defunct processor instances.

In contrast to conventional automotive systems with task-related, dedicated processor resources, the aggregation of driver assistance tasks on a virtualizable processor array offers considerable advantages. As tasks may transparently share processor resources by the virtualization procedure, overall cost is reduced, as not every task needs a dedicated processor instance. The design of completely disjoint task memories as well as the guaranteed task interruption at any point in time even enables sharing of a processor resource between a task relevant to safety and, e.g., a task of the car's entertainment system. While this is commonly strictly avoided in embedded design, a task cannot harmfully interfere with another task by design of the Virtualization Layer.

As the size of the virtualizable processor array can be scaled, the number of processor instance may be tailored according to the vehicle class. A compact car most often features less assistance systems and entertainment functions than an executive car. Even if the same amount of assistance systems and entertainment functions is supported by both car types, car manufacturers may want to spend a smaller processor array for the compact car, thus reducing overall cost of the car at the expense of processing power. While an executive car would feature smooth user interaction at any point in time, a cheaper compact car could show some lag in its entertainment functions due to the reduced size of the processor array. As the scheduling budgets can be set freely by the system designer, the tasks relevant to safety, however, could be tailored to react as fast and safe as in the executive car.

Besides cost reduction as prominent yield of the virtualizable MPSoC, concentrating tasks onto a centralized processor array may significantly simplify design, robustness, and maintenance of an embedded system. In contrast to a decentralized plethora of microprocessors and microcontrollers, all embedded tasks may exploit the same type of processor resource, thus harmonizing the set of programming languages and

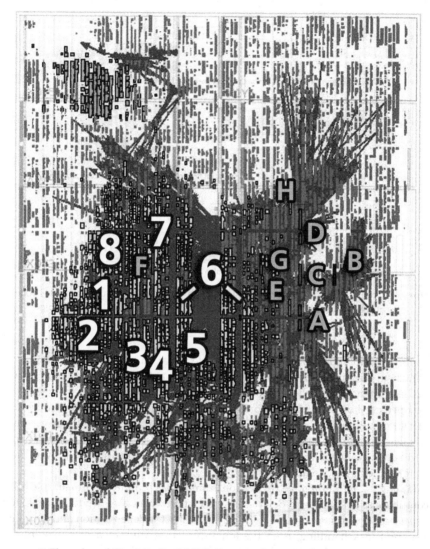

Figure 4.18: Floorplan of the virtualized MPSoC mapped to a Virtex-6 FPGA.

instructions employed. Furthermore, as each processor in the array is capable of replacing another processor by an update of the task-processor bindings, the allocation of spare resources in case of errors is trivial. Moreover, even if no dedicated spare resources are available, a complete re-organization of the task-processor bindings, possibly by discarding less important tasks, may restore the systems main functionality at the event of errors. This self-healing property was demonstrated by the iterative

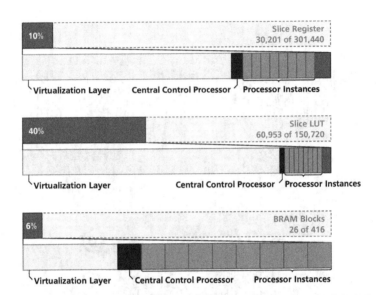

Figure 4.19: A Visualization of Device Logic Occupation. The combinatorial Task-Processor Interconnection Network accounts for about 99 % of the LUTs occupied by the Virtualization Layer.

reliability reshaping in the automotive example above. In an automotive environment, a permanent error in a processor resource could lead to the car's break down. However, with the employment of the virtualizable processor array, a defunct processor could be compensated by the virtualization procedure until the driver manages to visit a car repair shop. As the processor instances of the virtualizable processor array are at a centralized spot in the car, maintenance as well as the replacement of components is, in addition, simplified. The virtualization features could, thus, significantly increase a car's reliability and robustness.

Summing up the automotive application example has proven the virtualizable MPSoC to contribute to a reduction in device cost and complexity at a tremendous gain in terms of execution dynamism and reliability. Due to strict task separation and completely transparent task handling, even the long-avoided sharing of a processor resource between safety-critical tasks and other tasks becomes feasible.

4.2 Reshaping in an Energy-Constrained Quadrocopter System

Besides systems, in which reliability is the main optimization goal, the concept of a virtualizable MPSoC may also be exploited for embedded systems, which face other constraints. In the following application example, the virtualizable MPSoC will be tailored to be integrated into a Quadrocopter, a small unmanned aerial vehicle, cf.

Figure 4.20: A Quadrocopter with onboard Camera [Dkroetsch 2011].

Figure 4.20. A Quadrocopter may be equipped with a plethora of sensor devices, but has to cope with a limited supply of power. The application example will demonstrate the execution behavior of a virtualizable MPSoC in an energy-constrained system. Depending on the actual environmental situation as well as the energy supply, a dynamic system reshaping takes place. Furthermore, the Agile Processing scheme is exploited during the Quadrocopter's flight.

4.2.1 Envisaged Scenario

A Quadrocopter is a small aerial device, which usually features a low own weight. It may be equipped with some payload. While its motors are usually too weak to actually transport cargo, the payload may consist of sensor systems such as cameras or temperature sensors. A Quadrocopter combines the ability of autonomous, GPS-based flight with a fairly simple manual flight control. As small Quadrocopters are usually driven by electrical power rather than with combustion motors, their range is limited by the capacity of their battery. Typical operation times are in the range of about twenty minutes.

The ability for carrying sensors, autonomous flight control, as well as the comparable low device cost render a Quadrocopter to be an advantageous alternative to the employment of a manned helicopter in certain scenarios.

Such a scenario may be a rescue operation after a disaster, such as an earthquake. In the following scenario, an earthquake has hit a city. Buildings have collapsed and many

Table 4.2: Tasks present in the Quadrocopter System.

#	Task	Priority	Type
0	System Initialization (SI)	0	**Startup Routine**
1	Ground Communication (GC)	0	
2	Position Control (PC)	0	**Flight Control**
3	Autopilot (AP)	1	
4	Global Positioning System (GPS)	1	
5	Ground Heat Detection & Analysis (GHD)	2	
6	Microphone (MIC)	2	**Primary Casualty**
7	Analysis of Sources of Light (SOL)	2	**Detection Systems**
8	Visual Body Recognition (VBR)	2	*Agile Processing Task*
9	Environmental Temperature Tracking (TT)	3	
10	Air Pressure Tracking (APT)	3	
11	CO_2 Level Tracking (C2T)	3	**Auxiliary**
12	Radiation Level Tracking (RT)	3	**Sensor Systems**
13	Audio Response by Megaphone (AR)	2	**Casualty Comm.**

people are assumed to be buried alive or to be at least partially covered by debris. As streets are impassable by rescue parties, Quadrocopters are exploited to autonomously scan the environment for casualties and to guide rescue teams to them.

4.2.2 Sensors and Control Systems of the Quadrocopter

The Quadrocopter is assumed to be equipped with sensors, which provide information about the current position and environmental data, such as temperature, air pressure, or radiation levels. Table 4.2 lists the tasks present in the system of the Quadrocopter. These tasks may be divided into an initial startup routine, which configures the Quadrocopter for flight, the primary flight control systems, the system for the detection of casualties as well as a set of auxiliary systems, which provide additional environmental information. Last but not least, a task provides communication with found victims by exploiting the onboard megaphone and microphone.

For the casualty detection, the onboard camera is assumed to record images via the Visual Body Recognition (VBR) task. A microphone records environmental noise during flight. Furthermore, a heat sensor may detect body heat sent out by victims. Additionally, the Quadrocopter may recognize sources of light in the rescue area. If one or more of these sensors indicate a potential casualty on ground, the VBR task switches to another execution mode, which analyzes the last recorded image for human shapes. As this analysis may be parallelized, e. g., by partitioning the area of the image,

Table 4.3: Battery Level Thresholds and resulting Changes in the System's Configuration.

Battery Level Thresholds	System State
> 30%	No restrictions, Agile Processing with maximum Degree of Parallelism
≤ 30%	Shutdown of Auxiliary Sensor Systems, Agile Processing with three parallel Instances
≤ 5%	Shutdown of Casualty Detection Systems Initiate Return Flight to Ground Station
≤ 2%	Shutdown of Auto Pilot and GPS

VBR will act as an Agile Processing Task in the application example. As soon as the Quadrocopter has identified a human within the debris, the position is transmitted to the ground station. With an onboard megaphone, the victim may be informed about its imminent rescue.

Task Priorities and Battery

The tasks feature several priority classes, cf. Table 4.2, where a lower value represents a higher priority. During normal system operation, any task may be executed. The battery of the Quadrocopter is assumed to last for about 20 minutes of operation when all systems are active. Table 4.3 denotes the changes in the system's configuration depending on the battery charge level. With the battery charge level being above 30% of the battery's capacity, the Agile Processing task, cf. Section 4.2.2, may run with a maximum degree of parallelism in case a parallel execution scheme is selected. With a battery charge level between 5% and 30%, the degree of parallelism is limited to three instances. With a parallelization degree of three, a distinct speedup in comparison with a sequential execution is achieved, however, the energy consumption is lower than with the maximum degree of parallelism. It is assumed that the control processor receives information about the current battery charge level from the onboard battery. For the simulation runs, this information, i. e., the triggers for a system reshaping, is provided from the outside world by means of a UART interface.

Assumptions for the Agile Processing Task

VBR acts as an Agile Processing task, which searches for humans by analyzing pictures captured by the onboard camera. Computer vision algorithms, such as image segmentation [Felzenszwalb 2004] may be exploited. In order to parallelize this process the picture may, e. g., be cut into several sections. The size of a section depends on

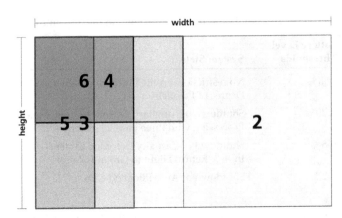

Figure 4.21: A Picture of the Camera may be cut into Sections depending on the Degree of Parallelism.

the desired degree of parallelism, which is denoted by numbers in Figure 4.21.[5] The parallelization of an Agile Processing task by the insertion of pragmas was detailed in Section 3.4.3.

It is assumed that the time needed to transfer the pixel data to the parallel instances is significantly lower than the computation time spent in the parallel instances. Section 3.3.5 has demonstrated that delivering the parallel parts in a pipelined fashion, cf. Figure 3.18 (b) further lowers the overall execution time. For the application example, the execution time of the task and its communication overhead are scaled accordingly. It is assumed that the result of a parallel instance is a binary yes/no decision, whether a human shape has been detected or not. As the execution time of the other tasks in the system is not of particular importance in this example, they run in an indefinite loop unless they are suspended because of a Task Group scheduling event or a reshaping procedure.

4.2.3 Example Mission Sequence

Figure 4.22 depicts the sequence of a rescue mission of the Quadrocopter, which is divided into several disjoint flight states, numbered from I to VII. The Quadrocopter is programmed to search in a certain area of the disaster zone. In Figure 4.22, this is the area spanning the rectangles from A0 to D4. It is planned that the Quadrocopter autonomously flies to the first rectangle (I). At startup, the system initialization task is executed. Until the Quadrocopter has reached its destination, just the flight systems are active. As soon as it enters its assigned application area, all casualty detection systems as well as the auxiliary systems are activated (II). The Quadrocopter now

---

[5]In doing so objects positioned at the edges of these sections might be missed. In a real world case, the designer possibly scales the sections to overlap each other.

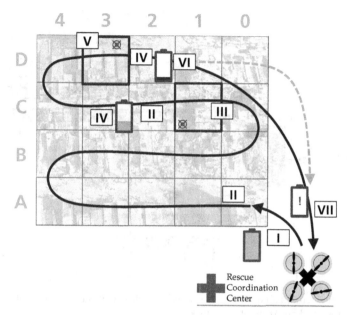

Figure 4.22: Sequence of a Rescue Mission of the Quadrocopter. Background Image taken from [Abassi 2010].

sequentially scans the rectangles in the map for casualties. The flight path is indicated by the arrow. In rectangle C1, the heat sensor indicates a ground temperature, which may hint to the existence of a victim. As a result, VBR starts to analyze the most recent picture in a parallel fashion (III). As result of processing this picture, the presence of a victim has been detected. Its position is transmitted to the ground station and the victim is informed by the megaphone about its rescue. The Quadrocopter returns to a sequential state of VBR and resumes scanning the next rectangle for further casualties. At some point in time, the battery level falls below the 30 % threshold. Consequently, the auxiliary systems are shut down in order to preserve energy (IV). In rectangle D3, the microphone records noises. Again, a parallel processing of the recorded pictures by VBR is enabled. (V) However, the degree of parallelism is limited to three instances due to the drowning energy supply, cf. Table 4.3. After successfully detecting a human, the Quadrocopter tries to resume its planned flight route. However, already in the next rectangle, the energy supply hits the 5 % mark (VI). Thus, the rescue mission is aborted and the casualty detection systems are shutdown. The Quadrocopter autonomously triggers the return to its ground station. However, the energy supply further diminishes. As the battery is in a critical state, with just 2 % of its charge level, the ground station is informed that the Quadrocopter will now disable its autonomous flight functions (VII). The rescue team now has to manually fly the Quadrocopter back to its ground station.

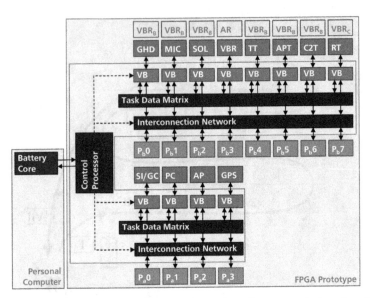

Figure 4.23: The virtualizable MPSoC is shaped to a close Cluster consisting of an Array of four and an Array of eight Processors.

After a recharge process, the Quadrocopter may resume its mission starting from the last rectangle, in which it searched for victims.

4.2.4 Role of the virtualizable MPSoC

As underlying architecture of the envisaged Quadrocopter application example, a virtualizable MPSoC is setup, cf. Figure 4.23. It consists of a close cluster, cf. Section 2.3.5, which features an array a of four processors P_a0 to P_a3 and an array b of eight processors P_b0 to P_b7. Array a will accomodate the tasks necessary for maintaining flight operation, i. e., the tasks SI, GC, PC, AP, and GPS will be executed. For the simulation runs, SI and GC reside in the same code memory. After SI is completed it calls the function of GC. Thus, these tasks are regarded as one task SI_GC. Array b will host all the tasks necessary to accomplish the search for victims. In Figure 4.23, the tasks, which have to be configured into task memories, e. g., by partial dynamic reconfiguration, are depicted in a lighter shade above the tasks initially present in the system. While partial dynamic reconfiguration may be evaluated during runs in hardware, this technique is not represented in system simulators. Thus, for the simulation runs, partial dynamic reconfiguration is mimicked by evoking a dummy function instead of the dedicated function, which would trigger a reconfiguration. In the simulation run a task memory consequently features both the dummy code for the task initially present in the system as well as the dummy code for the task to be configured at runtime.

The decision to exploit a clustered MPSoC instead of one larger processor array is not for safety reasons. Due to the strict memory separation of tasks, the tasks necessary for flight control could be bound to the other tasks in the system without the danger of malicious task interference, cf. Section 2.2.6. Nevertheless, larger processor arrays lead to a larger task-processor interconnection network, thus increasing the overall latency, cf. Section 2.3.4. The tasks relevant for flight management are assumed to feature timing constraints, which prohibit being scheduled with other tasks on the same processor instance. They are, therefore, mapped to a 4×4 array. The remaining tasks are bound to the 8×8 array.

A UART interface acts as a simulated battery. The drain of the battery is adapted to the measurements of the processors' energy consumption, cf. Section 2.7. Thus, the battery informs the control processor of the MPSoC in case a threshold is undershot and then the control processor will manage the updates of task-processor bindings. A reshaping may be triggered for several reasons:

1. The GPS task provides information about whether the rescue area has been entered or left. In this case, the casualty detection systems are being activated or deactivated, respectively.

2. A Casualty Detection System indicates the possible finding of a victim. Accordingly, the Visual Body Recognition is toggled to be executed in parallel at the expense of temporarily suspending other detection and sensor tasks. If the most recent pictures have been analyzed, the previously deactivated detection and assistance tasks are reactivated.

3. The battery indicates falling below a certain threshold and, thus, triggers a graceful degradation of the sensor tasks.

The initial binding of the system is as follows:

$$BV_{aI} = ((SI\_GC) \mapsto 0), (PC \mapsto 1), (AP \mapsto 2), (GPS \mapsto 3)$$
$$BV_{bI} = (GHD) \mapsto 0), (MIC \mapsto 1), (SOL \mapsto 2), (VBR \mapsto 3), (TT \mapsto 4),$$
$$(APT \mapsto 5), (RT \mapsto 6), (C2T \mapsto 7)$$

4.2.5 Analysis of Runtime Behavior

Figures 4.24 and 4.25 depict the simulated execution sequence during the eradication of the mission sequence detailed in Section 4.2.3. In case a new system state is entered, a reshaping procedure, cf. Algorithm 18, takes place. The setup of this new state takes 89 clock cycles. With decreasing energy level, processors are subsequently shut down by a reshaping of the system's configuration. Consequently, some of the least important tasks are being disabled. These are tasks, which are depicted in light green

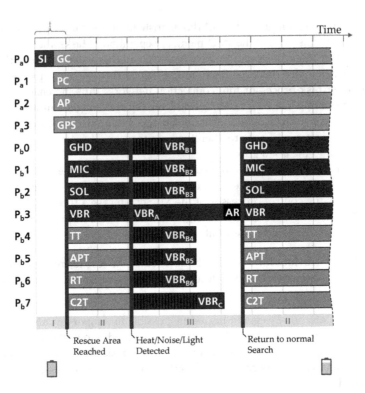

Figure 4.24: Execution Behavior of Flight Phases I to III according to Figure 4.22.

in Figure 4.25. Finally, just the most crucial tasks to maintain flight operation remain active.

Timing overhead for the partial reconfiguration when applying the Agile Processing scheme cannot be derived from the simulation. Furthermore, the actual speed is dependent on the speed of the off-chip memory containing the partial bitstream images. According to measurements in the scope of a Bachelor Thesis by Randolph Lieding [Lieding 2014], the protocol to set up the Agile Processing scheme for six parallel Instances, cf. Section 3.24, is executed within 510 clock cycles after reshaping the systems configuration for a parallel execution.

The diagram in Figure 4.26 depicts the relation between the measured power consumption of the virtualizable MPSoC and the Quadrocopter's simulated battery charge level. The power offset of the system as well as the assumed external sensor devices, which may be disabled as well, are not considered. Measurements were performed on the virtualizable MPSoC clocked to 10 MHz in the scope of the bachelor thesis of Antonio Gavino Casu [Casu 2013]. Vertical lines depict the points in time at which a reshaping of the system's configuration takes place. The small battery icons depict

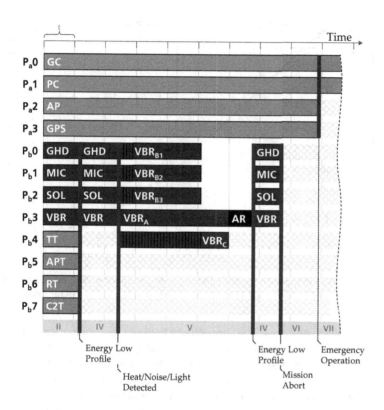

Figure 4.25: Flight Phases III to VII according to Figure 4.22.

energy-related reshaping procedures. The different mission states are depicted in Roman numbers, cf. Figure 4.22. When deactivating the number of active processors, the slope of the battery charge level becomes flatter, cf. phase IV in Figure 4.26. Running just the most critical tasks in order to maintain a stable flight further strechtes the Quadrocopter's battery life, cf. phases VI and VII.

4.2.6 Synthesis Evaluation

Figure 4.27 depicts a floorplan of the synthesized design for a Virtex-6 LX240T FPGA. The virtualizable MPSoC is scaled to a close cluster, cf. Section 2.3.5. However, as the communication is handled via dedicated Message Hubs in each processor array, the spatial separation of the two clusters on the chip is fairly distinct. The control processor depicted in green is interestingly closely placed to the 4 × 4 cluster instead of a balanced position between both clusters. As visible in grey and blue, large parts of the FPGA's resources are occupied by the widely distributed placement of the interconnection

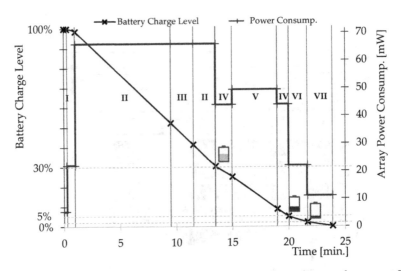

Figure 4.26: Drain of the Quadrocopter's Battery over Time depending on the current Power Consumption. Vertical Lines indicate a Reshaping of the Architecture.

networks and the virtbridges. The connectivity between task memories and processors is depicted in darker shades of blue and grey. Again, the clustering is clearly visible.

The resource consumption of the prototype design is depicted in Figure 4.28. The design of a close cluster of an 8 × 8 and a 4 × 4 array allows for a direct comparison of both array sizes. In terms of register count, the resource consumption scales linearly with the size of the array. Due to updates in the hardware description, the overall register use is lower than for the synthesized prototype in the previous application example. For the LUTs, with increasing array size the resource consumption increases in a faster pace. This is due to the structure of the interconnection network, cf. Section 2.3.4. For the sake of completeness, the BRAM consumption is given as well. In contrast to the automotive application example in Section 4.1, the individual task memory size has been increased in order to fit the corresponding software code. The overhead introduced by the virtualization solution in terms of BRAM is negligible. Summing up, the virtualization approach introduces a fair amount of resource overhead but, provides a decent yield in terms of execution dynamism. As motivated in Chapter 1, the availability of enough resources is indeed not a problem to worry about today. Instead, the resources spent for the Virtualization Layers allow to overcome this "Nulticore" effect as discussed in Section 1.

4.2.7 Conclusion

The exploitation of the Agile Processing scheme for an energy-constrained embedded system has demonstrated the yield in terms of execution flexibility gained by the

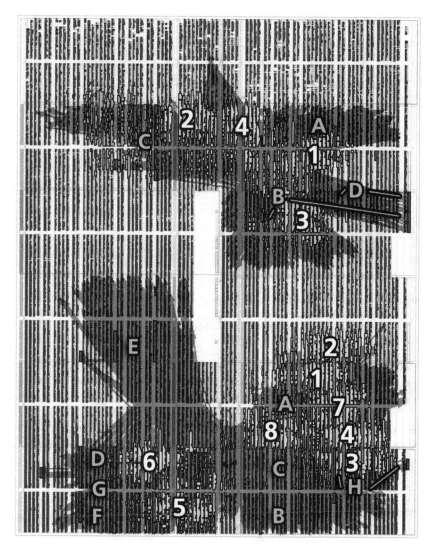

Figure 4.27: Floorplan of a close cluster consisting of an 8 × 8 and a 4 × 4 Array. Processors in yellow are marked by numbers. Task Memories in red are marked by Letters. The Control Processor is depicted in green Color.

virtualization properties. The embedded system may reshape its current configuration based on external factors such as sensor inputs as well as based on internal ones such as the energy remaining in its batteries. Due to the Agile Processing scheme, tasks may temporarily boost their performance by switching to an adjustable parallel execution

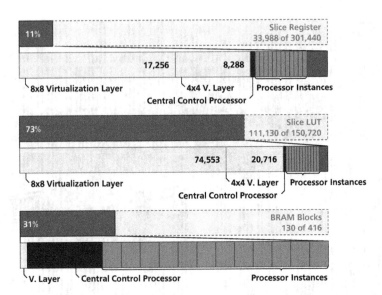

Figure 4.28: A Visualization of Device Logic Occupation:The Register Count scales linearly with the Size of the Processor Arrays. The LUT Consumption increases at a faster Rate when the Array Size doubles.

behavior. Other tasks in the system may be suspended by the virtualization procedure in the meantime. During parallel execution, the degree of parallelism may be adjusted transparently. In each execution cycle, the number of parallel instances may be varied up to $n - 2$, where n is the number of processors in the array.[6] The application example has proven the feasibility of the Agile Processing scheme in combination with the virtualization features in order to obtain self-awareness of systems regarding their energy management and execution behavior.

---

[6]One processor is needed to execute the A part, one processor to execute the C part of a parallelized task.

5 Conclusion and Outlook

This work has introduced several new concepts for the design of multi-processor systems in embedded designs, which rely on hardware virtualization. By exploiting a hardware-based virtualization concept, design flows for a variety of use cases, which span from highly reliable to parallel executable systems, are covered. In particular, the Agile Processing scheme allows the transparent switch between sequential and parallel execution of tasks, whereas the degree of parallelization can be scaled dynamically. Resolving the usually static task-processor bindings and keeping task memories strictly disjoint enables features known from software-managed operating systems without abandoning the requirements, which are often crucial for embedded systems: Predictable execution times, strict memory separation for safety reasons, and the availability of fault detection and fault recovery mechanisms, just to name a few. The virtualization concept is based upon a layer between tasks and processors, which provides the functionality of shifting task execution among the processor array in a very fast manner that outperforms existing software-based solutions.

In the Virtualization Layer a dedicated task-processor interconnection network, whose configuration is updated at runtime, manages the shift of task execution. Additionally, it provides intrinsic means for task group scheduling. Denoting task execution sequences as well as a self-organizing scheduling scheme evoked by tasks are techniques enabled by the proposed architecture without causing additional control overhead.

Besides the task-processor interconnection, the enhancement of a point-to-point task communication concept has been introduced. Here, a runtime code manipulation allows for transparent point-to-point communication despite the lack of knowledge, on which processor the communication partner is currently being executed or whether it is executed at this point in time at all. As a runtime code modification scheme is exploited, just minor changes to existing legacy code is to be made in order to enable the employment of this task in a virtualizable environment.

As reliability and safety are often optimization goals in the embedded world, the Virtualization Layer features generic redundancy modules as well as several self-healing means in order to recover from erroneous states. The ability to shift the execution of a task transparently to another processor resource is an essential prerequisite in order to allow for self-healing strategies. The application of existing binding optimization procedures, which produce bindings that are optimal in terms of reliability, has been demonstrated in the scope of a complex automotive application example.

Transparent task activation and deactivation as well as temporarily disabling processor cores as necessary are provided by the Virtualization Layer. These features may be exploited in order to conceive energy aware systems, which may tailor their execution behavior, i. e., the number and set of active tasks and processors, to the current supply of energy. This has been demonstrated for a quadrocopter, which faces harsh energy constraints and may profit from the energy awareness features introduced by the Virtualization Layer.

A dedicated development environment called FripGa accompanies the generic hardware architecture of the Virtualization Layer. Thus, the designer may construct virtualizable systems either by means of a graphic user interface or by scripted input. The design environment is built to work seamlessly with existing design flows. For the prototype implementation, the tool chain of the chip vendor Xilinx, Inc. is supported. As a consequence, existing designs may be edited in FripGa, virtualization features may be added and the entire system can be synthesized for an FPGA right out of FripGa.

The proposed virtualization concept has been implemented as a prototype for an FPGA platform and was successfully tested for systems consisting up to twelve array processors. It is worth mentioning that the proposed virtualization concept does not rely on a specific hardware architecture, such as an FPGA, or a dedicated processor type. In case a certain feature exclusively present on FPGAs, such as partial dynamic configuration, has been exploited, alternatives for other architectures were given as well. The instructions fed into the processor array by the virtualization procedure are taken from a standard set of instructions present in almost all common general purpose processors. As for the chip architecture, no feature of the processor has been exploited, which is unique to this processor type. Consequently, given the effort of code adaption, the approach can be exploited for any other processor type and tool suite. It is not limited to soft-core processors or the Xilinx workflow in any way.

As every optimization towards one property almost always inevitably lead to a deterioration of other aspects, the yield in execution dynamism introduced by the virtualization features leads to a drop in the system's maximum frequency. By scaling the virtualizable processor array down, by defining clusters, or by choosing another target chip architecture, this effect can be compensated. Consequently, it is up to designer to define the degree of execution dynamism needed for the specific application scenario.

Summing up, the virtualization concept introduced by this work covers a comprehensive concept for the design, setup, test, and implementation of virtualizable embedded designs. The design flows resulting from the adoption of the virtualization concept propose solutions to the common problem of nowadays multi-processor and multi-core computing, where the mere instantiation of many processor instances mostly raises many problems and solves just a few. The application examples taken from the automotive world and from systems with harsh energy constraints, of which each faces individual requirements, prove the versatility of the virtualization solution.

Taking the virtualization concept as a foundation, a plethora of new problem statements arises. In future work, virtualizable processor arrays might consist of processors, which indeed feature a common instruction set, but differ in terms of performance, energy consumption, resource consumption, or reliability. In such systems, advanced methodologies for the efficient mapping of tasks to heterogeneous arrays are needed. In return, systems could be designed, whose tasks run on small, energy-efficient processors most of the time. If changing operating conditions require a temporary increase in performance or a highly reliable execution, tasks could dynamically be re-allocated to suited processors depending on these needs. A further step in the level of abstraction is created by taking sets of small clusters of virtualizable arrays as foundation. The structure, layout, and interaction of these clusters will then raise another quality of problem statements. The execution dynamism may be advanced in future work by dynamically evoking and discarding entire clusters of virtualizable tasks. This enables a highly complex system-on-chip consisting of virtualizable sub-systems, which has the ability to shape itself perfectly to the requirements being setup by its surrounding. The virtualization concept is, thus, intended to provide a glimpse of aspiration to narrow the design gap and to catch up in the desperate race against the malice of Moore's Law.

List of Publications

[1] Alexander Biedermann and Sorin A. Huss. *Selbstheilende Strukturen in einem virtualisierbaren eingebetteten MPSoC* IBM Academic Lab Days, Böblingen, Germany, November 2013.

[2] Alexander Biedermann, Boris Dreyer and Sorin A. Huss. *A Generic, Scalable Reconfiguration Infrastructure for Sensor Networks Functionality Adaption.* 26th IEEE International SoC Conference (SOCC), Nürnberg, Germany, September 2013.

[3] Alexander Biedermann and Sorin A. Huss. *A Methodology for Invasive Programming on Virtualizable Embedded MPSoC Architectures.* 13th International Conference on Computational Science (ICCS), Barcelona, Spain, June 2013.

[4] Alexander Biedermann and Sorin A. Huss. *Hardware Virtualization-driven Software Task Switching in Reconfigurable Multi-Processor System-on-Chip Architectures .* ACM 5th Workshop on Mapping of Applications to MPSoCs (Map2MPSoC/SCOPES 2012), St. Goar, Germany, May 2012.

[5] Alexander Biedermann, Matthias Zöllner and Sorin A. Huss. *Automatic Code Parallelization and Architecture Generation for Embedded MPSoC.* ACM 5th Workshop on Mapping of Applications to MPSoCs (Map2MPSoC/SCOPES 2012), St. Goar, Germany, May 2012.

[6] Alexander Biedermann and Sorin A. Huss. *FripGa: A Prototypical Design Tool for Embedded Multi-Core System-on-Chip Architectures.* IEEE/ACM Design, Automation and Test in Europe, DATE'12, University Booth, Dresden Germany, March 2012.

[7] Alexander Biedermann and Sorin A. Huss. *Scalable Multi-Core Virtualization for Embedded System-on-Chip Architectures.* IEEE/ACM Design, Automation and Test in Europe, DATE'12, Friday Workshop: Quo Vadis, Virtual Platforms? Dresden, Germany, January 2012.

[8] Alexander Biedermann, Thorsten Piper, Lars Patzina, Sven Patzina, Sorin A Huss, Andy Schürr and Neeraj Suri. *Enhancing FPGA Robustness via Generic Monitoring IP Cores.* International Conference on Pervasive and Embedded Computing and Communication Systems, Vilamoura, Portugal, March 2011.

[9] Alexander Biedermann, Marc Stoettinger, Lijing Chen and Sorin A. Huss. *Secure Virtualization within a Multi-Processor Soft-core System-on-Chip Architecture.* The 7th

International Symposium on Applied Reconfigurable Computing, Belfast, UK, March 2011.

[10] Alexander Biedermann and H. Gregor Molter (Eds.). *Design Methodologies for Secure Embedded Systems*, volume 78. of Lecture Notes in Electrical Engineering. Springer, Berlin, Germany, November 2010.

[11] André Seffrin and Alexander Biedermann. *Cellular-Array Implementations of Bio-Inspired Self-Healing Systems: State of the Art and Future Perspectives*. Design Methodologies for Secure Embedded Systems, volume 78. of *Lecture Notes in Electrical Engineering*, Berlin, November 2010.

[12] André Seffrin, Alexander Biedermann and Sorin A. Huss. *Tiny-Pi: A Novel Formal Method for Specification, Analysis, and Verification of Dynamic Partial Reconfiguration Processes*. 13th IEEE Forum on Specification and Design Languages (FDL 2010), Southampton, UK, September 2010.

[13] Marc Stoettinger, Alexander Biedermann and Sorin A. Huss. *Virtualization within a Parallel Array of Homogeneous Processing Units*. 6th International Symposium on Applied Reconfigurable Computing, Bangkok, Thailand, March 2010.

[14] Felix Madlener, Sorin A. Huss and Alexander Biedermann. *RecDEVS: A Comprehensive Model of Computation for Dynamically Reconfigurable Hardware Systems*. 4th IFAC Workshop on Discrete-Event System Design (DESDes'09), Gandia, Spain, October 2009.

List of supervised Theses

Master Theses, Diploma Theses, and Bachelor Theses

[1] Randolph Lieding. *Dynamic Task Switching in a virtualizable Multi-Processor System.* Bachelor Thesis, TU Darmstadt, April 2014.

[2] Antonio Gavino Casu. *Power-Optimierung von Soft-Core-Prozessor-Virtualisierung.* Bachelor Thesis, TU Darmstadt, December 2013.

[3] Boris Dreyer. *Dynamisches Rekonfigurationsnetzwerk zur wechselseitigen Rekonfiguration heterogener, verteilter eingebetteter Systeme.* Master Thesis, TU Darmstadt, October 2013.

[4] Andreas Rjasanow. *Selbstheilende Strukturen in virtualisierbaren Multiprozessor-System-on-Chip-Architekturen.* Master Thesis, TU Darmstadt, June 2013.

[5] Steffen Fleckenstein. *Massiv-parallele Videofilterung für FPGA-Boards.* Bachelor Thesis, TU Darmstadt, April 2012.

[6] Wei Lin. *Virtualisierung von Soft-Core-Prozessoren.* Diplomarbeit, TU Darmstadt, January 2012.

[7] Matthias Zöllner. *Modellierung von Parallelisierungsstrukturen für sequenzielle Algorithmen in C.* Bachelor Thesis, TU Darmstadt, January 2012.

[8] Tobias Rückelt. *Implementierung eines Sensorsystems als Beispielapplikation für generisches FPGA-Monitoring.* Bachelor Thesis, TU Darmstadt, July 2011.

[9] Clemens Bergmann. *Design einer dynamisch rekonfigurierbaren FPGA-Architektur.* Bachelor Thesis, TU Darmstadt, May 2011.

[10] Maik Görtz. *FripGa - Software zur Codegenerierung von Many-Core-Architekturen auf FPGAs.* Master Thesis, TU Darmstadt, March 2011.

[11] Jan Post. *Implementierung und Evaluation eines massiv-parallelen Bildskalierungsfilters auf einem FPGA.* Bachelor Thesis, TU Darmstadt, February 2011.

[12] Andreas Rjasanow and Gregor Rynkowski. *Verteilte Triple-Voted-TMR-Architektur auf FPGA-Boards.* Bachelor Thesis, TU Darmstadt, February 2010.

Final Theses ("Studienarbeiten") and Practical Courses

[1]   Matthias Zöllner. *Parallelisierungstechniken für sequentiellen Code.* Final Thesis, TU Darsmtadt, February 2014.

[2]   Boris Dreyer. *Kommunikation in einem virtualisierbaren MPSoC.* Practical Course, TU Darmstadt, January 2014.

[3]   Boris Dreyer. *Entwurf eines JTAG-eACE-Players für Mikroprozessor-basierte Systeme.* Final Thesis, TU Darmstadt, November 2013.

[4]   Kevin Luck. *Ein virtualisierbares Automotive MPSoC.* Final Thesis, TU Darmstadt, May 2013.

[5]   Nicolas Eicke, Sebastian Funke, Kai Schwierczek and Markus Tasch. *Framework zur Modellierung verteilter, paralleler eingebetteter HW/SW-Designs.* Practical Course, TU Darmstadt, October 2012.

[6]   Wei Lin. *Ein skalierbares Multi-Processor System-on-Chip zur Taskvirtualisierung.* Practical Course, TU Darmstadt, October 2012.

[7]   Tobias Rückelt. *Graphischer Editor für Models of Computation.* Final Thesis, TU Darmstadt, October 2012.

[8]   Wei Lin. *Implementierung und HW/SW-Partitionierung eines skalierbaren, verteilten FIR-Filters.* Practical Course, TU Darmstadt, July 2012.

[9]   Kevin Luck. *Glue Logic für Board-zu-Board-Kommunikation.* Practical Course, TU Darmstadt, July 2012.

[10]   Antonio Gavino Casu, Kadir Inac, Randolph Lieding, Mischa Lundberg and Daniel Schneider. *Virtualisierung in eingebetteten Multi-Prozessor-Systemen.* Practical Course, TU Darmstadt, April 2012.

[11]   Michael Koch, Niels Ströher, Lucas Rothamel and Manuel Weiel. *Framework zur Modellierung verteilter, paralleler eingebetteter HW/SW-Designs.* Practical Course, TU Darmstadt, April 2012.

[12]   Andreas Rjasanow. *Generischer Monitoring-IP-Core für FPGAs.* Final Thesis, TU Darmstadt, April 2012.

[13]   Wei Lin. *Integration von partiell-dynamischer Rekonfugration in High-Level Design Tools.* Practical Course, TU Darmstadt, January 2012.

[14]   Jan Post. *Implementierung eines HW-IP-Cores für schnelles Pixel-Resampling.* Final Thesis, TU Darmstadt, October 2011.

[15] Hieu Ha Chi, Dan Le, Do Thanh Tung and Binh Vu Duc. *Graphisches Tool für parallelisierte HW/SW-FPGA-Designs*. Practical Course, TU Darmstadt, September 2011.

[16] Quoc Hien Dang, Johannes Decher, Thorsten Jacobi and Omid Pahlevan Sharif. *Graphisches Tool für parallelisierte HW/SW-FPGA-Designs*. Practical Course, TU Darmstadt, September 2011.

[17] Michael Koch, Niels Ströher, Lucas Rothamel and Manuel Weiel. *Graphisches Tool für parallelisierte HW/SW-FPGA-Designs*. Practical Course, TU Darmstadt, September 2011.

[18] Clemens Bergmann. *Attacken auf Android-Smartphones*. Practical Course, TU Darmstadt, June 2011.

[19] Peter Glöckner, Amir Naseri, Johannes Simon and Matthias Zöllner. *Framework für massiv-parallele Systeme in heterogenen FPGA-Netzwerken*. Practical Course, TU Darmstadt, April 2011.

[20] Christopher Huth. *Methodiken zur Bewertung der Güte von Security-USB-Token*. Practical Course, TU Darmstadt, October 2010.

[21] Tobias Rückelt. *Entwicklung eines redundanten Temperatursensors*. Practical Course, TU Darmstadt, October 2010.

[22] Christopher Huth. *Man-in-the-PC-Attacke auf einen Banking-USB-Stick*. Semesterarbeit, TU Darmstadt, July 2010.

[23] Joel Njeukam. *Partielle Rekonfiguration für Virtex-5 FPGAs*. Practical Course, TU Darmstadt, April 2010.

Bibliography

[Abassi 2010] L. Abassi. *2010 Haiti Earthquake Damage 4*. online: http://upload load.wikimedia.org/wikipedia/commons/a/a2/2010_Haiti_earth quake_damage4.jpg, accessed 07/01/2014, 9:00 am, 2010. 177

[Ackland 2000] B. Ackland, A. Anesko, D. Brinthaupt, S.J. Daubert, A. Kalavade, J. Knobloch, E. Micca, M. Moturi, C.J. Nicol, J.H. O'Neill et al. *A single-chip, 1.6-billion, 16-b MAC/s multiprocessor DSP*. IEEE Journal of Solid-State Circuits, vol. 35, no. 3, pages 412–424, 2000. 2

[Ajtai 1983] M. Ajtai, J. Komlós and E. Szemerédi. *An O(N Log N) Sorting Network*. In Proceedings of the Symposium on Theory of Computing (STOC), pages 1–9. ACM, 1983. 38

[Ambric Inc. 2008] Ambric Inc. *Am2000 Family Massively Parallel Processor Array*. online: http://web.archive.org/web/20080516200115/http://www. ambric.com/products/, accessed 12/11/2013, 11:40 am, May 2008. 107

[Amdahl 1967] G.M. Amdahl. *Validity of the single Processor Approach to achieving large Scale computing Capabilities*. In Proceedings of the April 18-20, 1967, Spring Joint Computer Conference, pages 483–485. ACM, 1967. 129

[ARM 2010] ARM. *AMBA 4 AXI4-Stream Protocol*, 1.0 edition, 2010. 79

[Arora 1990] S. Arora, T. Leighton and B. Maggs. *On-line Algorithms for Path Selection in a nonblocking Network*. In Proceedings of the twenty-second annual ACM Symposium on Theory of Computing, pages 149–158. ACM, 1990. 37

[Barthe 2011] L. Barthe, L.V. Cargnini, P. Benoit and L. Torres. *The SecretBlaze: A configurable and cost-effective open-source soft-core Processor*. In Proceedings of International Symposium on Parallel and Distributed Processing Workshops and Phd Forum (IPDPSW), pages 310–313. IEEE, 2011. 8

[Batcher 1968] K.E. Batcher. *Sorting Networks and their Applications*. In Proceedings of the April 30–May 2, 1968, Spring Joint Computer Conference, pages 307–314. ACM, 1968. 38

[Beaumont 2012] M. Beaumont, B. Hopkins and T. Newby. *SAFER PATH: Security Architecture using fragmented Execution and Replication for Protection against trojaned*

Hardware. In Proceedings of the Conference on Design, Automation and Test in Europe (DATE), pages 1000–1005. EDA Consortium, 2012. 14

[Beck 2001] K. Beck, M. Beedle, A. Van Bennekum, A. Cockburn, W. Cunningham, M. Fowler, J. Grenning, J. Highsmith, A. Hunt, R. Jeffries et al. *Manifesto for Agile Software Development*, 2001. 135

[Belanovic 2003] P. Belanovic, M. Holzer, D. Micušík and M. Rupp. *Design Methodology of Signal Processing Algorithms in Wireless Systems.* In Proceedings of the International Conference on Computer, Communication and Control Technologies (CCCT), pages 288–291, 2003. 1, 2

[Bell 2008] S. Bell, B. Edwards, J. Amann, R. Conlin, K. Joyce, V. Leung, J. MacKay, M. Reif, L. Bao, J. Brown et al. *Tile64-Processor: A 64-Core SoC with Mesh Interconnect.* In Proceedings of the International Solid-State Circuits Conference (ISSCC), pages 88–598. IEEE, 2008. 33

[Benini 2002] L. Benini and G. De Micheli. *Networks on Chips: A new SoC Paradigm.* Computer, vol. 35, no. 1, pages 70–78, 2002. 33

[Biedermann 2008] A. Biedermann and B. Meyer. *Theoretische und algorithmische Evaluation eines massiv-parallelen Multiprozessorarrays der Am2000-Familie unter Verwendung von Videoalgorithmen.* Diploma Thesis, TU Darmstadt, September 2008. 38, 107

[Biedermann 2011a] A. Biedermann, T. Piper, L. Patzina, S. Patzina, S.A. Huss, A. Schürr and N. Suri. *Enhancing FPGA Robustness via Generic Monitoring IP Cores.* In Proceedings of International Conference on Pervasive Embedded Computing and Communication Systems (PECCS), pages 379–386, 2011. 96, 120, 163

[Biedermann 2011b] A. Biedermann, M. Stoettinger, L. Chen and S.A. Huss. *Secure Virtualization within a Multi-Processor soft-core System-on-Chip Architecture.* In Proceedings of the International Symposium on Applied Reconfigurable Computing (ARC), pages 385–396. Springer, 2011. 17

[Biedermann 2012a] A. Biedermann and S.A. Huss. *FripGa: A Prototypical Design Tool for Embedded Multi-Core System-on-Chip Architectures.* In Conference on Design, Automation and Test in Europe (DATE), University Booth. IEEE/ACM, 2012. 110

[Biedermann 2012b] A. Biedermann and S.A. Huss. *Hardware Virtualization-driven Software Task Switching in Reconfigurable Multi-Processor System-on-Chip Architectures.* In Proceedings of the Workshop on Mapping of Applications to MPSoCs (Map2MPSoC/SCOPES), pages 32–41. ACM, 2012. 67

[Biedermann 2012c] A. Biedermann and S.A. Huss. *Scalable Multi-Core Virtualization for Embedded System-on-Chip Architectures*. In Conference on Design, Automation and Test in Europe (DATE), Friday Workshop: Quo Vadis, Virtual Platforms? IEEE/ACM, 2012. 39

[Biedermann 2012d] A. Biedermann, M. Zöllner and S.A. Huss. *Automatic Code Parallelization and Architecture Generation for Embedded MPSoC*. In Workshop on Mapping of Applications to MPSoCs (Map2MPSoC/SCOPES 2012), 2012. 123

[Biedermann 2013a] A. Biedermann, B. Dreyer and S.A. Huss. *A Generic, Scalable Reconfiguration Infrastructure for Sensor Networks Functionality Adaption*. In International SoC Conference (SOCC). IEEE, 2013. 54

[Biedermann 2013b] A. Biedermann and S.A. Huss. *A Methodology for Invasive Programming on Virtualizable Embedded MPSoC Architectures*. In Proceedings of International Conference on Computational Science (ICCS), pages 359–368. Procedia Computer Science, 2013. 135

[Bolchini 2007] C. Bolchini, A. Miele and M.D. Santambrogio. *TMR and Partial Dynamic Reconfiguration to mitigate SEU faults in FPGAs*. In Proceedings of International Symposium on Defect and Fault-Tolerance in VLSI Systems (DFT), pages 87–95. IEEE, 2007. 121

[Bonamy 2012] R. Bonamy, H.M. Pham, S. Pillement and D. Chillet. *Ultra-fast power-aware Reconfiguration Controller*. In Proceedings of Conference on Design, Automation and Test in Europe (DATE), pages 1373–1378. IEEE/ACM, 2012. 55

[Brebner 1996] G.J. Brebner. *A Virtual Hardware Operating System for the Xilinx XC6200*. In Proceedings of Conference on Field-Programmable Logic and Applications (FPL), pages 327–336. Springer, 1996. 6

[Brebner 2001] G.J. Brebner and O. Diessel. *Chip-Based reconfigurable Task Management*. In Proceedings of Conference on Field-Programmable Logic and Applications (FPL), pages 182–191. IEEE, 2001. 6

[Burke 2004] E.K. Burke, P. De Causmaecker and G. Vanden Berghe. *Novel metaheuristic Approaches to Nurse Rostering Problems in Belgian Hospitals*. Handbook of Scheduling: Algorithms, Models and Performance Analysis, vol. 18, pages 1–44, 2004. 67

[Casu 2011] A.G. Casu, K. Inac, R. Lieding, M. Lundberg and D. Schneider. *Virtualisierung in eingbetteten Multi-Prozessor-Systemen*. Practical Course, TU Darmstadt, April 2011. 112

[Casu 2013] A.G. Casu. *Power-Optimierung von Soft-Core-Prozessor-Virtualisierung*. Bachelor Thesis, TU Darmstadt, December 2013. 102, 180

[Ceng 2008] J. Ceng, J. Castrillon, W. Sheng, H. Scharwächter, R. Leupers, G. Ascheid, H. Meyr, T. Isshiki and H. Kunieda. *MAPS: An integrated Framework for MPSoC Application Parallelization*. In Proceedings of the Annual Design Automation Conference (DAC), pages 754–759. ACM, 2008. 127

[Cerone 2009] V. Cerone, M. Milanese and D. Regruto. *Combined automatic Lane-Keeping and Driver's Steering through a 2-DOF Control Strategy*. IEEE Transactions on Control Systems Technology, vol. 17, no. 1, pages 135–142, 2009. 152

[Chakrabarty 2009] A. Chakrabarty, M. Collier and S. Mukhopadhyay. *Matrix-based Nonblocking Routing Algorithm for Beneš Networks*. In Proceedings of Conference on Future Computing, Service Computation, Cognitive, Adaptive, Content, Patterns (Computationworld), pages 551–556. IEEE, 2009. 37

[Chandra 1997] R. Chandra, D.-K. Chen, R. Cox, D.E. Maydan, N. Nedeljkovic and J.M. Anderson. *Data Distribution Support on Distributed Shared Memory Multiprocessors*. ACM SIGPLAN Notices, vol. 32, no. 5, pages 334–345, 1997. 123

[Chen 2007] T. Chen, R. Raghavan, J.N. Dale and E. Iwata. *Cell Broadband Engine Architecture and its first Implementation – A Performance View*. IBM Journal of Research and Development, vol. 51, no. 5, pages 559–572, 2007. 1, 32

[Chen 2009] C.T. Chen and Y.S. Chen. *Real-time Approaching Vehicle Detection in Blind-Spot Area*. In Proceedings of 12th International IEEE Conference on Intelligent Transportation Systems (ITSC), pages 1–6. IEEE, 2009. 152

[Clos 1953] C. Clos. *A Study of non-blocking Switching Networks*. Bell System Technical Journal, vol. 32, no. 2, pages 406–424, 1953. 34

[Cohen 2010] A. Cohen and E. Rohou. *Processor Virtualization and split Compilation for heterogeneous Multicore Embedded Systems*. In Proceedings of Design Automation Conference (DAC), pages 102–107. ACM, 2010. 5

[Cordes 2013] D. Cordes, O. Neugebauer, M. Engel and P. Marwedel. *Automatic Extraction of Task-Level Parallelism for Heterogeneous MPSoCs*. In Proceedings of International Conference on Parallel Processing (ICPP), pages 950–959. IEEE, 2013. 123

[Cotret 2012] P. Cotret, J. Crenne, G. Gogniat and J. Diguet. *Bus-based MPSoC Security through Communication Protection: A latency-efficient Alternative*. In Proceedings of Annual International Symposium on Field-Programmable Custom Computing Machines (FCCM), pages 200–207. IEEE, 2012. 95

[Dagum 1998] L. Dagum and R. Menon. *OpenMP: An Industry Standard API for Shared-Memory Programming*. Computational Science & Engineering, IEEE, vol. 5, no. 1, pages 46–55, 1998. 123, 127

[Darms 2006] M. Darms and H. Winner. *Umfelderfassung für ein Fahrerassistenzsystem zur Unfallvermeidung*. In VDI Berichte, volume 1931 of *VDI*, page 207, 2006. 150

[Densmore 2006] D. Densmore and R. Passerone. *A Platform-based Taxonomy for ESL Design*. IEEE Design & Test of Computers, vol. 23, no. 5, pages 359–374, 2006. 109

[Dkroetsch 2011] Dkroetsch. *Aeryon Scout with Camera*. online: http://commons. wikimedia.org/wiki/File:Aeryon_Scout_With_Camera.jpg, accessed 07/01/2014, 9:10 am, 04 2011. 173

[Dreyer 2014] B. Dreyer. *Kommunikation in einem virtualisierbaren MPSoC*. Forschungsarbeit, TU Darmstadt, January 2014. 93

[Eicke 2012] N. Eicke, S. Funke, K. Schwierczek and M. Tasch. *Framework zur Modellierung verteilter, paralleler eingebetteter HW/SW-Designs*. Practical Course, TU Darmstadt, October 2012. 69

[Felzenszwalb 2004] P. Felzenszwalb and D. Huttenlocher. *Efficient graph-based Image Segmentation*. International Journal of Computer Vision, vol. 59, no. 2, pages 167–181, 2004. 175

[Ferger 2012] M. Ferger, M.A. Kadi, M. Hubner, M. Koedam, S. Sinha, K. Goossens, G.M. Almeida, J.R. Azambuja and J. Becker. *Hardware / Software Virtualization for the Reconfigurable Multicore Platform*. In Proceedings of the International Conference on Computational Science and Engineering (CSE), pages 341–344. IEEE, 2012. 6

[Figuli 2011] P. Figuli, M. Hubner, R. Girardey, F. Bapp, T. Bruckschlogl, F. Thoma, J. Henkel and J. Becker. *A heterogeneous SoC Architecture with embedded virtual FPGA Cores and runtime Core Fusion*. In Proceedings of Conference on Adaptive Hardware and Systems (AHS), pages 96–103. NASA/ESA, 2011. 6

[Franke 2003] B. Franke and M.F.P. Oboyle. *Compiler Parallelization of C Programs for multi-core DSPs with multiple Address Spaces*. In Proceedings of International Conference on Hardware/Software Codesign and System Synthesis, pages 219–224. IEEE/ACM/IFIP, 2003. 123

[Ganssle 2008] Jack Ganssle. *The Nulticore Effect*. online: http://www.embedded. com/design/mcus-processors-and-socs/4008183/The-Nulticore-effect, accessed 11/06/2013, 2:15 pm, 2008. 2

[Gericota 2005] M.G. Gericota, G.R. Alves and J.M. Ferreira. *A self-healing Real-Time System based on run-time Self-Reconfiguration*. In Proceedings of Conference on Emerging Technologies and Factory Automation (ETFA), volume 1, pages 4–pp. IEEE, 2005. 116

[Glöckner 2011] P. Glöckner, A. Naseri, J. Simon and M. Zöllner. *Framework für massivparallele Systeme in heterogenen FPGA-Netzwerken*. Practical Course, TU Darmstadt, April 2011. 112

[Goke 1973] L. Rodney Goke and G.J. Lipovski. *Banyan Networks for partitioning Multiprocessor Systems*. ACM SIGARCH Computer Architecture News, vol. 2, no. 4, pages 21–28, 1973. 34

[Goldberg 1974] R.P. Goldberg. *Survey of virtual Machine Research*. Computer, vol. 7, no. 6, pages 34–45, 1974. 5

[Green 2013] O. Green and Y. Birk. *Scheduling Directives for shared-memory Many-Core Processor Systems*. In Proceedings of the International Workshop on Programming Models and Applications for Multicores and Manycores, pages 115–124. ACM, 2013. 57

[Görtz 2011] M. Görtz. *FripGa - Software zur Codegenerierung von Many-Core-Architekturen auf FPGAs*. Master Thesis, TU Darmstadt, March 2011. 112

[Haase 2004] J. Haase, F. Eschmann, B. Klauer and K. Waldschmidt. *The SDVM: A self distributing Virtual Machine*. In Proceedings of International Conference on Architecture of Computing Systems (ARCS), volume 2981, 2004. 5

[Hansson 2011] A. Hansson, M. Ekerhult, A. Molnos, A. Milutinovic, A. Nelson, J. Ambrose and K. Goossens. *Design and Implementation of an Operating System for Composable Processor Sharing*. Microprocessors and Microsystems, vol. 35, no. 2, pages 246–260, 2011. 6

[Hübner 2006] M. Hübner, C. Schuck, M. Kühnle and J. Becker. *New 2-dimensional partial dynamic Reconfiguration Techniques for real-time adaptive Microelectronic Circuits*. In Proceedings of Annual Symposium on Emerging VLSI Technologies and Architectures, pages 6–pp. IEEE, 2006. 54

[Heiser 2008] G. Heiser. *The Role of Virtualization in Embedded Systems*. In Proceedings of Workshop on Isolation and Integration in Embedded Systems (IIES), pages 11–16. ACM, 2008. 5

[Hemani 2000] A. Hemani, A. Jantsch, S. Kumar, A. Postula, J. Oberg, M. Millberg and D. Lindqvist. *Network on Chip: An Architecture for Billion Transistor Era*. In Proceedings of the NorChip Conference, volume 31. IEEE, 2000. 33

[Henkel 2003] J. Henkel. *Closing the SoC Design Gap*. Computer, vol. 36, no. 9, pages 119–121, 2003. 1

[Henkel 2012] J. Henkel, A. Herkersdorf, L. Bauer, T. Wild, M. Hubner, Ravi K. Pujari, A. Grudnitsky, J. Heisswolf, A. Zaib, B. Vogel et al. *Invasive Manycore Architec-*

tures. In Proceedings of Asia and South Pacific Design Automation Conference (ASP-DAC), pages 193–200. IEEE, 2012. 33, 135

[Hofmann 2008] A. Hofmann and K. Waldschmidt. *SDVM^R: A Scalable Firmware for FPGA-Based Multi-core Systems-on-Chip.* In Proceedings of Annual Symposium on VLSI (ISVLSI), pages 387–392. IEEE, 2008. 6

[Howard 2010] J. Howard, S. Dighe, Y. Hoskote, S. Vangal, D. Finan, G. Ruhl, D. Jenkins, H. Wilson, N. Borkar, G. Schrom et al. *A 48-Core IA-32 message-passing Processor with DVFS in 45nm CMOS.* In Proceedings of International Solid-State Circuits Conference (ISSCC), pages 108–109. IEEE, 2010. 33

[Huang 2009] C.H. Huang and P.-A. Hsiung. *Hardware Resource Virtualization for dynamically partially reconfigurable Systems.* IEEE Embedded Systems Letters, vol. 1, no. 1, pages 19–23, 2009. 6

[Intel Corporation 2011] Intel Corporation. *Intel Refreshes Ultimate Enthusiast Processor Lineup with Six-Core Offerings.* online: http://newsr oom.intel.com/community/intel_newsroom/blog/2011/11/14/int el-refreshes-ultimate-enthusiast-processor-lineup-with-six -core-offerings, accessed 11/28/2013, 3:00 pm, 2011. 7

[Intel Corporation 2013a] Intel Corporation. *Desktop 3rd Generation Intel CoreProcessor Family, Desktop Intel Pentium Processor Family, Desktop Intel Celeron Processor Family, and LGA1155 Socket Thermal Mechanical Specifications and Design Guidelines (TMSDG).* Intel Corporation, 1 2013. 7

[Intel Corporation 2013b] Intel Corporation. *Intel64 and IA-32 Architectures Software Developer's Manual.* Intel Corporation, vol. 2 edition, 3 2013. 7

[Irwin 2004] M.J. Irwin, L. Benini, N. Vijaykrishnan and M. Kandemir. *Techniques for designing energy-aware MPSoCs*, pages 21–47. Morgan Kaufman, 2004. 102

[Israr 2012] A. Israr. *Reliability Aware High-Level Embedded System Design in presence of Hard and Soft Errors.* PhD Thesis, TU Darmstadt, May 2012. 117, 118, 154, 156

[Jozwik 2012] K. Jozwik, H. Tomiyama, M. Edahiro, S. Honda and H. Takada. *Comparison of Preemption Schemes for Partially Reconfigurable FPGAs.* IEEE Embedded Systems Letters, vol. 4, no. 2, pages 45–48, 2012. 6

[Jung 2005] H.G. Jung, D.S. Kim, P.J. Yoon and J.H. Kim. *Computer Analysis of Images and Patterns*, chapter Stereo Vision based Localization of free Parking Site, pages 231–239. Springer, 2005. 152

[Kalte 2005] H. Kalte and M. Porrmann. *Context Saving and Restoring for Multitasking in reconfigurable Systems.* In Proceedings of Conference on Field-Programmable Logic and Applications (FPL), pages 223–228. IEEE, 2005. 14

[Khronos OpenCL Working Group 2008] Khronos OpenCL Working Group. *The OpenCL Specification*. A. Munshi (ed.), 2008. 123

[Kistler 2006] M. Kistler, M. Perrone and F. Petrini. *Cell Multiprocessor Communication Network: Built for Speed*. IEEE Micro, vol. 26, no. 3, pages 10–23, 2006. 78

[Knuth 1997] D.E. Knuth. *The Art of Computer Programming*, volume 3: Sorting and Searching, chapter 5.3.4: Networks for Sorting, pages 219–247. Addison-Wesley, 1997. 38

[Koal 2013] T. Koal, M. Ulbricht and H.T. Vierhaus. *Virtual TMR Schemes Combining Fault Tolerance and Self Repair*. In Proceedings of Conference on Digital System Design (DSD), pages 235–242. Euromicro, 2013. 119

[Koch 2011] M. Koch, N. Ströher, L. Rothamel and M. Weiel. *Graphisches Tool für parallelisierte HW/SW-FPGA-Designs*. Practical Course, TU Darmstadt, September 2011. 112

[Koch 2012] M. Koch, N. Ströher, L. Rothamel and M. Weiel. *Framework zur Modellierung verteilter, paralleler eingebetteter HW/SW-Designs*. Forschungsarbeit, TU Darmstadt, April 2012. 112

[Kopetz 2008] H. Kopetz, C. El Salloum, B. Huber, R. Obermaisser and C. Paukovits. *Composability in the Time-triggered System-on-Chip Architecture*. In International System-on-Chip Conference (SOC), pages 87 –90. IEEE, 2008. 5

[Kuck 1981] D.J. Kuck, R.H. Kuhn, D.A. Padua, B. Leasure and M. Wolfe. *Dependence Graphs and Compiler Optimizations*. In Proceedings of the ACM SIGPLAN-SIGACT Symposium on Principles of Programming Languages, pages 207–218. ACM, 1981. 125

[Lala 2003] P.K. Lala and B.K. Kumar. *An Architecture for self-healing Digital Systems*. Journal of Electronic Testing, vol. 19, no. 5, pages 523–535, 2003. 116

[Lanuzza 2009] M. Lanuzza, P. Zicari, F. Frustaci, S. Perri and P. Corsonello. *An efficient and low-cost Design Methodology to improve SRAM-based FPGA Robustness in Space and Avionics Applications*. In Proceedings of the International Symposium on Applied Reconfigurable Computing, pages 74–84. Springer, 2009. 54

[Leiserson 2010] C.E. Leiserson. *The Cilk++ Concurrency Platform*. The Journal of Supercomputing, vol. 51, no. 3, pages 244–257, 2010. 123

[Leu 2011] A. Leu, D. Aiteanu and A. Graser. *A novel stereo Camera based Collision Warning System for Automotive Applications*. In Proceedings of International Symposium on Applied Computational Intelligence and Informatics (SACI), pages 409–414. IEEE, 2011. 152

[Leupers 2012] R. Leupers, G. Martin, R. Plyaskin, A. Herkersdorf, F. Schirrmeister, T. Kogel and M. Vaupel. *Virtual Platforms: Breaking new Grounds*. In Proceedings of the Conference on Design, Automation and Test in Europe (DATE), pages 685–690. EDA Consortium, 2012. 6

[Levinson 2000] L. Levinson, R. Manner, M. Sessler and H. Simmler. *Preemptive Multitasking on FPGAs*. In Symposium on Field-Programmable Custom Computing Machines, pages 301–302. IEEE, 2000. 14

[Lieding 2014] R. Lieding. *Dynamic Task Mapping in a virtualizable Multi-Processor System*. Bachelor Thesis, TU Darmstadt, March 2014. 180

[Lin 2012] W. Lin. *Virtualisierung von Soft-Core-Prozessoren*. Diplomarbeit, TU Darmstadt, January 2012. 38

[Liu 1993] J. Liu and V.A. Saletore. *Self-scheduling on distributed-memory Machines*. In Proceedings of the Conference on Supercomputing, pages 814–823. ACM/IEEE, 1993. 67

[Luck 2013] K. Luck. *Ein virtualisierbares Automotive MPSoC*. Final Thesis, TU Darmstadt, May 2013. 152

[Marwedel 2011] P. Marwedel, J. Teich, G. Kouveli, J. Bacivarov, L. Thiele, S. Ha, C. Lee, Q. Xu and L. Huang. *Mapping of Applications to MPSoCs*. In Proceedings of the International Conference on Hardware/Software Codesign and System Synthesis (CODES+ISSS), pages 109–118. IEEE, 2011. 118

[Meloni 2010] P. Meloni, S. Secchi and L. Raffo. *An FPGA-based Framework for technology-aware Prototyping of multicore embedded Architectures*. IEEE Embedded Systems Letters, vol. 2, no. 1, pages 5–9, 2010. 112

[Mentor Graphics 2013] Mentor Graphics. *ModelSim - Leading Simulation and Debugging*. online: http://www.mentor.com/products/fpga/model, accessed 12/18/2013, 10:10 am, 2013. 112

[Momtazpour 2011] M. Momtazpour, M. Ghorbani, M. Goudarzi and E. Sanaei. *Simultaneous variation-aware Architecture Exploration and Task Scheduling for MPSoC Energy Minimization*. In Proceedings of the Great Lakes Symposium on VLSI, pages 271–276. ACM, 2011. 75

[Moore 1965] G.E. Moore et al. *Cramming more Components onto Integrated Circuits*, 1965. 1

[Muller 2013] S. Muller, M. Scholzel and H.T. Vierhaus. *Towards a Graceful Degradable Multicore-System by Hierarchical Handling of Hard Errors*. In Proceedings of International Conference on Parallel, Distributed and Network-Based Processing (PDP), pages 302–309. Euromicro, 2013. 117

[Nassimi 1981] D. Nassimi and S. Sahni. *A Self-Routing Benes Network and Parallel Permutation Algorithms*. IEEE Transactions on Computers, vol. C-30, no. 5, pages 332–340, 1981. 37

[Nvidia 2011] Nvidia. *NVIDIA CUDA Programming Guide*, 2011. 123

[Ottoni 2005] G. Ottoni, R. Rangan, A. Stoler and D.I. August. *Automatic Thread Extraction with decoupled Software Pipelining*. In Proceedings of International Symposium on Microarchitecture (MICRO), pages 12 pp.–. IEEE/ACM, 2005. 123

[Parberry 1992] I. Parberry. *The pairwise Sorting Network*. Parallel Processing Letters, vol. 2, no. 2, page 3, 1992. 38

[Patel 1981] J.H. Patel. *Performance of Processor-Memory Interconnections for Multiprocessors*. IEEE Transactions on Computers, vol. C-30, no. 10, pages 771 –780, 1981. 34

[Paulsson 2006a] K. Paulsson, M. Hubner and J. Becker. *Strategies to On-Line Failure Recovery in Self-Adaptive Systems based on dynamic and partial Reconfiguration*. In Proceedings of NASA/ESA Conference on Adaptive Hardware and Systems (AHS), pages 288–291. NASA/ESA, 2006. 121

[Paulsson 2006b] K. Paulsson, M. Hubner, M. Jung and J. Becker. *Methods for runtime Failure Recognition and Recovery in dynamic and partial reconfigurable Systems based on Xilinx Virtex-II Pro FPGAs*. In Proceedings of Annual Symposium on Emerging VLSI Technologies and Architectures, pages 6–pp. IEEE, 2006. 54, 167

[Pionteck 2006] T. Pionteck, R. Koch and C. Albrecht. *Applying partial Reconfiguration to Networks-on-Chips*. In International Conference on Field-Programmable Logic (FPL), pages 1–6. IEEE, 2006. 56

[Plurality 2013] Plurality. *Plurality - Leading the Multicore Revolution*. online: http://www.plurality.com/technology.html, accessed: 12/16/2013, 11:15 am, 2013. 57

[Polychronopoulos 1987] C.D. Polychronopoulos and D.J. Kuck. *Guided Self-Scheduling: A Practical Scheduling Scheme for Parallel Supercomputers*. IEEE Transactions on Computers, vol. C-36, no. 12, pages 1425–1439, 1987. 67

[Portland Business Journal 2008] Portland Business Journal. *Ambric for sale*. online: http://www.bizjournals.com/portland/stories/2008/11/17/daily25.html?t=printable, accessed 12/11/2013, 11:50 am, November 2008. 107

[Post 2011] J. Post. *Implementierung und Evaluation eines massiv-parallelen Bildskalierungsfilters auf einem FPGA*. Bachelor Thesis, TU Darmstadt, February 2011. 113

[Quinlan 2011] D.J. Quinlan and C. Liao. *ROSE Source-to-Source Compiler Infrastructure*. In Proceedings of Cetus Users and Compiler Infrastructure Workshop in conjunction with PACT, volume 2011, page 1, 2011. 127

[Rückelt 2011] T. Rückelt. *Implementierung eines Sensorsystems als Beispielapplikation für generisches FPGA-Monitoring*. Bachelor Thesis, TU Darmstadt, July 2011. 120

[Rückelt 2012] T. Rückelt. *Graphischer Editor für Models of Computation*. Final Thesis, TU Darmstadt, October 2012. 112

[Research 2006] CORDIS Community Research and Development Information Service. *Information Society Technologies - Facts & Figures: Hardware*. online: http://cordis.europa.eu/ist/embedded/hardware.htm, accessed 11/01/2013, 9:30 am, July 2006. 7

[Rjasanow 2012] A. Rjasanow. *Generischer Monitoring-IP-Core für FPGAs*. Final Thesis, TU Darmstadt, April 2012. 120

[Rjasanow 2013] A. Rjasanow. *Selbstheilende Strukturen in virtualisierbaren Multiprozessor-System-on-Chip-Architekturen*. Master Thesis, TU Darmstadt, June 2013. 100

[Rudolph 1985] L. Rudolph. *A Robust Sorting Network*. IEEE Transactions on Computers, vol. C-34, no. 4, pages 326–335, 1985. 38

[Runge 2012] A. Runge. *Determination of the Optimum Degree of Redundancy for Fault-prone Many-Core Systems*. GMM-Fachbericht Zuverlässigkeit und Entwurf, 2012. 120

[Seebach 2010] H. Seebach, F. Nafz, J. Holtmann, J. Meyer, M. Tichy, W. Reif and W. Schäfer. *Designing Self-Healing in automotive Systems*. In Proceedings of Conference on Autonomic and Trusted Computing (ATC), pages 47–61. Springer, 2010. 120

[Seffrin 2010] A. Seffrin and A. Biedermann. *Cellular-Array Implementations of Bio-Inspired Self-Healing Systems: State of the Art and Future Perspectives*. In Design Methodologies for Secure Embedded Systems, volume 78 of *Lecture Notes in Electrical Engineering*, pages 151–170, Berlin, 2010. Springer. 116

[Sidiropoulos 2013] H. Sidiropoulos, P. Figuli, K. Siozios, D. Soudris and J. Becker. *A Platform-independent runtime Methodology for mapping multiple Applications onto FPGAs through Resource Virtualization*. In Proceedings of Conference on Field-Programmable Logic and Applications (FPL), pages 1–4. IEEE, 2013. 6

[Simmler 2000] H. Simmler, L. Levinson and R. Männer. *Multitasking on FPGA Coprocessors*. In Proceedings of Conference on Field-Programmable Logic and Applications (FPL), pages 121–130. IEEE, 2000. 6

[Singh 2013] A.K. Singh, M. Shafique, A. Kumar, J. Henkel, A. Das, W. Jigang, T. Srikanthan, S. Kaushik, Y. Ha, A. Prakash et al. *Mapping on multi/many-core Systems: Survey of current and emerging Trends*. In Proceedings of the International Conference on Computer-Aided Design (ICCAD), pages 508–515. IEEE/ACM, 2013. 118

[Stoettinger 2010] M. Stoettinger, A. Biedermann and S.A. Huss. *Virtualization within a Parallel Array of Homogeneous Processing Units*. In Proceedings of the International Symposium on Applied Reconfigurable Computing (ARC), pages 17–28, 2010. 6

[Sunderam 1990] V.S. Sunderam. *PVM: A Framework for parallel distributed Computing*. Concurrency: Practice and Experience, vol. 2, no. 4, pages 315–339, 1990. 5

[Tang 1986] P. Tang and P.-C. Yew. *Processor Self-Scheduling for Multiple-Nested Parallel Loops*. In Proceedings of International Conference on Parallel Processing (ICPP), volume 86, pages 528–535, 1986. 67

[Tcl Developer Xchange 2013] Tcl Developer Xchange. *Welcome to the Tcl Developer Xchange!* online: http://www.tcl.tk/, accessed: 13/11/2013, 13:00 am, 2013. 111

[Teich 2008] J. Teich. *Invasive Algorithms and Architectures*. In it - Information Technology, volume 50, No. 5, pages 300–310, 2008. 135

[Teich 2012] J. Teich, A. Weichslgartner, B. Oechslein and W. Schroder-Preikschat. *Invasive Computing - Concepts and Overheads*. In Proceedings of the Forum on Specification and Design Languages (FDL), pages 217 –224. ECSI, 2012. 135

[Ullmann 2004] M. Ullmann, M. Hübner, B. Grimm and J. Becker. *On-demand FPGA runtime System for dynamical Reconfiguration with adaptive Priorities*. In Proceedings of Conference on Field-Programmable Logic and Applications (FPL), pages 454–463. IEEE, 2004. 54

[Varanasi 2011] P. Varanasi and G. Heiser. *Hardware-supported Virtualization on ARM*. In Proceedings of the Second Asia-Pacific Workshop on Systems, page 11. ACM, 2011. 5

[Vector Fabrics 2013] Vector Fabrics. *Pareon*. online: http://www.vectorfabrics.com/products, 2013. 127

[Ventroux 2005] N. Ventroux and F. Blanc. *A low complex Scheduling Algorithm for Multi-Processor System-on-Chip*. In Proceedings of the Conference on Parallel and Distributed Computing and Networks, pages 540–545. IASTED/ACTA Press, 2005. 75

[Waksman 1968] A. Waksman. *A Permutation Network*. Journal of the ACM, vol. 15, no. 1, pages 159–163, 1968. 34

[Wichman 2006] S. Wichman, S. Adyha, S. Ahrens, R. Ambli, B. Alcorn, D. Connors and D. Fay. *Partial Reconfiguration across FPGAs*. In Proceedings of the Military and Aerospace Applications of Programmable Logic Devices and Technologies Conference, pages 26–28, 2006. 54

[Wirth 1995] N. Wirth. *A Plea for lean Software*. Computer, vol. 28, no. 2, pages 64–68, 1995. 1

[Wolf 2008] W. Wolf, A.A. Jerraya and G. Martin. *Multiprocessor System-on-Chip (MPSoC) Technology*. IEEE Transactions on Computer-Aided Design of Integrated Circuits and Systems, vol. 27, no. 10, pages 1701–1713, 2008. 2

[Wu 2009] J. Wu, M. Si, F. Tan and C. Gu. *Real-time automatic Road Sign Detection*. In Proceedings of International Conference on Image and Graphics (ICIG), pages 540–544. IEEE, 2009. 152

[Xilinx, Inc. 2011] Xilinx, Inc. *LogiCORE IP Fast Simplex Link (FSL) V20 Bus (v2.11e)*. Xilinx, Inc., Oct. 2011. 79

[Xilinx, Inc. 2012] Xilinx, Inc. *MicroBlaze Processor Reference Guide*. Xilinx, Inc., v14.1 edition, 04 2012. 7, 80, 85

[Xilinx, Inc. 2013a] Xilinx, Inc. *MicroBlaze Soft Processor Core*. online: http://www. xilinx.com/tools/microblaze.htm, accessed: 10/01/2013, 11:45 am, 2013. 9

[Xilinx, Inc. 2013b] Xilinx, Inc. *PicoBlaze 8-bit Microcontroller*. online: http://www. xilinx.com/products/intellectual-property/picoblaze.htm, accessed: 10/01/2013, accessed 11:55 am, 2013. 8

[Xilinx, Inc. 2013c] Xilinx, Inc. *Vivado Design Suite*. online: http://www.xilinx. com/products/design-tools/vivado/, accessed 12/18/2013, 10:45 am, 2013. 109

[Yamauchi 1996] T. Yamauchi, S. Nakaya and N. Kajihara. *SOP: A reconfigurable massively parallel System and its Control-Data-Flow based compiling Method*. In Proceedings of Symposium on FPGAs for Custom Computing Machines, pages 148–156. IEEE, 1996. 33

[Zhang 2003] X. Zhang, G. Dragffy, A. Pipe, N. Gunton and Q. Zhu. *A reconfigurable self-healing embryonic Cell Architecture*. In In Proceedings of the International Conference on Engineering of Reconfigurable Systems and Algorithms (ERSA), volume 1, page 4. Citeseer, 2003. 116

[Zöllner 2012] M. Zöllner. *Modellierung von Parallelisierungsstrukturen für sequenzielle Algorithmen in C*. Bachelor Thesis, TU Darmstadt, January 2012. 127

[Zöllner 2014] M. Zöllner. *Parallelisierungstechniken für sequentiellen Code.* Final Thesis, TU Darsmtadt, February 2014. 137